Amanda Minnie Douglas

Sydnie Adriance

Trying the World

Amanda Minnie Douglas

Sydnie Adriance
Trying the World

ISBN/EAN: 9783744709361

Printed in Europe, USA, Canada, Australia, Japan

Cover: Foto ©Thomas Meinert / pixelio.de

More available books at **www.hansebooks.com**

SYDNIE ADRIANCE.

SYDNIE ADRIANCE;

OR,

TRYING THE WORLD.

BY

AMANDA M. DOUGLAS,
AUTHOR OF "IN TRUST," "STEPHEN DANE," "CLAUDIA," ETC.

Student. How does the book begin, go on, and end?
Festus. It has a plan, but no plot. Life hath none.
BAILEY.

BOSTON:
LEE AND SHEPARD.
· 1869.

Stereotyped at the Boston Stereotype Foundry,
19 Spring Lane.

SYDNIE ADRIANCE;

OR,

TRYING THE WORLD.

CHAPTER I.

"Our birth is but a sleep and a forgetting;
  The soul that rises with us, our life's star,
Hath had elsewhere its setting,
  And cometh from afar.
Not in entire forgetfulness,
  And not in utter nakedness,
But trailing clouds of glory do we come
From God, who is our home."
                    WORDSWORTH.

I BELIEVE I shall keep a journal.

It is one of those sullenly rainy days in summer when Nature seems determined to maintain a perpetual drizzle without accomplishing much; a purposeless, vague, dreamy day. An indistinct presence fills the silent spaces with phantoms half human, and my mood, speculative and questioning, chimes in with it. Since my little bark of life, freighted with one human heart, is about to commence her voyage on the broad ocean of the world, it may interest me to note the incidents.

Three months ago I was eighteen. Now it is July. I have graduated at school, and am awaiting the arrival of my guardian, who is doubtless an elderly, good-natured, prosy sort of man, of whom I know absolutely nothing, except that I am to be brought out under the auspices of his sister, who is a widow. My dear, kind Mr. Anthon, whom I *did* love, has been dead two years, and these St. Johns are distant relatives of his.

Some curious spell has followed me thus far. A life not wanting in incident, but deficient in all the brightness and glad hopes that make childhood a fairy land, — an enchanted country that one can retire to when the cares of the world press hard and close. But if the tales of poets are true, I do not think I had any childhood.

My first remembrance seems to be of a deep forest, so thickly wooded that the light penetrated only at rare intervals. A ledge of rock ran through it, threaded by a small rivulet, whose trickle made a pleasant melody. I believe that spot was my birthplace. No matter where my mortal eyes first saw the light, my soul sprang into existence there, baptized in floods of solemn glory, and my natal hymn chanted by winds that blew "gales from heaven."

After this comes a picture of a dark, gloomy house, with great eaves shadowing the windows; trees, tall and straight; old-fashioned flower-beds, stiff and formal, unlike the freedom and grace of nature. I wonder now if they never felt tempted to rebel? *I* did when my opportunity came.

The place was roomy, but only three apartments were in general use. Once a year, when the clergyman came to tea, the parlor was opened. The furniture was all heavy and dark, every article kept strictly in its place. Here I lived with my two great-aunts and a serving man. The former were maiden ladies, always old to me, reticent to sternness, yet not harsh. They were invariably dressed with the utmost neatness; they never talked loud or fast; went about the house quietly, and performed the same tasks day after day with

Aunt Mildred was a trifle the smaller. I think, too, she
• had a gentler nature; and though I never clung to her, I
had a different feeling concerning her. Children soon
learn to make distinctions. They were not tender women.
Neither ever caressed me. I did not miss it, for all those
early years my life must have been mere negation.

One day an incident occurred that changed the tenor
of my thoughts. A lady visited us, bringing a little girl
of my own age. I was shy at first, but she most gracious.
Golden-haired and fair as a lily, I took her at once as a
type of the angels of my Bible stories. But, alas! she was
vain, self-willed, imperious in temper, and full of petty
deceit. My creed up to this time had been very simple,
and the child astonished me. Her mother kissed and
petted her continually, and there came to my heart a
strange want.

Being a novice in the art of entertainment, I took her
to my nook in the woods, and I certainly must have
amazed the poor child by my eloquent description.

"Is it your play-house?" she asked. "Have you dollies
and dishes in it? Why doesn't your aunt give you some
cake and sweetmeats to take there?"

"It's like a cathedral," I returned, though I confess my
notions on the subject of cathedrals were exceedingly
vague. "If I had a doll I shouldn't take it. Dolls can't
see nor think."

"I'm afraid," she said, shivering. "There are ghosts
and witches in such dark places. I don't want to go."

"It's so beautiful!" I returned. "And I never saw a
ghost. I don't believe there are any."

We trudged on. I half carried her, in spite of her desire to return. At length we reached the summit of the
rock, and I waited for her to be entranced with the weird
beauty. She stared around with a look of blank wonder.

"I don't see anything but rocks and trees," she exclaimed, pettishly. "It's a dismal place, and I want to go. home."

Taking her in my arms, I walked down with an indignant heart. It seemed sacrilege to let her feet so much as touch a dead leaf. Ah! I did not know then that some souls were born deaf and blind, except as to material wants. And when, a few days after, as I was enjoying the grandeur of a summer shower, with its vivid lightning and heavy tread of thunder, she buried her face in her mother's lap, and shrieked with terror until the shutters were closed, the measure of my contempt for her was full.

Yet that brief visit worked a great change in my childish ideas. My mother was dead. I had seen her grave in the churchyard; but I had never heard my father spoken of. I speculated a while, and one day, as I sat sewing, I said, suddenly, —

"Aunt Mildred, where is my father?"

She let her work fall, and started in surprise; but aunt Hester answered sternly, —

"He is dead."

"Why is he not buried with my mother?"

"He did not die here," aunt Mildred said, recovering herself. Then, carelessly, "Sydnie, run, find Peter. I want to see him before he goes to the village."

My errand did not detain me a moment. Crossing the hall I heard aunt Hester say, in a louder key than usual, —

"I tell you she shall be brought up to despise her father as much as her silly, infatuated mother loved him."

"You forget that in two years she can have her choice to go or stay."

"She shall hear *my* story first. I mean to keep this girl. She is the last of *our* family, and who has a better

right? Her father and grandfather have caused us suffering enough."

When I entered they subsided into their usual gravity.
I was afraid to ask any further questions; but that evening, meeting Peter in the garden, I said, eagerly, —

"Did you ever see my father, Peter?"

"What do you know about him?" the man asked, in
surprise.

"I know that my mother loved him," was my confident
reply; and love was no longer an idle term with me.

"Poor child, it would have been better for her if she
had never seen him."

"Why?" was my importunate question. "Is he really
dead? and why did he go away when my mother loved
him?"

"It's no story for little girls. Your aunts will tell you
about it some day."

I had to content myself there. Trained to habits of
implicit obedience, I had not the confidence to venture
upon any overt act, and there really seemed nothing to do.
So I wondered what would happen in two years. It was
like a lifetime. But I went on with the old routine.
Studying and sewing at stated hours, reading aloud, rambling about the woods, taking occasional drives with my
aunts, and going to church on Sundays, were the events
of my life. I began to realize that I was shut away from
the world, as it were, — the world that I learned about in
my books, — and I longed for some change with an intensity that fairly exhausted my strength. Aunt Mildred
grew tenderer towards me; but I needed more than passive kindness.

One incident alone broke the vague dreaminess of those
years. There was a room adjoining the parlor that I had
never seen open; but finding the door ajar during the an-

nual cleaning, I ventured in with great trepidation. I
remember it being a perfect May morning, with floods of
sunshine falling everywhere. Even here it had penetrated.
Of furniture or arrangement I took little note. On the
wall hung a portrait of such exquisite beauty that I was
transfixed. Some strange and subtile intuition thrilled me
at once. "Edith, aged 19," sleeping in her churchyard
grave, became a sudden reality to me. I clasped my hands
with a low cry, "Mother! mother!" Hardly more than a
whisper, yet my own voice frightened me. I stood there
until a hand touched my shoulder. Turning, I saw aunt
Mildred.

"It is my mother!" I exclaimed, almost angrily.

"Yes. Hush; come away. Some time I will tell you
about her," and the vision was shut out of my longing
sight.

"Tell me now," I cried.

"Hush. I have promised that I would not. When you
are twelve years old you shall know the story. Be patient
until then."

How was I to be patient a whole year? I cannot tell
now how I endured it, but never was year so long. I used
to have a fancy that aunt Mildred shunned me; that as
the time approached she grew colder and more distant.
What change was impending?

How clearly I remember the day! With earliest dawn
I was awake. Birds were twittering among the trees,
breezes odorous with the peculiar freshness of spring swept
through my room as I opened the window. I no longer
shared my aunts' apartment, and here I reigned sole mistress. Twelve years old! What would happen to me
before night? It fairly annoyed me that everything
should be unchanged. The breakfast table, the same light
household tasks, the quiet orders. Presently I brought
my books.

"We will not have any lessons, since it is your birth-day," aunt Hester began, graciously. "Your aunt Mildred and I have been preparing some gifts for you, and after dinner we will take a pleasant drive. You are growing a large girl now, and will become more and more of a companion to us."

I was amazed and delighted. Some new dresses, that looked lovely to my inexperienced eyes, a hat with a beautiful wreath of flowers, books, a work-box in complete order, a drawing-book with a set of pencils, and a small gold locket. I broke into the wildest enthusiasm; and though I thought of my mother, and the story I was to hear, it seemed like ingratitude to remind them of it now. Indeed I was busy enough arranging my treasures, and noon came before I was aware.

A little while after dinner I stood on the porch, dressed in my new finery, waiting for aunt Mildred. A man came briskly up the path, and, in answer to my exclamation, aunt Hester turned. Even now I can recall the ashen hue that overspread her countenance.

"Miss Adriance," the stranger said, holding out his hand, "I hope I find you in good health. Is this my little ward?"

Something in his face and voice attracted me wonderfully. The health, vigor, and cheerfulness, the breezy ring in the tones, the bright smile, were like letting the sunshine into a dark room.

"You seem to be in great haste," aunt Hester said, sharply.

He laughed. "I believe the stipulation was that I should come to-day. Isn't it her birthday?" nodding to me.

"Yes," I answered, with sudden boldness.

Aunt Mildred made her appearance, but started back in dismay when she observed the visitor.

"If you were going out, I will not detain you now," he said. "We can have our talk afterwards."

"It makes no difference," was the haughty reply. "Peter,"—as he was driving around,—"we shall not go this afternoon.—Will you walk in?"

We all followed aunt Hester to the state parlor. She opened the shutters, and begged the guest to be seated. Then she would have dismissed me.

"You have told her how she is situated, I presume," he said. "Have you decided whether you will try the world, little girl, or stay here in your cloister?"

"She knows nothing," aunt Hester interrupted. "A child like her could not understand."

"I mean that she shall understand fully," he said, decisively. "I certainly shall keep the promise I made to her dying mother. At the age of twelve, you know, she was to have her choice — to remain here, or to go away to school."

"Sydnie," my aunt said, "go to your room and lay aside your hat. You can return presently."

I obeyed, but remained up stairs thinking of what I had heard. How many times during the last year I had felt cramped and fettered in this narrow life! And to get out of it with a bound, to be free, to see something besides this lonely house! The idea carried me captive.

Aunt Hester broke in upon my reverie. The story that I had longed for was given in a bitter, resentful manner. My mother, after years of care and kindness, had eloped with a poor, miserable wretch, who had married her simply for her money, and, failing to obtain possession of that, had deserted her. She had come back to them broken-hearted, and they had received her, or rather they had gone to her in her extremity, and at her death, which had occurred shortly after, taken sole charge of me. Mr. Anthon had also been appointed my guardian, and, as he had already said, at the age of twelve I should be at liberty to go to school if I chose. She set forth the hardship and trials of school life, the duty I owed them for their years of kindness, the impossibility of my leaving them, and presently allowed me to go to Mr. Anthon.

I was in a whirl of confusion, my bright visions sadly dimmed. I must have betrayed it in my face, for Mr. Anthon drew me near him and soothed me with his kindly voice.

"It will be a hard fight, little girl," he said, "and but for one or two reasons I should not urge you to make it. Your mother was most anxious you should be brought up with companions of your own age. She traced some of the misfortunes of her life to her lack of knowledge and experience, and she wished you to be forewarned. She was left a babe, in the charge of her father's sisters. I believe he had disappointed them a good deal in his marriage. They loved her with a jealous, extravagant fondness; but a younger heart won her; and when they forbade her lover the house, she listened to him and eloped. It was unwisely done, poor child. The story is too sad for one so young as you. Suffice it that they are both dead. It was her wish that at twelve you should go to school, and see more of the world than is possible in this secluded corner. I think it best also. Your great-aunts are past the prime of life; and, though it would be pleasant for them to keep you, at their death you would be altogether unfitted for occupying the position you might take. They consult their wishes instead of your good."

A child is easily won perhaps. I thought of the last two dreary years, and how constantly I had wished for a change. If I only dared to go! But what if I should not like it?

2

He laughed genially.

"No fear of that, I think; and if you're tired of it in three months' time, I'll promise to bring you back."

Mr. Anthon staid all night. During the evening I could not help contrasting him with my aunts. How prim and austere they seemed! How sharp aunt Hester's tones were!

"Aunt Mildred," I said, the next morning, "what would you do?"

A strange, pained look came into her face.

"Child," she answered, huskily, "do as you like."

"I should *like* to go," I said, slowly.

She came quite close to me, and I observed how tremulous her tones were.

"It will be hard to part from you, but I think you are right. Aunt Hester has all the Adriance pride. She would like you to stay here, and carry on the old place after we are dead. You couldn't do it — one woman alone. You need something different from this. What happiness or pleasure would there be in it?"

"You will not think me ungrateful," I said, hesitatingly.

"No, no; unless the after years prove you so. I will not advise, for it seems traitorous to go against my own sister, but —"

We looked at each other. I understood what she meant. We were not in the habit of giving confidences, nor was I a demonstrative child; but she stooped and kissed me, and I felt armed with her approval.

My wardrobe was arranged with a sort of sullen indifference. I believe I was really glad to go at the last, though grieved at parting with aunt Mildred. But Mr. Anthon kept me in fine spirits during the journey; and when we reached my new home I found my courage equal to the emergency. Two of Mr. Anthon's nieces were there, rosy, laughing girls, resembling him so nearly that I soon felt at ease with them; and though shy to a degree that only a child accustomed to a solitary life could realize, in the course of a few weeks I began to feel contented and satisfied. My tasks were not hard, and music, being an entirely new pleasure, enraptured me.

My vacation came in October, and Mr. Anthon took me home. The place chilled me. I wondered how these two women could go on in such an apathetical round. Glad enough was I to get back to school. I began to realize how wide a gulf there was between us, made not only by years, but habit, prejudices, and perhaps blood; for I confess I felt a little akin to my father. Mr. Anthon had once said that my mother never blamed him; and that was enough for me.

One bleak midwinter day I was suddenly summoned to the drawing-room, and found my guardian quite unlike his usual cheery self. Indeed, I had never seen him look so grave.

"I am the bearer of bad news, little girl," he said, slowly. "You must go home immediately. Your aunt Mildred is very ill, and desires to see you."

My heart yearned towards her instantly.

"Aunt Hester is well?" was half question, half assertion.

"I don't want to shock you; but there have been sad times in the old house. Miss Hester was taken with paralysis a fortnight ago; but she rallied very soon, and was thought improving until yesterday, when she had another attack, which proved fatal in a few hours. Your aunt Mildred, worn out with nursing her, is now ill with a fever. She despatched a messenger to me early this morning. It is too late to start to-night, but we will go to-morrow as soon as you can get ready."

Mrs. Derwent, the principal, was summoned to a consultation, and all arrangements made for my journey. I know now that I must have seemed a most peculiar child to her. I was more stunned than grieved; and then even the idea of death was new to me.

It was nearly dusk of the short winter day when we reached home. I shivered as I walked slowly up the garden path. The frozen ground gave back a sullen thud to my tread, and the hoarse wind sang dismally among the leafless trees. No matter how quiet a place may be naturally, the presence of death renders it more solemn. I felt the oppression in every nerve, for I had become so accustomed to stir and tumult, and the glad voices of children.

A strange woman received us, but I went up to aunt Mildred's room as soon as I took off my wrappings. I was shocked by the change in her. The face was wan and ashy pale, the soft eyes preternaturally bright with the fever that was consuming her. There was some passion in my heart, although it had been dwarfed by the absence of nourishing sympathies, and now it rushed to the surface like a flood. I threw my arms over the pillow, and kissed her with remorseful tenderness, exclaiming, in tones of anguish, —

"O, aunt Mildred, you must not die! Only live, and I will never, never leave you again. I was wrong in wanting to go away."

"Child," she said, "do not distress yourself. Remember that I am an old woman, and could not expect much more of life. God is wiser than we, and knows best."

Something in her tone awed me.

"We are the last of our race, and it is well," she went on, slowly. "There is a different current running through your veins. Mine was warmer in youth; and yet the bright hopes of life never prospered with me. We were both proud, too proud. One sees it at the last. Has Mr. Anthon come? I want to talk with him."

"You are not able," the nurse said.

"As able as I shall ever be. After supper I want him sent to me. There is a little business to transact."

I sat by the bed, holding her hand, until called down stairs. I saw no more of her that evening; but Mr. Anthon spent nearly an hour with me, trying to comfort and advise.

The next day aunt Hester was buried. A lonesome funeral, for she had in her lifetime secluded herself from friends and neighbors. I took one glance at the rigid face, but it looked so unlike my remembrance of her that I could hardly realize the fact of relationship. Aunt Mildred had seemed improving, though her recovery was considered impossible.

This second evening set in chill and rainy. My supper was sent away untouched, and presently I was summoned to the sick room.

Aunt Mildred dismissed her nurse, and drew me to the very edge of the bed. I kissed the wrinkled cheek, and took her hands in mine.

"I have a long story to tell you," she began, "and I will not defer it until too late. When you are older you will understand it better, but I shall not be here then. Try to judge us both leniently."

She moved uneasily upon the pillow, and I felt her clasp tighten.

"You asked me once about your mother. Your grandfather married, abroad, a Spanish woman of wonderful beauty. He brought her home soon after your mother's birth; and he came back only to die, for his health had been delicate many years. He had wasted the larger part of his fortune, and his wife and child were left to our care. Between Mrs. Adriance and Hester there was a strong antagonism. She remained with us simply because she had no other home; but it was only for a few years. She died suddenly, and her child was ours. My sister exulted in this. She watched the little one with a more than mother's fondness and jealous care. We were comparatively young then, and had not so completely given up society. Your mother was beautiful and attractive, and was barely seventeen when she announced her engagement with a young man of whom we knew nothing. Aunt Hester was very angry. She dismissed him herself, and bade your mother forget him. Being high-spirited, this led to a bitter quarrel, which was ended at length by your mother leaving her home and becoming a wife. I tried to intercede for her, but it was useless. She wrote two or three very sweet letters, but Hester remained implacable, and declared her disowned forever.

"Some fifteen months afterwards she wrote again, begging that her small fortune might be advanced, as they were in pressing want, and her husband's health had failed. Hester paid no attention to this; but in a few weeks another letter was received, imploring us to hasten to her immediately. I was not well, so Hester went alone, and shortly afterwards returned with your mother and yourself, then but two months of age. How changed from the bright girl who had once been our delight! Your father had gone to his relatives, and died after a short illness, though she confessed that he had overtasked himself by some exertion that had brought on one attack of hemorrhage before he left her. His relatives had discarded her altogether, and she was indeed broken-hearted. She wasted away rapidly, and soon added another to the list of early deaths. One day, shortly after the burial, a stranger visited us and held a long conversation with Hester. Whatever the subject was she kept to herself, only when she came in the room afterwards I noted that her face had a strange, set look, and her lips were nearly colorless.

"'This child is all ours,' she said, fiercely. 'The world shall be shut out from her as rigidly as if she were in a convent. She shall have no chance for friendship or love beyond us.'

"I should have told you that your mother appointed Mr. Anthon your guardian, and arranged that you should go to school for two years when you had reached the age of twelve, and after that choose whether you would remain with us, or henceforward battle with life yourself. Aunt Hester resolved to bring you up in such seclusion that you would be unhappy among strangers, and wish to return, knowing well that Mr. Anthon would not insist upon your staying if it rendered you really miserable. I made some weak attempts to interfere, but she was always the stronger and overruled me; and, though I loved you, I was helpless. Besides, you appeared cheerful and contented, and I was afraid of rendering you dissatisfied, without being able to place any better aliment in your way. Forgive us both — my weakness and her jealous coldness. Old blood does not warm easily. I want you to have a happier life than we ever knew. This place is to be sold. Mr. Anthon will tell you the rest. Kiss me, child, and remember me kindly when I am gone. Mine has been a poor, wasted life."

I kissed her with a strange awe, and hardly understood the full import of what she had said.

"Call the nurse."

The woman would have sent me away, but I felt that aunt Mildred wanted me, for the wistful eyes watched me unceasingly. I promised to be very quiet, and kept my seat, still holding her hand. She was very much exhausted, and scarcely seemed to breathe.

That was a weird, ghostly night, and haunts me yet. The red blaze of the logs upon the hearth, the fitful glare of the candle, the winds moaning outside, dashing fierce gusts of rain against the windows, and the awesome silence within. I tried to think of my mother, but all in my brain was chaos. The nurse seated herself by the fire, and presently fell into a doze. I was not a coward, yet a peculiar fear seemed to pervade every nerve, and I watched breathlessly for something that I could not define or shape into thought. The candle burned dimly, the blaze on the hearth began to smoulder, and the room was peopled with phantoms.

There was a stir, and a feeble voice murmured, " Sydnie ! "

I bent over aunt Mildred until my cheek touched hers. It was unlike anything I had ever felt.

" One thing more. Forgive her — poor, worn heart, distracted with its own jealous longings. I know she was sorry afterwards; but she destroyed it in a moment of fierce passion. The picture — "

I was too much frightened to comprehend, or utter any cry.

" Is it morning? "

" No," I said; " it must be near midnight."

" God help us all, for we are weak, and the way is thorny. Child, Sydnie, let us go, for the day breaks."

She clutched my hand, and partially raised herself, then fell back. I understood the struggle, yet could not stir, fascinated by the very terror. How many moments I know not, but the candle gave an expiring flash, and went out. The nurse roused herself, and lighted another.

Coming to the bed, she glanced at the set and stony eyes.

"Why, miss, she's dead!" was her terrified exclamation.

It was blindness, darkness, nothingness to me. I knew they took me out of the room, but for days after that I was ill for the first time in my life.

Mr. Anthon staid until I was sufficiently recovered to go back to school. I was thankful to leave the dreary place, and glad to hear that it was to be sold. My mother's portrait had been destroyed by a ruthless hand, so there was nothing I cared to retain.

"There'll be a brighter life before you," my guardian said, kindly. "Those two old women moped themselves to death, and were full of whims and cranks. It was enough to kill any child. And I don't think Miss Hester did the right thing by you or your mother. However, that's all over now."

It was not all over with me for a long while; but I did outgrow those impressions with the years. Three were spent with Mrs. Derwent, then a change was deemed advisable. In my quiet, self-contained way I had learned to love Mr. Anthon dearly. Every vacation was made delightful by some pleasure trip, wearing away more and more the isolation produced by my childhood.

Two years ago he died, as I have said. I missed him sorely, and am afraid I shall not take kindly to my new guardians, Mr. St. John and his widowed sister, Mrs. Lawrence. She called, shortly after her relative's death; but all I seem to remember was a glitter of silk and lace, and a shimmer of blonde curls. I am to enter society under her auspices.

I wonder how I shall like the great world! Most of the girls are eager to try it; but I dread leaving my cloister. We have gossiped over it in a thoughtless fashion, as if love and marriage were all.

It is curious to stand on the threshold of a new life, not knowing whither one is to go.

The silent night falls over me as I write. The rain has ceased, and through the rifted clouds the stars are shining.

CHAPTER II.

"Do you not know I am a woman? When I think I must speak."
ROSALIND.

I AM at Laurelwood.

Let me go back to the day on which I commenced my journal. The next morning I received a note, stating that Mr. St. John would call for me at four, as the· boat left at five.

I believe Dr. Johnson somewhere says we can never do a thing consciously for the last time without a feeling of sadness. I experienced the truth of this remark. Though the long dining-hall was nearly deserted, there was a homelike charm about the place. Even the vase of colored grasses, grown tiresome on other days, held a certain sense of beauty. The walks I had paced, the room in which I had studied and dreamed, wore the look of a familiar friend. "Farewell," I said, with a pang, for it was hard to dissever my thoughts from them.

At the appointed time I was summoned to the reception room, and introduced to Mr. St. John. He was not at all what I had expected, and the difference made me positively shy and awkward. A man about thirty, tall, compact, and full without being stout, with a chest and limbs one gives to the old athletes. He impressed me as having a peculiar strength, and his 'face completed the suggestion. I did not think him handsome at first. I watched him as he talked to Miss Deforrest, and found an odd, piquant charm in his face. A broad, full forehead, and a really magnificent head, hair of a nondescript

color, brown in one of its variations, I suppose, fine and
silky, the ends curling in dainty rings. I set that down as
too girlish ; beard of a little deeper color, almost black underneath ; a fair, fresh complexion, with a smooth, soft skin,
like a child's ; eyes of a blue or gray, with a curious, steely
gleam ; straight, delicate brows above them ; a straight
nose, Grecian in type ; a small mouth, with curved, scarlet
lips. But the sense of power and will grew upon you. In
some moods this face could be very tender ; in others, bitter, perplexing, imperious and indifferent.

Miss Deforrest was called away. Mr. St. John glanced
down to my end of the sofa with the good-natured smile
one gives a child.

"The rain interfered with my plans yesterday," he said,
and the voice was like the man — not what one usually
meets with. "I expected to come for you. I dare say
you had the blues shockingly."

"I am not much troubled with that malady," I answered,
curtly.

"How odd! I thought all school-girls were subject to
it. But of course rainy days make you cross."

The assurance in the tone vexed me.

"I have no particular dislike to rainy days ; on the contrary, I think some are positively enjoyable," I said, coldly.

"I shall watch the next stormy day with great interest ; "
and there was a little gleam in his eye that provoked me.
I would not make any answer.

"I believe I shall have to send you to make your
adieus," he said, presently, glancing at his watch. "It is
quite a ride to the landing."

I merely bowed, and left him. There were a few farewells and kindly wishes, and then I put on my bonnet and
mantle, and took one last glimpse of myself in the little
mirror. Was the face I saw crude and school-girlish ?

Our drive was a very quiet one. I had an uncomfortable consciousness that Mr. St. John's eyes were studying me, yet if I turned mine to his vicinity, his expression was grave and absent. Some of the girls had been fond of discussing faces and predicting character, a subject that always interested me deeply. I wondered what any other person would think of him; and because I could not please myself in an analysis, I was fairly annoyed. Indeed, he seemed to make his face express very little just then; but I had a misgiving that it was only like a crouching lion, the power held in reserve.

He was most kind and gentlemanly, not with any excess of politeness, but the peculiar ease that makes one feel thoroughly comfortable. We found our way through the crowd at the wharf, and my belongings were soon safely deposited in my state-room. The whole scene was novel to me, because my own position in it was so new.

After supper we went on deck. The shores we were leaving behind made suggestive pictures in their lengthened perspective. Yellow fields, heavy and ripe for harvest; clumps of woods, dense and shadowy; clustering villages; boats skimming the river, and an occasional flock of homeward-bound birds. The air was fragrant with the spicy breath of summer and the dewiness of coming night.

Just as the sun was setting, the moon rose, and the effect of the double light upon the water was indescribable. The clouds, rolling off to the horizon, made long, low islands of purple and sapphire, that seemed floating in a sea of pearl, while now and then a crimson arrow shot up, leaving in its wake a long trail of golden glory. The river was calm, with slow, regular swells, except where the boat flung upward a line of foam. A light mist crept along the curves of the shore, like a troop of fairy phantoms. Here we passed dusky ravines, there a rock where the water dashed up in playful passion, making its gray sides sparkle as if set with gems. My companion pointed out some spot lovelier than the rest, with the eye of one who had studied nature closely.

"How grave you have grown," he said, at length. "Do you grieve for what you are leaving behind?"

"Not quite that," I made answer; "and yet one does shrink a little from an untried life, with its stern realities."

"Are you given to conjuring up giants in the way? As if life was likely to be anything but rose-color to a girl who holds as much in her hands as people usually do!"

"It *is* sometimes," I said, positively.

"You have been cultivating imagination largely."

"I may have had some reality, although you seem so doubtful about it," I answered.

"No life is all sunshine, nor was it so intended. And yet I think God doesn't mean us to fear the future. We are to take up daily events with hopeful hearts, and shape them into a higher form than crude fragments."

"But how few live in earnest!" for somehow the rare inflection of his voice touched me.

"What is your idea of an earnest life?"

"Something better than mere froth and foam, or selfish enjoyments; an existence in which one leaves enduring marks of having labored to benefit his kind, to strengthen the weary, comfort those who are tried and tempted, and point out a better path for them to walk in."

"You have been reading German metaphysics, Miss Adriance."

"Surely the strong angel of the useful loses none of his power when joined to the spirit of the beautiful."

"Few care to unite them thus upon the bridge of life. The useful angel too often goes about clad in coarse raiment, and people instinctively shrink from him. Where will you begin with your mission?"

"I have not decided."

"Like a woman! People in the moon are generally benefited most by these visionary schemes."

"I can commence with myself," I said, "since you seem to commiserate the people in that distant locality."

"Ah, I thought you were through with yourself, and ready to .undertake the salvation of others. You should have lived in the past centuries, when crusades were fashionable."

"I am content to live now, but I shall try to live in earnest."

"Be a sort of reformer, martyred on the cross of public opinion. You will gain some glory that way."

"I am not ambitious of such glory," I said, indignantly.

"Take up the sins and follies of society. There is a wide field. But I am afraid this wicked old world is bent upon rushing to destruction, in spite of sages and prophets."

I was ready to cry with vexation. He stood there in the moonlight, looking really handsome, but cool and provoking; and I had a dim suspicion that in his heart he was laughing at me.

"You'll improve on these romantic notions after a little," he said, gravely. "Young men and young women have a great fancy for fighting impossible giants. It's a kind of mental measles. But they get over it, and come to the stage where they are interested in each other, when the Lancers at night or a bouquet in the morning is sufficient to restore the balance of the most vacillating mind."

"I shall endeavor to reach something higher than these trifles."

"Miss Adriance, I have seen a good deal of the world, and have the advantage of you by more than a dozen years. I know what most women's lives are. A good deal of dressing and display, some flirting, harmless, of course, for in society one plays a sort of give and take game, with the heart left out, and a good marriage at the last. That is the great stake; and failing there, your life will be pronounced unsuccessful."

The girls used to talk of this at school; I can't tell why, but it invariably annoyed me. And to have him take it up in such a cool, tantalizing manner!

"Marriage is not the great aim and end of all lives," I said, indignantly.

"Isn't it? Miss Adriance, I *do* begin to believe you were meant for a reformer. When a young woman has sufficient courage to dare the terrors of going down to posterity as *Miss* somebody or other, she must be stronger than the majority of her sex. Let me see — what will you do? There's the Woman's Rights question. I have not sufficient brain to take in all its bearings; in fact, when I go over it, I invariably get muddled; but I dare say you have given it a good deal of attention. Women, being tired of reasonable employments, have a desire to soar to the unreasonable. They want to manage the business part, and generously propose that the sterner sex shall stay at home and enjoy themselves."

"It is you who are unreasonable," I interrupted, angrily. "A man always exaggerates when he undertakes to express a woman's opinions. Are we blind and deaf to those higher calls of the soul? When we are held in bondage to the false and unsubstantial, and see above us the gleam of truth, and purity, and loftiness, do you suppose no pulse is ever stirred, no desire awakened that leads us to struggle after the fine gold, instead of the base counterfeits the world offers us? If it is right for a man to make his life grand and noble, why cannot a woman *try* at least?"

"*Is* truth at the bottom of these struggles? I believe

it is oftener some paltry ambition. It jars against one's idea of a woman to see her so eager for contests that must render her harder, even if she escape the coarseness."

"You don't understand me," I said, trying to keep calm.

He laughed again; such a provoking, cynical, yet, withal, musical sound! I believe I almost hated him.

"You do not make yourself at all intelligible. Here you are with your head full of school-girl nonsense, ready to do battle for some great cause of which you are beautifully ignorant, and — shall I make a prediction — in six months you will be so deeply engrossed with pomps and vanities and a lover, that you will be quite willing to let the world jog on at its old rate. It has stood a good many such assaults, Miss Adriance."

I lost all my patience, never very extensive, perhaps. I was not hoping for unattainable good, not trying to make a martyr of myself, but willing to take the world as I found it, having an even chance with others for happiness. I did not mean to kneel at the shrine of fashionable follies and make them my highest good. There was a better aliment for human souls. The contention grew warmer, he irritating me beyond endurance. All this under a sky of soft splendor, and at our feet the murmurous waves beating time to chants of melody, while the very air seemed blowing out waves of liquid light. The sense of harmony all around made me feel more indignant with him. I rose haughtily, and bade him good night.

I had taken a step or two, when he said, softly,

"Miss Adriance!"

I stood irresolute, and then — I am ashamed to confess it — turned partially. His face had changed wonderfully, and I had the feeling of being drawn into some vortex.

"Come, Miss Adriance," he said, "I am not going to let

3

you leave me in such a mood. This is the first night of
our acquaintance, and I want you to have pleasant dreams
of me. Remain until you are good-humored."

He had taken my hand, but I drew it away with an impatient gesture, and left him. He had been barbarously
unjust, and he would find that I was no child to be coaxed
into agreeableness with a word. If I found his sister as
captious and irritating, my life would not open very delightfully. I wished myself back at school, or anywhere,
in fact, where I should not see him. I had acted unwisely in allowing him to provoke me, but he might have
had a little generosity, if our beliefs were dissimilar. "*I*
never can like him," I said to myself as I fell asleep.

The sun rose gloriously the next morning. I watched it
through my little window, longing for a more extended
view, and debating within myself upon the propriety of
seeking it, when a waiter stopped at my door with Mr. St.
John's card, on which was written, in pencil, —

"If Miss Adriance will come on deck, she will be amply
repaid by the beautiful scene."

Obeying my first impulse of resentment, I returned an
answer, declining. It was a pitiful gratification, after all,
for I was tormented with mere bits and fragments of glowing dawn. I had a passion for these changeful pictures of
sea and sky. The tremulous rays of gold and crimson
wandered fitfully through my little room, and the soft light
brought visions of the greater glory beyond.

The noise and commotion recalled me to common life.
I felt awkward and nervous about meeting Mr. St. John,
and wondered how he would get over our dispute of last
night. I might have spared my speculations and the resolves with which I fortified my mind. He was calm and
gracious, totally ignoring all the disagreeable incidents that
had passed between us. I absolutely became confused.

Mrs. Lawrence was awaiting us at a hotel, and we drove thither. She was not up yet, so we both waited in her little parlor. Mr. St. John brought me a book and some papers, and occupied himself in reading. Well, the man certainly was a Sphinx!

After a while Mrs. Lawrence made her appearance. She was thirty-five, I afterwards learned, three years her brother's senior, but one would readily have believed her ten years younger. A remarkably beautiful woman, pure blonde in type, barely medium size, and gracefulness itself. To watch her was like listening to music. I felt ugly and overgrown beside her.

"My dear Miss Adriance!" and her voice had something of the peculiarity of her brother's — a kind of liquid sweetness, that attracts one involuntarily. I could not help being won by the charm.

She scanned me from head to foot, but I did not read disapproval in the languid, purple-blue eyes, so I ventured to breathe and to smile.

"How bright and fresh you look," she said. "I can believe that you heeded my injunction, Stuart," glancing at her brother, "and did not keep her up half the night watching the moon."

"As that seems to be my pet employment, there was some danger."

His voice was just dashed with irony, reminding me of the delicate flavor of bitter almonds. I colored at the remembrance of our evening's conversation, but returned, carelessly, —

"I believe I do not usually carry traces of such simple dissipation in my face."

"It's folly to waste one's good looks when it amounts to nothing;" and she smiled in a charming fashion. "Now, if you please, we will have some breakfast, and then Miss

Adriance and I can afford to dismiss you, as we are going on a shopping expedition."

There was a little, expressive curl to his lips, as his face settled into an indifference that made it positively cold.

She was very gracious and entertaining, and I could not help feeling at home with her, indeed, could not help liking her; but I had a misgiving that there was the least spice of contempt in the approval Mr. St. John gave. When we returned to the parlor, he bade us " good morning," and sauntered out.

"Now we will hold a little consultation," Mrs. Lawrence said, with a girlish interest and enthusiasm that was not affectation, although it seemed to border upon it. "I am going to take you to Newport, and I expect you to create quite a sensation."

"Don't expect too much of me," I said, with a sudden fear.

"My dear, you don't know your own power at all. How should you, indeed?. With your style and looks you ought to make a decided impression. Rest assured that I shall give you every advantage."

"I do not question your generosity," I returned, "but my own —" desire, I was about to say, then changed it to " ability."

"You will feel different about that presently. Then you are quite an heiress, another item in your favor; and when you do fairly take your place, and feel at home in it, you will like the triumphs. Only you must not fall in love too soon."

"I believe I am not very susceptible."

She smiled approval. "The first thing will be to get your wardrobe in order," she continued. "I know you have nothing available, so we will go out and supply ourselves. Your dresses will be made at home, under my own supervision. I have a maid who is worth fifty modistes. Are you ready to go now, or would you rather rest for an hour or two?"

I signified my willingness, and we set out immediately. It was my first induction into the mysteries of fashionable life, and I yielded to Mrs. Lawrence's suggestions the more readily in order that I might not betray my own ignorance. But I really wondered when and how I should find use for half the articles she purchased, and now and then gave a thought to my resolves of the evening before, comprehending that it would be more difficult to assimilate the two lives than I had believed. And yet I could not help being interested. When a shopkeeper places before you elegant goods in their most enticing light, how can you fail to admire?

Mrs. Lawrence knew the routine well, and before night had spent what seemed to me a quarter of my fortune at least; but the shopping was done. Thirza, a quadroon maid, hardly less beautiful than her mistress, was busy all the evening packing, and the next morning we resumed our journey, stopping at night to rest, for Mrs. Lawrence had no idea of unduly fatiguing herself.

Mr. St. John I hardly saw at all, but we felt his care and attention in many ways. Now and then I experienced the sensation of being watched by the cool eyes that I knew fathomed much more than they chose to reveal.

From the station it was a long drive to the St. John mansion — through broken woodlands where rugged old trees were moss-grown and festooned with brilliant wild vines, contrasting vividly with the silvery river flowing in and out, here widening to a lake, there a mere thread; the deeper green of the forest bathed in a soft haze of sunshine, and mellowed by frequent breaks of light and shade. The air was fragrant with the spiciness of the dis-

tant pine woods, and occasionally some weird song, quite
new to me, broke from the throat of an unseen warbler.
It seemed like going into an enchanted country.

The road became clearer presently, and at a little distance
I espied a great gray stone mansion, ivy covered, and apparently in the midst of the most picturesque confusion —
turfy glades, dreamy, mysterious nooks, clumps of shrubbery, fountains trickling over miniature rocks, and flowers
in the wildest profusion. The house was an old, quaint
mixture of different styles of architecture, and had probably been constructed at different periods. The front was
broken by recesses and balconies and deep windows, and
at one corner rose a turret, that added to the general effect.
It was so cosy and roomy-looking, so really homelike, for
all its strange beauty, that my heart gave a quick, involuntary thrill. I leaned out of the carriage, eager to take in
every aspect of loveliness.

"You like it," Mr. St. John said, under his breath, and
something in his voice startled me.

"Like is a poor word;" and I felt the warm color rising
to my face.

"And in six months you will weary of it."

"No," I said, impulsively; "I could never weary of it.
Why, I question if Paradise was more lovely!"

"And Eve was not content without the forbidden fruit.
There's something unattainable to every life."

I glanced furtively at his face; it had gloomed over
with some unseen thought, and the eyes seemed weary and
wistful.

"Home!" he said, as he sprang out lightly, and gave his
hand to his sister.

"Well," he continued, assisting me, "are we to be
friends, Miss Adriance? Have you forgiven me for ruth-
lessly demolishing some of your airy fabrics?"

"I should be generous to my worst enemy now," I replied, softly. "Who could hold malice in this world of bewildering beauty?"

I did not dare glance up again, for some strange spell seemed to shadow me. Was I really entering an enchanter's realm?

CHAPTER III.

"Our aspirations, our soul's genuine life,
Grow torpid in the din of worldly strife."

FAUST.

THE interior at Laurelwood was not less charming than the scenes without. I was lost in a maze of beauty, fairly bewildered with spacious halls and stairs, niches out of which some graceful old-world goddess smiled, or bore her burden of fragrant flowers. A kind of tropical, sensuous ease pervaded every spot. You heard the murmur of the fountains, making a dim, lulling music, and were wooed insensibly to repose.

I was shown to an elegant suit of rooms next to those of Mrs. Lawrence. The quaintly carved furniture, the light, delicate carpets, and the luxurious couches and chairs, gave me visions of delight. There was an æsthetic side to my nature certainly. And then I went back to my childhood, with its hardness and plainness, its long, solitary days. Was it really I who had a right to these lovely rooms; who was to be waited upon, and queen it as royally as I liked? For nothing would please Mrs. Lawrence better.

Thirza came in to arrange my hair while her mistress was resting from the fatigue of her journey. "How magnificent!" she said, as she took it down.

It was handsome — fine, soft, and abundant, a perfect midnight mass.

"Miss Adriance has a little foreign blood," she continued.

"A Spanish grandmother;" and I laughed.

"It is in your figure and carriage as well. And your eyes show it."

Some of the girls at school had envied me my eyes and complexion. They were both dark and wild, I thought.

The deft fingers wove wonderful braids, and compacted them in strange devices. Then she broke off a spray of white jasmine, and twined it in and out. After that she took an inventory of my dresses, and decided upon white. Perhaps the contrast made it so becoming; at all events it was my favorite.

"But there's no style to it," she said, disdainfully.

"Up to this time I have been only a school-girl," I replied with a little smile. "There was not much need of style."

"Look at yourself, and see if I have not improved you."

I turned to the full-length mirror. What wraith or vision met me! Tall, rather inclined to slenderness, but not thin; drooping shoulders, the head proudly poised, the forehead low and broad, the features regular, but too immobile, I thought, and a soft, roseate flush warming up the clear, fine skin. I had not considered the subject greatly before, but I was glad to look as well, especially in a place like this where all the surroundings were exquisite.

Some time afterwards Mrs. Lawrence entered, fresh from the hands of her maid. There was a strong contrast between us: she was so finished, so elegant, a perfect embodiment of grace.

"How much you have been improved," she said, in a pleasant tone. "You need a little more brilliance and vivacity to your face, though under some circumstances that air of indifference would be superb."

I flushed deeply, not with pride, but rather with a sense

of humiliation. I fancied that I should soon hate having every slight change in looks commented upon.

"Society will soon give you the tone you need. I am determined upon having you a perfect success."

"Do not count too confidently upon my charms," I said, slowly. "All persons may not judge me with your lenient eyes."

She smiled, and nodded sagaciously.

"I believe I know the world pretty well. You must not spoil your triumphs by any girlish *gaucheries*. I think I shall enjoy having a *protégée* amazingly, though at first I was quite unwilling that Mr. Anthon should leave you to our care. He always talked of you as a little girl, and I am not especially fond of children."

Frank at least. Dainty, and sweet, and tender as she seemed, I felt that she had no warm, human heart.

"What if I had been irredeemably ugly?" I asked.

"You were not, so we will not trouble ourselves with suppositions," she returned, with charming amiability. "Truth to tell, plain people always offend a certain sense of mine."

"But one cannot help it if one grows plain, or was born so."

"It is a great misfortune," and she shrugged her fair shoulders with infinite grace.

The summons to dinner interrupted the conversation, and I was not sorry, for I found myself warming with the sort of injustice she displayed. Would I not have needed a home and friends under any circumstances?

Afterwards Mr. St. John asked me to walk through the grounds, and I was delighted to comply, for I had only taken tantalizing glimpses of them.

"Don't keep her out too long in the night air," Mrs. Lawrence said, as we went down the broad steps.

A peculiar expression passed over his face that tempted me to smile. How unlike they were—this sister and brother.

"One always pays the penalty for superior refinements," he said, in a low tone, and with a touch of sarcasm.

"I have not arrived at that stage where it is of momentous importance to me," I returned, laughingly.

He made no reply, but seemed lost in contemplation of the gravelled walk. Then we turned into a winding path. The lovely night, with its great glowing stars and silvery moon, the air heavy with fragrance, filled my soul with a sense of unutterable beauty. Some tasteful hand had vied with nature here, and produced marvellous perfection. Dells that were so thickly wooded they seemed miniature forests, nooks with an old gray rock shaded by a border of shrubbery at the back, and a tiny stream purling its way along or tumbling over some resistance and forming a cascade of pure spray, everywhere a variety: the grounds made to look much larger by this arrangement, and something to attract the eye continually. One wandered on and on.

Presently Mr. St. John thawed a little, though his silence had not been at all uncomfortable. I don't know that I could have talked at first, for I was filled with the solemn awe a sense of affluent beauty always gives me. I want to be quiet, and take large draughts of measureless content. Once or twice he had glanced at me, and I felt that my mood had been perfectly understood. It is a comfort to be with people who do not insist upon your explaining every phase of feeling.

He spoke of the night first, and then called up some foreign remembrances. He had the faculty of making perfect pictures in description; every subject was tinted and textured by a mind not only vivid, but refined and discriminating. I listened like one under the spell of a charmer.

I don't know how it came around at length, but in some manner Mr. Anthon's name was mentioned. I noticed how the voice that I had thought exquisitely modulated before softened to a peculiar pathos. They had been very dear friends it seemed, and after Mr. Anthon's illness commenced, he had spent some time at Laurelwood. I felt that he had interested Mr. St. John some way in my behalf. How kind and thoughtful he had always been for me!

I liked Mr. St. John much better for this glimpse of tenderness. The man was not all cynicism or sarcasm then. In fact I began to reconsider my hasty judgment. Was it anything more than anger because he had teased me?

We staid out quite late, in spite of Mrs. Lawrence's entreaty, but I think my bright eyes and glowing face disarmed her.

She would have been inexpressibly shocked had she known that after Thirza was gone I left my bed and sat for a long while by the open window. The glorious night tempted me, but I could not have slept. Everything was too new and unreal. This ease and luxury, these lovely sights and entrancing sounds, swayed me powerfully. I was almost afraid that, like Abou Hassan's palace, it might vanish presently, and I find in its stead some cold, gray reality.

The next day I was in constant demand. Shawls, scarfs, bonnets, laces, and gloves were inspected and duly tried, altered and arranged until they pleased Mrs. Lawrence's critical eye. Then the dresses! I confess I did begin to tire of the finery after a while. It was like being fed upon sweets until one is surfeited.

I did try to feel grateful for the pains she was taking,
and I found a curious interest in watching her. Always
cool and unruffled, patient to the last degree; quick-
sighted to discover the least flaw or imperfection. Had
the woman no soul beyond this?

Mr. St. John was pretty closely occupied with some
business, as the estate was large, and he gave it a very
thorough supervision. Now and then he laughingly inquired after the dresses; and one morning sauntered into
his sister's sitting-room, where I had ensconced myself in
the deep rose-embowered window, and was lazily reading.

"How cool and delightful," he said. "But are you not
playing truant?"

"From what?" and I glanced up, rather amused.

"I supposed you would devote every moment to the
work-room. What if your dresses are spoiled?"

"They are in better hands than mine, and do not altogether engross me."

"I am afraid your education is incomplete. And essays
too!" for he had taken up my book.

"One needs something to preserve the mental equilibrium."

"It should be a 'Mirror of Fashion,' or 'The Art of
making one's self agreeable.'"

"Because you consider me particularly disagreeable and
antiquated?"

He colored.

"I am anxious to have you succeed as well as possible."

"What is to be the test of my success?"

"Scores of lovers, and a rich husband, I suppose."

"I am afraid I shall not meet your expectations," I returned, gravely. "If I should come to be considered an
incumbrance at Laurelwood —"

Somehow I could not resist the temptation of saying it;

but I saw that I had angered him. One of those subtle flashes came into his eyes, and a white line about his mouth. He looked steadily at me for an instant. ·

"Pardon me," I said, in some confusion. "But you do vex me when you pretend to think that I have no higher aim in life than mere frivolity — that I can be content with fine dresses and admiration, or that I look upon marriage as the only termination to be desired."

"How you run over these things," he returned, with a curious inflection, "and you don't understand one of them. What girl ever did at eighteen?"

"Am I more ignorant than the generality of women?" I asked, nervously.

"More utopian, perhaps, Miss Adriance; I am rather anxious to see you fairly launched in the world of fashion. You will find it very different from your fancies. And you will do just about as your neighbors."

I took up my book again and opened it, but my pulses were racing along at an angry speed. How was it that he managed to vex me so easily?

"Miss Adriance," he said, presently, "you carry your feelings too much in your face. In time you will learn to wear a society mask, which you will find very convenient."

"I shall never wear a mask, or think it necessary to hide the truth, or any of my beliefs. I do suppose I can find people generous enough to make allowance for youth and inexperience. Human nature is not altogether unjust and faithless, or suspicious."

"Nearly every one sets out with high hopes, Miss Adriance. The voyage looks fair at the commencement — the sky is clear, the winds balmy, the shores bright with vivid pictures, and the siren, Hope, lulls you on and on with glowing visions. By and by the stream grows dull

and muddy, the overladen barks go lumbering along in
a dead wind, or get utterly becalmed. Then comes the
trial of patience. One can work better than one can
stagnate."

"I shall find my life-work somewhere," I said, confidently.

"But who finds what he wants?"

He turned towards the opposite window with a weary
face; indeed it was almost moody. What had come to his
life?—for he seemed to have all of this world's good gifts,
and yet I could not help feeling that he was not as happy
as Mrs. Lawrence, though her mind was continually occupied with trifles. He had missed something, and yet he
seemed to me a strong, self-centred man, not easily
touched by passing events.

Shortly after this we were surprised by a visitor, or
rather *I* was, for Mrs. Lawrence did not mean to introduce
me to her ordinary callers until after our return. But
Thirza announced to me that Mr. Graham was in the
drawing-room, and would remain all night.

"I am glad enough," she said. "It must be lonesome
for you, this being secluded like a nun."

I had experienced no special want in that direction. In
fact I had not half examined the place yet.

Mr. Graham was two or three and twenty, with stray
remnants of boyish beauty that had not yet settled into
maturity. He had a soft, pleasant voice, and a certain
enthusiasm that made him an interesting companion. He
was taking the world in quite a different manner from Mr
St. John, though the latter made an admirable host.

There is an unconscious affinity between the young. I
strayed through the grounds with Mr. Graham, talking of
everything that came in our way, in that pleasant, chatty
fashion bordering upon friendship. I felt at home with his

genial mood; and though the subjects might not have been
wise or profound, we went over them very agreeably.

Later in the evening he asked me for some music. Mrs.
Lawrence had listened to my playing and singing with due
regard for what it would do for me in society. But it was
a passion with me, and when I found that I could kindle
another soul, it gave me a sudden inspiration. I saw his
eyes dilate with pleasure, and a fitful color wandered over
his face. How strangely those pathetic old ballads stir
one's heart! — love, sweet for all its pain, tempting in
spite of thorny ways; men and women content at having
drained the cup of bliss, and asking no more of life. Had
we fallen upon more material days and desires?

I felt glad and happy that night — why, I could not tell.
When Mr. Graham left us the next morning, it seemed as
if some brightness had gone out of the place.

I stood on the balcony, gathering up stray threads of
memory, when Mr. St. John approached, having been to
the gates with his guest.

"You deserve to be congratulated," he said; and
although I understood the tone, I returned, simply, —

"For what?"

"Upon your conquest. But to save a broken heart, I
will tell you that Mr. Graham is engaged to his cousin — a
kind of convenient family arrangement, I believe, she being
an heiress."

"I do not think that fact would weigh a particle with
Mr. Graham," I said as earnestly as I felt.

• "O, you have unlimited faith."

"And your warning was altogether unnecessary," I retorted, scornfully.

"It was merely pastime upon both sides, then! Well,
you acquitted yourself admirably. You will not have much
to learn at Newport."

"I believe I did only what common courtesy required," I said, haughtily.

"A woman's excuse for trifling."

"It is well there are some whose fine perception enables them to distinguish between ordinary politeness and the gratification of a foolish vanity. While there are such cool, clear-eyed people in the world, we need not fear for society."

"Undoubtedly;" and his voice was irritatingly sweet. "Neither may we apprehend any Quixotic reform when the prophets of the new faith are diverted by a word or a look from some fanciful sentimentalist."

If I could have annihilated him with a glance, I should have done so: and he looking calm and handsome, with that baffling smile playing about his face.

"You ridicule my high aims, and if I find any satisfaction in ordinary pleasures, you sneer. What is your ideal?"

"And you are a fiery radical," he said, ignoring my question. "I wonder"—a little lower, as if he was thinking to himself—"if you mean to play with hearts in that fashion?"

"Will it do any harm? Are men so sensitive and delicate?"

"O, no," he said, dryly. "It may go hard with some of them at first, but they soon get used to the warfare. It does damage faith a little, but those old-fashioned virtues are at a discount in modern life."

"I think you wrong us all," I said, more hurt than I cared to show. "If we wound any one, it is because we have first been pained ourselves."

Mrs. Lawrence crossed the hall, and I took shelter under her kindly wing. She put her slender white hand over my shoulder, and presently we walked away together.

4

"What was Stuart saying?" she asked; but I could see it was not from any curiosity. "You must not mind his queer notions; he has always been odd. I think it was living here so much alone, and the St. Johns are peculiar people. I married very young, and went away; and have only been back since the death of Mr. Lawrence, which occurred a few years ago."

I was silent.

"My dear," she continued, in her soft, musical tones, "you really surprised me by your self-possession. You will be a very fascinating woman, only you must not ruin your success by falling in love immediately."

"Why? In what manner would it interfere?" and I smiled.

"O, it breaks up the general interest. When a girl becomes engaged, the real strife for her is over, and she is soon superseded by newer attractions. You need not marry for a year or so. I think I can make it very pleasant for you; and I confess to liking you a great deal. But I came near forgetting my chief errand: Thirza wants you."

Afterwards I went to my own room. How lovely it looked, and how really delightful life was! Somehow I cannot help enjoying it. Is it worth while to strive against the current? Surely youth and pleasure go hand in hand, and one may find elements of truth and beauty in any existence. Why, then, torture one's self with a scourging sense of duty in continually grasping at the unattainable? Could I not take the richness of life without stooping to its dross?

I think Mr. St. John must dislike me. He is very kind to his sister — listens to her plans without making one objection; does many things for her pleasure, and never sneers or shows the bitter side of his nature: for he is bitter and stern, a strong, masterful man, and yet his very power attracts,

I wonder if I am unstable. Sometimes I feel afraid of myself. After all, how much can one help or hinder! If I only had a patient, trusty friend that I could go to in these weak moments! But I should as soon think of confiding in this marble Clytie as Mrs. Lawrence. Both are sweet, but cold.

CHAPTER IV.

"Well, well,
But you must cultivate yourself; it will pay you.
Study a dimple, work hard at a smile;
The things most delicate require most pains."
                                        FESTUS.

WE were in perfect order at last, and started on our campaign. To say that I was *not* interested, would be untrue. There was a fascination about seeing the world in this guise. Several of the girls at school had counted largely on a season at Newport or Saratoga, while I held my peace, knowing nothing of my future.

Mr. St. John had engaged a suit of rooms, so all we had to do was to enter in and take possession. While Thirza unpacked, and Mrs. Lawrence indulged in a rest on the sofa, I sat by the window enjoying the changeful scene below, that looked to my unpractised eye like irremediable confusion, and yet it attracted me wonderfully. I was to join this gay throng, and take my share of pleasure.

We did not go down to the parlors until evening. Mrs. Lawrence looked exquisitely lovely, and I fancied almost as youthful as I. Thirza had not over-dressed me, and I felt quite at home in my new attire. But the scene rendered me nearly breathless with surprise. Elegant women, stately and well-bred men, grouped together, talking, smiling, and posing themselves with the rare grace of statuary. What a brilliant picture it made!

In ten minutes Mrs. Lawrence and her brother were surrounded by a throng of old friends, and warmly welcomed. I responded to introductions that I felt sure I should never remember, and was rather confused, I am afraid. Mr. St. John was so kind that I almost wanted to express my gratitude. He answered questions for me, and warded off anything like awkwardness, until I began to talk quite naturally.

Presently the circle widened a little. I was standing by an open window, when I felt my arm clasped, and a familiar voice exclaimed, scarcely above a whisper, —

"In the name of all that's remarkable for wonders, how did you come here, Sydnie Adriance?"

I turned and found a school friend, Laura Hastings.

"Are you speechless?" she continued, laughingly. "Or are you out on a masquerade, where confessing one's identity breaks the charm, and resolves you back into a Cinderella?"

"Neither. Silent from surprise only."

"Didn't I tell you that I expected to make my début in the world of fashion? How happens it that you were not equally communicative?"

"Because I had no idea what my destiny would be."

"Let us walk up and down this piazza, for I want to catechise you. In the first place, when did you arrive?"

"This morning."

Laura Hastings was an odd, vivacious girl, who always seemed to carry everything her own way. We had been very good friends, without the slightest spark of affection. She occasionally ridiculed me, and I retorted by pronouncing her heartless.

"Who brought you here?" she went on.

"My guardian, Mr. St. John, and his sister, Mrs. Lawrence."

"Pretty well, so far. What kind of a woman is Mrs. Lawrence? Young, rich, and handsome?"

"All three."

"The gods are unjust to bestow so much upon one person. Do you aspire to belleship, Miss Adriance?"

I laughed at her piquant manner, and said, "I have no such ambition."

"Then you are not as sensible as I supposed. With your face and style I would have half Newport in love with me, and the other half dying with envy."

"That would not be a very high gratification."

"Don't be saintish and nonsensical! You should have left all that at school. However, if you are generous, I may stand a better chance. I've been here only a week, and had an offer already, besides strongly interesting a New York millionnaire — but he is old enough to be my father."

"You refused the offer?"

"Of course. He was a young artist, my cousin Carrie's bright particular. She put on airs, and went to a stupid little country place, but he seemed to have a fancy for hovering in the flame. He was only singed a little, and will go back to her with more devotion than ever, so no one was hurt. I believe I rather tempted him to come here."

"O, Laura! Why, when you did not mean to marry him?"

"To tease Carrie a little. She has an idea that goodness is all the capital one needs in this world. It is a poor investment, to my thinking."

"But truth, and honor, and generosity ought to meet with some recognition," I said, warmly.

"You cling to your first love pertinaciously, I see. A month at Newport will convert you to the true faith. Plain women may carry about a list of virtues as long as their sober faces, but the handsome ones all believe alike.

And you are rather magnificent. You've had some help,
for I know you never possessed all these ideas of your
own."

I flushed a little and was silent, for we paused at one
of the windows. She gave a quick glance around and
said, —

"Can you see your Mrs. Lawrence? I'm wild to know
what sort of a chaperone you have."

"She is sitting by that table yonder, between two
ladies, wears blue crape, and has golden ringlets."

"My dear Sydnie, I'm delighted. I can foresee a charming family party. The lady on her left, in mauve silk, is
my august mamma, and the other, Mrs. Westervelt, from
New York, an intimate friend. And your beautiful Mrs.
Lawrence — why, Sydnie, you live in Virginia, don't
you?"

I answered in the affirmative.

"You are the most fortunate girl alive! Think how
you used to study, as if you expected to teach for a living!
I've heard Philip Westervelt talk of this Mr. St. John.
They're immense friends. He is as rich as a Jew, and lives
elegantly, doesn't he?"

"Laurelwood is a lovely place," I said.

"I'm afraid you'll make me envy you, after all. Why,
you have only to captivate your bachelor guardian, to become mistress of one of the handsomest estates in the
country."

I blushed to my very finger ends, and for an instant
was positively angry at her boldness. She saw it.

"My dear," she said, good-naturedly, "please exercise
your Christian forbearance a little. Simplicity is very
charming, but it is a woman's duty to make the best marriage she can. We have this advantage over Eastern
women in that we are not absolutely sold to the highest

bidder, but make ourselves attractive and win him gently."

"Marriage must be something better than that with me," I answered, curtly.

"Now here is a modern hero that I should like to fascinate," she recommenced, with animation; "though I have a fancy that he could make a good fight. There's so much in his face — a sort of strength and defiance that always rouses one; and in figure and carriage he is splendid. He has just spoken to Mrs. Westervelt."

"That is Mr. St. John."

She turned her eyes full upon me, and studied me curiously.

"You're in love with him, of course?"

."I am not in love with him." I tried to say it calmly, but I had a misgiving that my voice was not quite steady; not because her accusation was true, but from its suddenness.

"Then you are a greater dunce than I imagined. Why, he cannot be much over thirty; just a good age. Was he at home when you went to Laurelwood?"

"He came for me at school. Mrs. Lawrence was in New York awaiting me," I said, coldly.

"You *do* mean to marry him? Honor bright, now."

"I have no expectations of the kind, neither will I discuss him in that fashion."

"Don't get vexed. You will not mind if I flirt a little with him?"

"As you like." My tone was calm enough then, but my face burned with secret annoyance.

"I am dying for my introduction. Let us go in."

"O, my dear," Mrs. Lawrence exclaimed, in a relieved tone, "I had begun to wonder where you were when I saw Mr. St. John alone. I am glad you have met a friend."

She looked Laura all over, and I had begun to understand her so well that I knew her verdict was favorable.
Mrs. Hastings was a stylish and rather haughty-looking
woman; Mrs. Westervelt very sweet and gracious. Somehow I was drawn to the latter at once.

Laura and Mr. St. John fell into a light skirmish. Without being absolutely witty, she was quick and piquant, and
it appeared to me never enough in earnest to be vexed if
any one demolished her opinions. He was not severe, and
kept back the sarcasm with which he had treated me on
our first meeting. She certainly amused and interested
him.

I had never thought Laura handsome at school. She
was showy, vivacious, and possessed the art of adapting
herself to any person. She had all sorts of beliefs, enthusiasms, and graces, and was very generally admired. To-
night, amid this brilliance, she did appear unusually attractive.

Presently Mr. St. John took us for a promenade and
ices. They had all the conversation, for I only spoke when
either appealed to me; but I tried to decide what Laura's
fascination for such a man was, and failed. It was altogether beyond my ken.

After quite a ramble we found the party discussing a
hop that was to take place the next evening. Afterwards
our circle widened, and I found myself enjoying the gay
talk, the music, and the changing groups. The newness
interested me strongly.

The next morning we went to ride. A friend of Mr.
St. John's sent the horses, and accompanied us himself — a
very agreeable gentleman withal, and a rather distinguished-
looking cavalier. The day was delightful. The sun went
in and out among masses of dreamy, floating cloud; the
fragrant air seemed to throb to the beating of the ocean

waves beyond.   All around was life — blissful, hopeful life.
A kind of auspicious beginning; yet now and then I
thought of the solitary child who had first learned to love
nature while scrambling over lonely, moss-grown rocks.
In those restricted visions how could she dream what the
dawn of womanhood would be?

It was curious what a listless air the hotel took on about
midday.   Young men lounged in the shadiest corners of
the balconies, finding it too warm for billiards.   Bathing
was over, dowagers were taking an after-dinner nap, young
ladies had disappeared to renew their beauty and freshness
for the evening.   A droning sort of stillness, rather enjoyable after all the crowd and confusion.

Laura insisted that I should come and look over her
dresses, and help her choose one for the hop.

"I suppose you'll be magnificent.   That comes of having a fortune.   What a splendid manager Mrs. Lawrence
is!   Your ride of this morning was just the thing, and
created a sensation.   That salmon-tinted plume in your
hat nearly drove me crazy; and you sat like a duchess.
She has given you a royal entrée."

"The ride wasn't managed at all.   Mr. Blanchard proposed sending his horses over.   We simply accepted the
invitation."

"Well, if you had taken immense pains, you couldn't
have played a better card.   I shall have to look well to my
laurels, in spite of your meek protestations.   Half a dozen
young men are counting upon an introduction to-night.   I
was quite in demand because I happened to be at school
with you."

"I wish you would find other things to talk about," I
said, pettishly.

"You can't make me cross with you, my dear.   I want
you for a confidant.   I must have some one with whom

I can talk over my conquests. In return I will allow you to give me high moral lectures. Perhaps I may profit. But if I stood in your place, wouldn't there be one tremendous sensation! You don't half appreciate it. I mean to make love to Mrs. Lawrence, and get myself invited to Laurelwood."

I smiled in spite of my annoyance.

"Confession number one will begin to-morrow," she said, as I went out of the room.

The hop was enchanting. Thirza made me supremely elegant. Mrs. Lawrence was in a radiant mood, and I was pleased, delighted, charmed. So many handsome and polished men, and lovely women, such brilliant lights and delicious music—low talk behind fans and in corners, dancing, compliments, and enjoyment to the very brim of pleasure's chalice. To know one is capable of inspiring others with admiration, to attract and satisfy insensibly, to see faces brighten at a word, does give one a peculiar contentment. It was my first real entrance into the world of fashion. I used to consider most of the school receptions a bore, and perhaps had based my ideas of parties upon those. That was weak claret to this Moselle.

Laura looked, acted, and danced in a most bewildering fashion. Everybody thought her beautiful, and she is a general favorite. Mrs. Westervelt pets her like a daughter. Mrs. Lawrence admires her style and spirit exceedingly. She is considered frank and amiable, and gains credit for hosts of virtues that she sneers at in private in her flippant way.

What avails it to struggle against the continual temptations that beset one, trying and failing, repenting and making new resolves, when a little surface gilding carries off the palm? Do those who exhort us to be earnest and pure in heart, simple and truthful, really believe these

homely virtues win a bright reward? The approval of
one's conscience is something, to be sure; but are not the
people who seem to be utterly deficient in conscience the
happiest? At least they take the smaller share of suffering.

Moralizing over a ball! Well, I *was* happy. The compliments and small talk did not seem as vapid as I expected. Mr. St. John appeared to enjoy it, though he did
not dance — never does, his sister says. He was very
attentive, introducing people to me; yet he was just as
kind to Laura.

"Such a conquest!" and Laura, fan in hand, threw herself on the sofa by the window. "Put away your writing
and listen to me, if it isn't a love letter."

"I am all attention," and I shut my tiny desk with a
sharp click. "What fortress have you laid in ruins now?"

"First — wasn't it superb last night! The handsomest
woman in the room was acknowledged to be Mrs. Lawrence; the two girls who bore off the palm were Miss
Adriance and Miss Hastings: the one with her dusky, oriental magnificence, eyes of slumberous fire, and vivid
southern temperament, the other with her cooler northern
blood, that gives a touch of frost, melting at the first advance of summer. Shall I go on?"

"Spare your nonsense," I said. "If I hear so much of
the ball I shall be sick of it."

"There is no use of airing your humility before me.
You did enjoy it, I know. I was glad to see you be-
have so respectably."

"I don't imagine a ball-room triumph is worth a great
deal," I returned, with a doubtful smile.

"Take the goods the gods provide, and make a feast
over them all. That is the only true philosophy. I enjoy
being considered handsome, though I do call in the assist-

ance of art. I'm thankful to the Bloom of Youth for my radiant complexion, to the hair-dresser for making the most of my scanty locks, and the dress-maker for improving my figure. When society praises you, take it as your just desert, and people will pride themselves upon telling you the truth. It is pleasanter to be overvalued than undervalued."

"But your conquest?" I said, impatiently.

"You were so engrossed with your own admirers that you missed the fun. Of course you were introduced to the poet, H——? The *on dit* is that he is engaged to Miss Conway, who really does write delightful stories, and is a very fine, intellectual woman. She was determined to keep him within her charmed circle of congenial minds, and I threw out a little bait. My sweet simplicity captivated him, and he has asked me to drive with him this afternoon. I wonder how Miss Conway will take it!"

"O, Laura, how could you?"

"All is fair in love and war, you know. I have improved the seventeen years and five months of my life. I think he is desperately smitten."

"Suppose he should fall in love?"

"Then he must fall out again."

"You will not marry him?"

"My dear simpleton, he is poor, and I am looking for a fortune."

"Whether you love or not?"

"When you come to take the census you will find that love matches do not pay. All I ever knew turned out miserably. Love in a cottage is charming to talk about, and I shall improve upon the theme this afternoon most eloquently."

"And you can deliberately resolve to throw away happiness for a mere show!"

"Put it 'substantial,' and I'll risk the happiness. You are too romantic, Sydnie. Your ideals and dreams will never be realized in this world of shams."

"There must be some truth, some reality."

"Nonsense! Society is a very fine humbug, and it won't do to drag in Truth by the hair of her head. It does not ask what is under the satin, but it does insist rigorously upon the satin. You will find that the chief end of woman is to make a good marriage. What else can she do? Old maids are laughed at, quizzed, sent about from pillar to post, and made the slaves of everybody, unless they happen to have a fortune. Not to marry well is a capital sin against society."

"But no true woman could degrade herself by marrying without affection."

"Of course it would be a crime to confess it. Here, with the mask off, we can show honest faces. What does a man marry for? He wants an elegant mistress to his establishment, or an income that will help him sustain one. In six months he wouldn't be able to tell his wife from other women, if it wasn't that she asked him for money occasionally. And if she was weak enough to pin her faith on his love, she can spend the rest of her days in the shadow of a dead hope, grow old and miserable at home, while society adores him, and pities him for being tied to such a log."

"You will admit that people *can* love?"

"One feels in one's novel-reading days as if there was a tender place in the head or the heart, that love alone could fill; yet few of the people who marry for love are happy. It has a miserable faculty of turning to dross. I choose to look at the facts. Here is the world, pretty fair if you are sharp enough to take advantage of it; otherwise you drift about to no purpose. When you have a good position you can dictate to your neighbors, and it is much pleasanter to rule than to be ruled."

"How much nobler we should all be if we took as much pains to do right as some do to be false and unnatural."

"O, it would wear me out in a month to practise so many virtues."

"And you are willing to receive credit for qualities you don't even desire to possess?"

"O, my dear girl, you go too deeply into these matters. Life in general is like French flowers. Brilliancy and beauty at the top — underneath, a little cotton and painted muslin stuck together by paste. It is not wise to go into details."

"I can never be satisfied with such an existence," I said, warmly.

"You had better ask for a missionary appointment, and go to foreign lands, for I think the majority of the people here do not desire to be converted from the error of their ways. You are a little too good for this world; yet I don't quite despair of you, under Mrs. Lawrence's judicious training. But I must run away now. Wish me success."

How much her views were like Mr. St. John's! Was there no real nobleness and generosity in the world? I would not judge it so harshly, because I felt in my own soul that I was capable of higher joys than dressing and flirting. And yet, what else was there to do in such a life? One read novels in a desultory fashion, or sketched, or crocheted a little, the rest of the time being devoted to pleasure.

Laura took her drive, and made a new engagement. She laughingly begged me to comfort Miss Conway, and fate threw us together. A fine, pure soul was hers, full of high aspirations. I liked H—— also. I could understand the harmony there might be between them, and it vexed me that he should neglect her for Laura.

How the girl managed that her many flirtations should not interfere I cannot divine. Most of the gentlemen seemed to consider her a charming and almost irresponsible child, and more than one matron excused her on the ground that she really did not mean any harm, but was frank and impulsive, and always ready to please. She was not unmindful of the main chance, however, and kept Mr. Varick within reach constantly. He was a widower, but childless; and for many years a sister, now dead, had superintended his establishment. Others besides her cast longing eyes towards the possessor of such a fortune.

As a whole, I believe my month at Newport was a success. Mrs. Lawrence approved, Mr. St. John took care that I should not lack for pleasures. Riding, bathing, dancing, and merriment of all kinds, that youth cannot resist. I honestly tried not to flirt, and was thankful that I had not come husband-hunting.

Not that there were no men worthy of loving. But in the glamour of such gayety who can see soul to soul? I felt that I would hardly risk a love born under such auspices. One could not tell the tinsel from the pure gold, if indeed there was any.

With all these gayeties there was little time to cultivate friendships, yet I did spend many pleasant hours with Miss Conway and Mrs. Westervelt. The latter was such a sweet, kind, motherly woman. I really wondered what attraction there was in the place for her, and found that her son had made her promise to join the Hastings party, as he expected to be away nearly all summer on business. Her passion for him was one of the rare romances of life. He was the last of quite a large family.

"A good young man," said Laura, with her peculiar little laugh. "Devoted to his mother, and all that. I don't know but I should marry him, only I am not of the goody sort, and want a little liberty to breathe now and then."

At last we reached the grand ball of the season — a masquerade. Such an endless discussion as to characters and dresses, and guesses hazarded about every one! The scene itself was beyond description. One felt transported to strange countries. Cavaliers, dukes, kings, historical characters, pages, and knights of romance jostled one another, and jested gayly. Laura personated Byron's Leila, looking the coquettish girl to perfection, the Oriental dress and fillet of pearls making her absolutely beautiful. The poet paid court to her as the Giaour. Mr. St. John chose the costume of a Spanish woman for me; and I wondered if my grandmother ever stepped more stately in flowing robes and lace mantle. Somehow I felt wondrously at home, and fancied that I acquitted myself very well.

It was near dawn when the revellers began to disperse. The night had been one of unusual enjoyment, but now crape, illusion, and flowers began to droop.

"Let us go," I said to Mrs. Lawrence; "I don't want to remember the scene in ruins."

"You are right," Mr. St. John returned. "The last gala night here. Are you not sorry?"

"No," I answered, a little wearily; "the whole month has appeared like a masquerade. I shall be glad to get back to sober life."

"Laurelwood will seem dull and tame."

"If it is as bright as my remembrance of it, I shall have no fear."

He turned me suddenly round, and gave one long, searching glance into my face; then, with a hurried good night, we parted.

5

CHAPTER V.

"It is sweet to feel by what fine-spun threads our affections are drawn together."   STERNE.

THE next day was one of farewells. No more rambles
in the tender, throbbing moonlight, with the great swells
of the ocean rising and sinking with their thunderous
rhythm, and foam phantoms chasing one another far up
the shore. No more drives in softest twilight, where the
purple air was all alive and quivering with the glory of
the departed day. No more brilliance and flirting in the
long hall, thronged with porters bringing down hosts of
trunks. The revel was surely over, and the place already
wore an air of desolation.

Mrs. Westervelt had insisted, and Mrs. Lawrence had
accepted an invitation for a few weeks in New York.

"Miss Adriance will not want to keep straight on with
dissipation, I think," Mr. St. John said. "Suppose we
take a quiet little turn about the country for a fortnight."

"O!" I exclaimed, in a delighted tone; and I know the
gratification in my face finished the sentence.

So we said good by to the party. I should have been
very lonely for the remainder of the day if I had not
heeded Mrs. Lawrence's fervent injunction, and gone to
bed. I was really tired and sleepy.

The parlors looked lonely enough in the evening. Two
or three lingerers sang at the piano, but I fancied the
voices had a pathetic touch.

"Let us go out for a short walk," Mr. St. John said. "There is no moon, but we shall not lose our way."

"Well," he began, after a long, long while, just as I fancied that he was not going to talk at all, "how do you like this phase of life? I think its gayeties have not proved tiresome."

"It seems a sort of hot-house existence," I answered; "and, though it is delightful for a while, I shouldn't want it continually."

He laughed sharply, with a curious sound in his voice that displeased me.

"You still cling to the old notion. Your friend should have turned your thoughts into a more practical channel."

I knew he meant Laura.

"I think neither of us would be likely to influence the other. We are as widely different as one can well imagine." Then, after a pause, which he seemed in no hurry to break, I said, "Mr. St. John, have you any faith, any creed, any rule of conduct?"

"My beliefs are not for a woman fair and young;" and I knew the expression of his face must be bitter by the tone he used. "But we will not spoil our last night here by disputing. We surely can find some pleasanter topic of conversation."

And, to do him justice, he did. I confess I do not understand the man at all. Every change in him surprises me. When he seemed firmly fixed as the rock of Gibraltar, and hedged about with thorns, and while you are considering in what manner you can best meet his mood, he suddenly becomes as calm and as fair as a summer sea.

Our little tour was very delightful, taking in Niagara. My pen almost stops, my very thoughts stand with uncovered, reverent heads. Sublimity and grandeur are meaning words, but they are tame when applied to this resistless

tide, nature's magnificent organ, whose tones seem akin to
the full choral of that morning when the stars all sang together. Every dash of spray is deeply tinctured with a
sense of mysterious loveliness, amber, opal, and frost-white
with the warmer hues born of sunshine. A sacred pilgrimage that ought to make one's soul better and nobler.

I liked Mr. St. John so much while we were there! He
seemed to throw off the mask he wears continually, and
give one a glimpse of the real man, royally sweet, appre-
ciative, and enjoyable.

I was glad to see Mrs. Westervelt again. She welcomed
us all warmly, with that genuine hospitality which is always beyond question. Home is preëminently her place.
Her gentleness, her affection, her comprehensive charity
charm me. I wonder how it would have been with me if
I had shared such a mother's love!

Philip, the son, was still away when we first came. I
own that I was positively anxious to see him, and it was
delightful to have his mother talk of him in her fond, half-
girlish manner — for she is one of the women who will
never grow old. Mr. Westervelt, though not much her
senior, seems quite aged beside her. He is still hale and
hearty, though, with his mind completely engrossed by
business.

Mrs. Lawrence had gone out one afternoon, and I sat in
Mrs. Westervelt's room, reading to her. This was a great
pleasure to me; and coming occasionally to a passage
marked, I lingered over it with peculiar interest. She
would recognize it with a quick smile, and for a few seconds lose herself in happy remembrances. During one of
these pauses I heard a servant's exclamation in the hall,
the quiet shutting of the door, and a light, springing step
mounted the stairs, two at a bound.

She gave a little cry of joy, and started from her chair,

to be clasped to a heart fond and warm as her own. I had a glimpse of a frank, youthful face, blushing in surprise, and a head of tawny, chestnut curls, and then I ran away, feeling that the scene was too sacred for stranger eyes. And it saddened me to know that in all the wide world there was no such love and no such welcome for me.

Presently I was sent for to the drawing-room, and introduced formally; but Mr. Westervelt laughed as he said,—

"My mother insists that I shocked you half an hour ago, Miss Adriance, by my sudden appearance. Not having the grace of an angel, I suppose I ought to apologize. I expected to find her alone."

"Not a very complimentary apology, when you saw how I was entertained," Mrs. Westervelt said, deprecatingly.

"Mother, do you mean to keep me from making peace with Miss Adriance? Did you expect me to send a telegram, with date of hour and moment, when I came flying upon the wings of the wind myself? Suppose we do it all over again? Newport has put some grand ideas in your head. I shall have to take a turn there next summer. Miss Adriance, am I forgiven? Please don't think me a bear. I am more like a great, shaggy Newfoundland dog."

"There certainly was nothing to pardon;" and I smiled.

"Mamma mine, you see she doesn't hold malice. I'm glad, Miss Adriance, for I want to be friends with you, since you have a claim on some one very dear to me. If you had not started quite so soon, I should have dropped down upon you at Laurelwood, for I have been rambling about Virginia the last six weeks. It would have been Tara's halls deserted."

"But 'Beauty's reign' was not over."

"Ah, you have been conquered by its potent spell. Did

you ever see so lovely a place, Miss Adriance? St. John
goes on adding to it year by year, and yet to me it has
always been perfect."

Mrs. Westervelt rang for a servant to light up the room.
I ventured to take my first real glimpse of Philip then.
Frank and manly, without being regularly handsome; a
rather full figure, with remnants of boyish grace, and a
face good and sweet, rather than strong. Not that it was
weak; but it lacked the sense of maturity and power that
always pleased me so in Mr. St. John. I don't know why
I should compare other men with him, as if he were a
standard of excellence, and yet I often find myself doing
it. There was nothing bitter nor satirical in this face; and
I felt how genial and warm his heart must be.

Mrs. Westervelt left us to give some orders about the
dinner. Philip eyed me in an odd, amused fashion for a
moment, then said, with his bright smile, —

"You must pardon me, but I have had a great curiosity
to see what Mr. St. John's ward would be like. Guardianship seems a new phase for him."

"He did not choose her," I returned; "she was 'great-
ness thrust upon him.'"

"How does he bear his honors — meekly?"

"I have a fancy that meekness is not one of his strong
characteristics."

"You are right. Well, do you like him?"

"Sometimes." I made a slight grimace for the rest.
He laughed.

"Don't think me impertinent. He is peculiar, and so
are you."

"Peculiar!" I echoed.

"Yes; you carry it in your face; a kind of mystery that
perplexes one."

"I was not aware of that," I said. "I always fancied
my feelings came quite readily to the surface."

"Do they? Not those that you care the most about. Did you ever think, Miss Adriance, of the different stories people carry in their faces? Some writer says, 'We come at length in ourselves to express the spirit within us. The physical fact has its perfect moral respondent.'"

"But that cannot apply to faces."

"I believe no general rule applies to all. But some faces do express at a glance the contents within. They are never difficult natures to read. Others set one wondering what their possessors will do in the great straits of life, when some emotion, magnetized by its own strength, sways and thrills them, and hurries them impetuously through contests. You ask if they will be bitter in anger, defiant, and uncompromising; or if through all the power and strength runs a fine stream of rarest love, like the glowing veins in an agate, and tells you what the draught would be if the right hand held the key to the fountain."

I was growing strangely interested, and asked, —

"What do you see in my face?"

"I'm not going to tell you now; but some time, when the friendship warrants the frankness, you may ask me; though I assure you I do not boast of my skill. You see that I count upon being friends;" and he smiled.

I held out my hand with a sudden impulse.

"Thank you. I have another fancy about names, Miss Adriance. If you have been wrongly called, we shall have a new christening. Now my mother, you see, must have had a presentiment. Philip would call up a vision of hazel eyes, chestnut curls, a laughing, careless fellow, with small regard for extreme conventionalities, fond of gay, social life, and home love. And Stuart is just the name for St. John — proud, stern, and suggestive."

"I will give you three guesses," I said, as his eyes questioned me.

"Margaret or Eleanor?"

"No."

"You are so tall and stately, and with that wealth of dusky hair, that you ought to have a queenly appellative. Softness and gentleness will not do for you."

"Why shouldn't I have a gentle name? Do you think I have nothing appealing in my nature?"

"Think of May, or Grace, or Jessie —"

"Or Ellen. Yet I am sure Ellen Douglas had some spirit and character."

A strange light wandered over his face, softening it indescribably.

"Your black eyes, with their slumberous fire, would spoil an Ellen. She should be small and slender, with loose, brown curls, and shy, downcast eyes of heaven's own blue; her voice should be smooth and cool, like the murmur of a midsummer stream through flowery meads. What strange dreams sometimes get tangled with one's life! But my last chance," and he roused himself with an effort — "Elizabeth?"

"It would be cruel to torment you. My mother loved my dead father so well that she gave me his name — Sydnie."

"Excellent. That heightens the mystery of your face."

"You insist upon that?"

"It is a cardinal point of faith with me. There's St. John's voice in the hall, so we will append to our conversation a 'to be continued;'" and he laughed lightly as he went out to meet his friend.

What a contrast the two men were! I could not help remarking it at the dinner table. How they had ever become such warm friends puzzled me. And this night Mr. St. John blossomed into a geniality and richness that was absolutely fascinating. How handsome he was, with a bright glow in his eyes and a flush upon his cheek! for although in the enjoyment of perfect health, he had very little color. We had a really delightful evening, and the picture remains in my mind as one of those perfect home scenes that I, at least, had rarely witnessed. Mrs. Westervelt's joy was complete; the sweet face was serene and content.

Mrs. Lawrence has a wonderful adaptableness. She seems at home everywhere, and enjoys all pleasures in the same refined and delicate manner. I suppose she has some choice, but none of her feelings are ever roused into active opposition. I wonder if she doesn't grow tired, living the same life over day after day. I should want some great event to happen, some incident that would stir my blood now and then.

After Philip's return we were a good deal gayer, or at least he gave to all delights his peculiar zest. His love for his mother was like a tender romance, and he treated her with a deference and devotion any wife might have been proud of. She appreciated it thoroughly; but I think she was most generous in that she did not seem to fear the time when she would be called upon to share it with another. Indeed, Philip's wife was rather a pet idea of hers. I smiled as I thought how Laura had discarded him from her future.

There was a series of small dinner-parties, concerts, and several operas to take up our attention; beyond this, rambles with Philip, who haunted picture galleries and artists' studios. He was not lacking in cultivation, as well as love for all things beautiful.

"It puzzles me how you can have learned so much," I said, late one afternoon, as we were sauntering through a quiet street.

"I believe nearly all the good things in my life came from Laurelwood," he returned, seriously.

"Love for art, for music, for home, and all refined enjoyments. You must have been an apt scholar, and Mr. St. John a most generous preceptor."

"When you know him better you will scarcely wonder. You have hardly seen his real character yet, and perhaps he might not show his heart as readily to a woman. I think he is a little suspicious of the sex; but he is noble enough to honor goodness when he meets with it."

"I have not been sufficiently noble to justify his appreciation, then — a rather mortifying conclusion."

"You don't believe that: I can tell it by the compression of your lips and the little shadow that comes in your eyes."

"Then my face has ceased to be mysterious."

"I understand some of its moods. Shall I tell you how I came to love St. John?"

"Yes," I answered, diverted from the question I meant to ask.

"Of course you can imagine how I was indulged through my boyhood, especially after I became an only child. My father was very proud of me. At college he kept me liberally supplied with money, and I ran into many temptations; youth is so taken with the glitter of show and power. I liked to be admired, and called a generous fellow; and that I did not plunge into absolute excesses was owing to the influence of my sweet mother. But, as you see, there was scarcely any restraint upon me. When I came home my father took me into his counting-house. It was merely a nominal position, and I might have idled my time shamefully; but I took quite a fancy to business. I squandered enough as it was, frequenting theatres, billiard halls, club-rooms, and champagne suppers, and driving a fast horse. You cannot realize the power of such influences, and how they blunt the finer feelings. One becomes accustomed to hearing the names of women he had respected bandied about in toasts and idle jests; truth, affection, and purity sneered at, and love perverted — bought and sold in market-places, — until one loses all faith in the holiness of human nature.

"After a while I was dangerously ill with a fever. I had never been sick before, and in the long convalescence there was plenty of time for thought. I used to watch mother, with her noiseless steps, smoothing pillows, arranging flowers, interpreting the slightest glance, and ministering unto me with unwearied devotion. How poorly I had requited her love and my father's unbounded confidence! I had wasted my energies in an idle, unprofitable life, and a weight like a mountain lay upon my heart. How could I escape walking in the old paths?

"St. John, happening to have some business with father, was at the house quite frequently, and we used to drive together. I suppose I must have moped and betrayed my want of spirits, for he took great pains to interest me. I found him so different from the men I had known, that at last I was won into betraying my secret uneasiness. A grand, rich nature, full of power, intellect, and courage, living the great truths he teaches to others, and offering no draught, be it ever so unwelcome a tonic, that he is not willing to test himself."

"He doesn't impress me in that manner," I said. "I have seen him sneer and be very bitter over some things."

"He *is* intolerant of shams. Having seen much of the world, he can readily distinguish between the false and the true. And, though gentle, there is a rigid side to his character. No man is ever wholly developed until he comes to the grand passion of his life. I want to see St. John fairly in love with a woman worthy of the regard such a man can give."

"But your own story."

"He persuaded mother to let him take me to Laurel-wood. It was my first visit, and in the spring. The glory of the place touched me deeply. It seemed to me that field and wood were never so beautiful. Quivering lights and trooping shadows; a perfect splendor of life in the flowers that shook out clouds of incense as a morning hymn; birds whose soaring crescendo broke into a thousand wild, sweet echoes; skies fretted with silver bars at mid-day, and glowing with purple and golden sunsets at night. Everything was instinct with a sense of quick, vital fresh-ness. Do you wonder that I found my soul? We used to have such long, delightful talks; and in the tender twi-light he would play on the organ many of those ineffable harmonies of the old masters. It was being 'born again.' I came back to my mother, her child."

"And you discovered the true secret of life," I said, musingly. "Some souls have a more difficult search. It seems to me half the things in this world are at war with the other half. How is one to distinguish?"

"By being true to God and one's self. The way is not so hard, after all; but we are blind and dull until some shock rouses us."

"It is more trying for a woman," I returned. "She is expected to pay some regard to the claims of society. I believe female reformers are at a discount."

"But patient, noble, high-toned women never are."

We had reached the house by this time. The breezy autumn wind had inspirited me. I felt strong and glad in every pulse, and ready to begin anew.

"I never can tell you all the reasons why I love St. John," Philip said, in a softened tone. "A month ago I was thankful for the lesson I had learned in self-denial and true manliness. Life isn't always fair and smooth.

There are thorns in nearly every path. Have I tired you with my confidences?"

"O, no." I experienced a quick, joyous, friendly feeling towards him. It was the first rare emotion of my life.

Running up stairs eagerly, — for we were a little late, — I met Mr. St. John on the landing — a cool, quiet, polished gentleman; a picture there in the light, mellowed through the ground globe: Philip Westervelt's hero — a Sir Galahad.

"Truant," he exclaimed, in a tone that influenced me curiously, "where have you been so long?"

"Walking with Mr. Westervelt, and talking. He isn't bitter, and cynical, and unjust, as you are."

Then I stood still, quite frightened. My thoughts had clothed themselves with words too soon.

"I am glad you have been well entertained," he returned, coldly, allowing me to pass without further comment.

What a bright, glowing face I saw in the glass! It *was* beautiful, and I could not help feeling glad. I had a presentiment that there were people in the world who could appreciate me, be patient with my faults, strengthen my earnest desire for what was best and highest in life, and help me to mould my character into that symmetry so much to be desired, where soul and body should not war with one another, but become a harmonious whole.

I was a little nervous as I went down to dinner; but Mr. St. John's face wore its usual serene expression. He never betrays any feeling to me.

CHAPTER VI.

"This is the excellent foppery of the world."
HAMLET.

WE saw Laura Hastings frequently, and I was surprised at the readiness with which she adapted herself to any position. The girl was a born actress. It was a mystery to me how she could appear so completely at home in any kind of mental garb in which she chose to clothe herself.

Mrs. Hastings smiled very complacently upon her child. Their rooms were generally thronged of an evening, and Laura queened it royally. I began to think Mrs. Hastings fully as good a manager as Mrs. Lawrence; and, though they were not really wealthy, everything was carried on with an air of elegance.

I called one day with Mrs. Westervelt, when Laura insisted I should remain to lunch, and carried me off to her room.

"My dear," she said, "I've been wild to see you all the morning. I had a most magnificent present last night, which I am sure you can appreciate;" and opening a casket, she displayed a pair of emerald bracelets of rare and exquisite workmanship. They seemed to make a glitter of sunlight in the small apartment.

"I leave you to guess the donor."

"Mr. Varick, I suppose: such gifts must be measured by the length of one's purse."

"Are they not splendid? You can have every lovely

thing you want; but to me they are perfect treasures.
And with them a card for Mrs. Thurston's ball. She is
his only sister, and immensely aristocratic. I fancy it was
a *special* permit."

"In what manner?"

"O, we plebeians haven't the *entrée* of that golden circle
by right. Mamma was hugely astonished. Of course you
know what it means."

"Not an engagement?"

"The next thing to it. We haven't progressed that
rapidly. Indeed, I'm sorry it's coming quite so soon."

"Do you really mean to accept him?"

"O, I shall accept, of course. Mamma would feel
tempted to sew me up in a sack and drop me in the Hud-
son if I didn't. And I must be married by next summer."

"What's the urgent necessity? You will not be ancient
by that time."

"But I have a handsome sister who is to be introduced.
We are too nearly of an age for comfort."

"I should think a sister would be a pleasant companion."

"Obtuse mortal: if a sister is handsome, she will rival
you; if plain, she will envy you and be spiteful. Gertrude
is a brilliant brunette, with great, lustrous eyes, and rich,
crimson cheeks, dashing, piquant, and glowing — just the
kind of woman that men go wild over. Mamma predicts
wonderful things for her. So, you see, after this winter
my reign will be at an end. I could comfort myself with
the pleasure of seeing her married first, and, perhaps, pick
up some of her old lovers."

"After she was married, you could reassert your sway."

"And be merely a side ornament in fashion's drawing-
room, holding a candle that my sister may see the better
to put on airs and patronize me. O, I know the world to

the last chapter; and no younger sister marries before
me."

"You do not take a very amiable view," I said.

"And you cannot realize my situation. Mamma will
expect me to make my old finery do next summer, and
spend everything upon Gertrude. I shall look faded,
passée, and, very likely, be ill-natured. People will wonder why I didn't marry, and try to make me out half a
dozen years older than I am. The world is a good enough
slave, but a hard master."

"The other would be galling slavery to me."

"We are altogether different, my dear. A comfortable
husband and a luxurious life are my ambition."

"But he is so much older, — rather stiff and formal, it
seems to me."

"I'd like to have him younger; but it will not do to let
the chance go by. So I shall accept him; and, if something better offers, I shall do the pathetic in a graceful
fashion."

"How heartless you are, Laura!" I could not forbear
saying.

She laughed.

"It doesn't pay to be sentimental. I am determined to
make a good match; but if anything better than this offers
I shall surely take it."

"And circumstances only will keep you from trifling
with Mr. Varick. I think he has *some* regard for you."

"Don't look so horrified. I shall manage it admirably.
A charmingly frank confession, in which I shall bewail my
mistake, amid tears and blushes, and appeal to his mag-
nanimous heart. There's nothing like flattering men a
little; they all have a weak spot. The secret of being
fascinating is only keeping people pleased with themselves.
When you rub them up the wrong way, it makes their eye-

sight ever so much keener, and they are able to detect every flaw in you."

"But think of the home hallowed by no affection!"

"It will be rendered brilliant by money, nevertheless. I should soon tire of the humdrum existence you worship. Goodness is invariably stupid; and love becomes, in time, a bore. If I was insane enough to marry some one who insisted upon my gracing the domestic fireside, and thought holding my hand and reading poetry sufficient compensation, I should elope with the first dashing fellow who presented himself."

"And you suppose no such temptation will occur to Mrs. Varick?"

"My dear, I have a great regard for the proprieties of life. I shall have an elegant house, an indulgent husband, and hosts of company. I can invite Gertrude to my parties, drive her out in my carriage, share honors with her next summer at Newport; so I fancy my time will be sufficiently occupied. I may do a little flirting on the sly, but it will be of the most harmless kind."

"And after you have gone through with the round of pleasures?"

"I'll go over them again, of course."

"The life looks bald, and heartless, and uninviting to me," I said.

"Sydnie," she began, suddenly, "why don't you take Phil? He is one of the good, fireside kind."

I colored with conscious shame; for somehow I could not bring myself to discuss my preferences in this flippant manner.

"Confess!" She knelt before me, and looked steadily into my face.

"There is nothing to confess. We are simply friends. If you need any further assurance, I *like* him very much."

"I absolutely despair of you. What do you intend to do with yourself?"

"I may find some place and employment."

"I will read your fortune. You are starting out with impossible theories, which men will tolerate now because you are young, handsome, and rich. But when you begin to fade, grow disappointed in the failure of your fine ideas, and possibly a little sharp in temper, you'll marry like the rest of us. Wouldn't it be grand to meet in about ten years and compare notes?"

The bell rang for lunch, and we went down stairs. A friend of Mrs. Hastings had come in, and Mrs. Thurston's ball was the great topic of discussion. Mrs. Hastings talked of their invitation with most aristocratic nonchalance; but she was too well-bred to hint at Laura's prospects, though I could not help but feel that they were both secretly elated.

After that we went down Broadway. When we parted she gave a dainty little nod of her head.

"I shall be sure to see you after I have distracted every one with my emeralds and my rich lover," were her parting words.

I walked slowly to Madison Square, wondering what changes ten years would bring about. How strange it seemed, to stand upon the threshold of life with so many pleasant things about one! I could afford to wait to marry for love if I chose. But *would* I ever find the ideal affection that lighted up the visions of my brain?

I was expatiating on the richness and beauty of Laura's bracelets the next morning, as we three ladies lingered over the breakfast-table. Going to the library, Philip met me with a question in his eyes that made me smile.

"Don't be vexed," he began, deprecatingly; "I heard part of your story. Do you know who gave Laura those emeralds?"

"Yes," I answered.

"Was it a Mr. Varick?"

"Why do you think so?" I was in no hurry to betray the secret.

"I saw him in Ball & Black's purchasing just such a set, and he left an order for them to be marked and sent to his residence. I heard he had taken Laura out driving several times."

"He was the donor. They are to wear at his sister's ball."

"A man like Mr. Varick doesn't go so far unless he is in earnest, and Mrs. Hastings is too much a woman of the world to let such an opportunity go by unimproved. Poor Laura will be relentlessly sacrificed. Why do you smile?"

"I was thinking that Laura might feel quite comfortable about it."

"She cannot. I have known her from a child. Her training has not been of the highest order, but she is capable of enjoying a better life than that will be. Why, Mr. Varick must be nearly fifty, pompous, and, I was going to say, soulless. If left to herself, she would be immeasurably above such traffic."

She had succeeded in deceiving Philip as to her real character. Indeed, what *was* real about her?

"I fancy she will be comparatively happy as Mrs. Varick," I said.

"Happy! The word is a mockery in that connection. I could forgive a girl who married for the sake of saving her family from want, but even then it would be a miserable farce. Laura is young, and has not the shadow of an excuse. Yet I can see how her mother will persuade, and get her entangled before she is hardly aware of it. Does every door turn only with a golden key?"

"I hope not," I said.

"I wonder what you will do!" looking past me rather than at me.

"Believe in all sorts of obsolete goodness, and spend my days hunting the impossible."

"It is *not* impossible; and for a woman to lose her faith in love seems monstrous. Poor Laura! You are her friend; why do you not try to incline her to better things?"

"I am afraid I should make a poor missionary."

"They are best who hold the faith firmly;" and he smiled.

I felt it would be dishonorable to portray Laura as I knew her, and was silent. She spoke the truth when she said it was as well to affect virtues as to possess them. How few people could penetrate the veil, unless brought into most intimate contact! And I believe, in her way, Laura was happy.

She went to the ball, and was enthusiastic over Mrs. Thurston's style and elegance. Shortly after we heard a rumor of the engagement, which Mrs. Westervelt contradicted out of pure generosity, and, the next time Laura called, asked her what could have given rise to such an absurd story.

Laura looked up with charming *naïveté*, and declared the report true.

"My dear child — to throw yourself away in the very bloom of youth!" and Mrs. Westervelt's face expressed all the astonishment and disapproval of which it was capable.

"I am aware that I shall be misunderstood;" and Laura made her voice soft and touching, while her eyes drooped a little, a trick in which she was well versed; "but Mr. Varick has proved himself a kind and generous man, and not incapable of winning a woman's regard. I liked him at Newport, and since then, when I have seen him in

contrast with too many of the vapid and conceited cox-
combs that frequent society, I have been led to pay him a
higher respect than before. I rate good sterling sense and
a mature mind higher than a mere pleasing exterior."

"If you can be happy," Mrs. Westervelt said, doubt-
fully.

"I think I shall, and not only that, but render him happy
also. That will be my highest study;" and she blushed
most becomingly. I confess I felt positively indignant.

"Didn't I go through with it capitally ?" she whispered,
in the hall. "I like to keep in Mamma Westervelt's good
graces. I depend upon you not to repeat my idle gossip."

"It was shameful!" I said; "I actually blushed for
you."

"Your virtue is altogether too violent. You must
train it to a more high-bred elegance. Mamma is up to
the seventh heaven of bliss. Mr. Varick proves a warmer
lover than I supposed, and thinks a three-months engagement long enough. So I suppose I must resign myself to
my fate; but I mean to go to Europe as a reward."

I brushed her kiss off of my lips in a strange heat of
passion. It was seldom that she offered such a caress,
and I knew she must be in a charmingly complacent
mood.

That evening we were gathered around the grate — for
the nights had grown chilly. There being no visitors,
Mrs. Lawrence had yielded to a headache, and gone to
her own room. Mr. St. John had been reading from a
new volume of poems, but presently closed his book, and
we fell into a desultory conversation.

Mrs. Westervelt spoke of Laura. My friendship, for all
it was but a name, kept me silent. Mr. St. John made
some generous excuses for her in her training and home
influence.

"What a pity," Philip said, sadly, "that marriage, the noblest and sweetest boon to humanity, should be perverted to unhallowed uses — degraded into mere barter for station and wealth. It gives faith a cruel wound. How can one make advances in the higher principles of life when the heart is fed upon husks?"

"Yet how little of the better aliment we find! Marriages are rare where hearts are united for a lifetime," Mr. St. John returned.

"If united at all, it must be for a lifetime."

"I don't know;" and his voice fell a trifle, while a shady look came into his eyes. "I have seen love last for years, and then perish miserably."

"It was not love. St. John, your faith is perfect everywhere except upon this point. I wish you knew. Love comes with truth in her heart, and constancy in every pulse, to sit down an everlasting guest in the hearts of those who truly welcome her. If there are sorrows and storms, she spreads her wings for an ark of shelter; if toil and care, she lightens it with her blessed smile. No room for regrets or jealousies, for both are true in deed and thought; no coldness, for she stands between them and the frosts of time. Year by year they grow into perfect accord, bringing heaven nearer with every dawn. Can such love ever fail?"

"You are right. This is love in its highest purity. God help us all to find it."

Philip sighed softly, and we all lapsed into silence. In the shade stealing over his face there was something that made one sad to see — a hope missed, or, perhaps, dropped out of life. It startled me for a moment.

And then I wondered if I should ever find such a star to light me on my way. Existence would be bare and bleak without it. I was capable of loving with passionate intensity; and yet, standing here upon the shore, I trembled with nameless apprehension. What if I should wreck this precious bark? There were so many ingulfing tides and quicksands. I longed to dare its mystery, and yet shrank from that fateful time.

Our stay had been prolonged on account of the opera, which had been unusually fine. It was mid-October before a day for our return was appointed.

I had grown warmly attached to the Westervelts. Between Philip and myself there existed a warm regard, too generous for love, and yet singularly comprehensive. I had a faint misgiving that his mother expected it to ripen into the rare bloom of that passion; and Mrs. Lawrence smiled an unqualified approval.

I had a fancy, too, that another watched. Was it for his sake? That thought annoyed me. Did Mr. St. John fancy that I should take pleasure in idly coquetting with such a heart, or did he believe me not worthy of so high a regard?

I had been lingering in the library a long while with Philip one afternoon, and fallen into a pleasant reverie, when a light step brought me back to reality; or, rather, the peculiar presence which I felt with a vivid presentiment. I turned, and our eyes met. Mr. St. John crossed the room, and stood beside me.

" Well?" I said, at length, wishing to break the powerful spell.

" Would one dare to be friends with you?" It was uttered in a low tone, and did impress me singularly.

" Mr. Westervelt doesn't find it a difficult matter," I answered, coldly.

" It is about that; and if I take a friend's privilege, pardon me. You are young, and have turned but few pages in the book of experience: I have read it to its bitter end. Am I not right in thinking you would avoid giving pain to one who is susceptible to deepest anguish as well as dearest joy?"

His voice was grave, but gentle in its inflection, as if somewhere in the darkness a chord of music had been touched, and sent back a responsive thrill.

I made no answer with my lips, but I think he saw assent in my eyes.

"Philip is affectionate, confiding, essentially truthful. Is it quite right to encourage a love that you do not, cannot return?"

"Why can I not?" I said, almost defiantly, yet scarcely above a whisper.

"Because your soul was cast in a different mould."

"You do not understand. I have given no encouragement of the kind you mean."

"Not intentionally. I acquit you of that. But a ship may be lost by following a stray light from some distant hill. Child, it is saving you as well. Tell me that I may trust you."

His hand touched mine: the strength and power magnetized me into a yielding mood. It was like being borne along by some swift current.

"You may trust me."

I said it almost without any volition of my own. The eyes, dusky with a luminous light, transfixed mine, reading my inmost soul, an unwritten page as yet. Then our lips met just an instant. If he had willed, he could have carried every pulse captive. What hidden cause restrained him?

I knew then that I could not love Philip Westervelt with the strength and passion of my slowly dawning nature. He was manly to the heart's core, tender, susceptible, and the woman of his choice would be twice blest — when she gave and when she received. But this chalice was not for me; it would be held to some other lips. My draught might be perilously sweet, yet there would be in it a flavor keen almost to bitterness.

I sat there in silence long after he left me, trembling with strange anticipations. I fancied my life was not to be as other lives, but filled with extremes, as it had been in childhood. I felt like one who has been long in darkness, and whose pulses flutter at the first tremulous ray of light. I would go whithersoever it led.

CHAPTER VII.

"I do believe,
Though I have found them not, that there may be
Words which are things, hopes which will not deceive."

CHILDE HAROLD.

I AM delighted to be at Laurelwood again.

In the ripened flushes of gold and crimson the season seems to gather up its trailing garments, and sweep imperiously through fields of mellow sunshine, groves of flowers, and clustering trees, leaving the maple scarlet and glowing with the warm embrace, and lighting the whole landscape with tawny flames. I thrill at the splendor, and long to hold the days in some giant clasp, that they fly not too rapidly. Long, inspiriting rides bring a flush to my cheek, and sometimes I can almost feel the fire that I know must flash from my eyes.

Mrs. Lawrence left me alone with nature while she prepared the house for a ball, that I might not lack in-door entertainment. I thought there was nothing to improve, but she did find some alterations to make. She has a remarkable eye, certainly. I don't wonder that Mr. St. John admires her: she is so quiet and elegant in all she does. I believe she could have everything taken out of the drawing-room and replaced, without a person suspecting it from any noise or bustle.

The house was a marvel on the night of the ball. The spacious hall, with its marble floor polished anew, every niche surprising you with a tall vase of flowers, or some dainty statue gracefully posed ; the wide stairs, with their soft carpet, a mass of delicate climbing vines, and moss that seemed to have been just gathered from rank, shady woods, yet dripping with moisture. The lights were softened, in order to give it a dreamy, suggestive look, rather than a brilliant glare.

If possible, the drawing-room was still more magnificent. At any time it was a storehouse of rare treasures, so exquisitely arranged that it never seemed crowded, and yet lured you on and on with a sense of undiscovered beauty. On the opposite side of the hall the library displayed its choice stores, and the gilded organ pipes made bright one shadowy corner. A large reception room for ordinary purposes had been turned into a cosy nook by bringing out some curious little stands, exquisitely carved or inlaid, until they looked like pure mother-of-pearl. A vase of flowers, a book of engravings, or some odd foreign toy won you to look, and then a luxurious chair wooed you to stay.

Mr. St. John asked me to go through the rooms before the revel began, never checking my enthusiasm in its wildest flights. I think he has been more friendly of late; some of his moods absolutely startle me, for I feel as if I were drifting down some weird, entrancing shore, and long to reach out my hand to cling to solid rock or tree. I am afraid of him, and yet I never appear to have the power to rescue myself. I am not sure but I like that bright, generous geniality best; it has less power in it, and does not give one the sense of hurrying on breathlessly — whither?

All the neighboring gentry had been invited, and some guests from a distance. By dusk there was a trooping through the halls, and a low, pleasant confusion of voices. I obeyed Mrs. Lawrence's injunctions, and kept to my room. Thirza, it seemed, would never have done with me.

I had grown quite used to her pleasant service; but now she dallied unconscionably.

A servant came up from Mr. St. John. He had sent me a few Cromatilla rose-buds and lemon-blossoms to wear, and I thanked him from the depth of my heart for his interest.

At last I was dressed. Mrs. Lawrence pronounced me perfect. I hardly knew myself, I was such a marvel of tulle and wraith-like blond lace, that must have been woven in Arachne's loom, and still seemed glittering with dew-drops.

"This outshines Newport," I said, with a gay laugh.

The rooms were filling rapidly when Mr. St. John escorted me down. Two or three familiar voices restored my mental equilibrium, but it seemed to me a perfect chaos of silk and satin and jewels, with waves of lace, and shimmer of curls like sunshine. The band was stationed in the hall, and was giving some low, suggestive airs, that made the scene appear more than ever like enchantment.

Mr. Graham came to claim me for the first quadrille. I felt quite at home with him, and he was delighted with the favor.

"What has happened to you?" he asked, in the earliest pause. "You have blossomed like some magnificent tropical plant. I could hardly have believed my sight at the first glance."

I had grown accustomed to admiration, and only smiled.

"What a day that was in the summer! I wonder if you remember it?"

"I have a pretty good memory," I said.

"I thought of you at Newport, and was tempted to make a flying visit. Only it wouldn't have been half the pleasure to you that it would have proved to me."

It was our turn now, and I was glad. But if his lips were silent, his eyes still spoke. I couldn't help thinking about his engagement with a sort of dim misgiving. Had I been unwise that summer day? Mr. St. John had lectured me about it crossly enough, but then my conscience had acquitted me.

"I will be very careful," I said to myself, as a crash of music announced the quadrille ended.

"Have you been introduced to father?" Mr. Graham asked, instead of seating me. "They were quite late in coming down. I believe mother thought she must make herself especially grand in order to do honor to Miss Adriance."

"Then I must reward her," I said, smilingly, and we took our way through the crowd.

General Graham, stout, rosy, and undeniably Scotch without his strong accent, pleased me at once. Mrs. Graham, fair, round, and motherly, with a sweet face and silvery voice, and beside them a petite fairy, with soft brown curls, and eyes like the starry flax flower.

"My cousin — Miss Keith," Hugh Graham said.

I ventured another look. It seemed to me as if I must have seen her somewhere before — one of those dim impressions that affect the brain so singularly.

Mr. St. John came in sight. "I believe there is an inquiry for you in the hall," he remarked.

"I'm to have another quadrille," Mr. Graham said, in a whisper.

Miss Keith was dancing opposite this time. What a tender, loving little face! what entreating eyes! I wondered if she was fond of her cousin. Somehow, it wasn't a marriage at all to my fancy. Were people continually misplaced?

There was not much time for speculation, however. The

gay scene was delightful, and appealed to every sense.   I
danced, chatted, and promenaded the rooms and hall, listened to flatteries that were delicate, and some that were
distasteful; and as a ball, I fancy it was a brilliant success.
People strayed away in little groups, and lingered in shady
corners, laughed and talked, looked at the pictures, and
examined the curious articles of foreign *virtu* in that in-
formal manner, as if they felt entirely at ease.   The supper
passed off delightfully.   I had never seen anything so
beautiful as the table.   The china, brilliant and thin,
glasses ground and cut until they caught the light at
every point, an epergne of frosted silver, in which flowers
and fruit were one tangled mass of color and beauty, and
two vases of malachite, festooned around the edges with
hanging clusters of luscious purple grapes, forming a glows
ing contrast.   I absolutely wondered how any one could
eat in that dazzle of loveliness.

It had not palled upon me when it ended.   Indeed, I
had been in unusual spirits all the evening.   The gayety
seemed less frivolous here, where there was no gossip of
lovers and good marriages.   At least, if there was I did
not hear it.

The Grahams were among those who remained all night;
and we had a cosy breakfast late the next morning, with
the dining-room quite in its usual trim, and no faded fragments of our night's dissipation visible.   I found Miss
Keith very shy, but with an odd charm, I might say quaint-
ness, that gave me a desire to know more about her.

General Graham gave us a most cordial invitation to
visit Mont Argyle, his residence, some distance from
Laurelwood.   A kind, courtly old gentleman, that I confess
I admired exceedingly.   Hugh seconded his father, with
an entreating glance.

"I wish you would come real soon, Miss Adriance," Miss

Keith said, shyly raising her eyes from the glimmer of their long lashes. "We are quiet people, and cannot promise you so much magnificence, but out of doors the country around us is grand. There are some splendid rides."

"And of course you ride, Miss Adriance," Hugh exclaimed. "It is one of my passions. We have some magnificent horses, at any rate;" and he laughed.

Miss Keith evidently was not given to jealousy. I experienced a strong inclination to take her in my arms and kiss the sweet face; but I was a little afraid of Mr. St. John's distant eyes, and so behaved discreetly.

After that episode, or rather plunge, into society, I floated upon the topmost wave. I am ashamed to chronicle the little progress I made in more solid matters. I found no time for study, very little for reading, and the merest point for reflection, though so much gayety does not tend to sharpen one's faculties, unless it may be in the matter of dress. The lazy languor of mornings abed, when the brain still lingers in cloudy dreamland, evenings filled with music, conversation, and the pleasant nothings that pass between well-bred and genial people. One thing gave me a secret little pain; I am almost ashamed to confess it; but Mr. St. John and I drifted apart; I seemed to lose the little hold I had once gained. We did not quarrel; indeed, he was considerate and polite, solicitous for my enjoyments, and left me at the fullest liberty; as if he did not seem to care, or thought my pleasures quite too frivolous for him.

I believe Mrs. Lawrence took unbounded satisfaction in my dawning career. The house was thronged with visitors, and we were besieged by invitations. I did try to hold myself aloof from more meaning attentions, for the triumph in such cases would not pay me for the pain, I well knew.

We met Hugh Graham frequently, sometimes with his cousin, oftener without. I had a consciousness that he took especial pleasure in these encounters. To dance with me, take me to supper, or any attention where he could clasp my fingers for a moment, was a delight which he did not care to conceal. It made me nervous, for I knew he had no right thus to display fondness for another woman, and I feared it was but working unhappiness for himself. He could never awaken within me the friendship that had been given to Philip so spontaneously, and no warmer sentiment would ever have been possible. There were many pleasant traits in his character, but it possessed no vital attraction for me. I was learning to make some fine distinctions.

Mrs. Lawrence saw no danger. Perhaps she had too much faith in her own creed to believe heresy possible. One morning when we were alone, I said, —

"When does Mr. Graham expect to marry his cousin?"

"O, I suppose there's no hurry. Although she is past twenty-one, she still looks a very child, and he seems fond of his liberty. As they have always known each other, there is no extravagant romance about the engagement."

"I wonder if they love each other!"

"As much as is necessary, I suppose;" and the placid eyes just lifted themselves from a dainty bit of crocheting.

"My dear Mrs. Lawrence, how much *is* necessary?" I said, with some impatience.

"Not as much as you think. They are very well matched indeed, and having been brought up together, their regard is a matter of gradual growth. She will make a quiet little wife, and never annoy him by any foolish officiousness. He will keep up his house in the style of his father, and lead a happy, easy, social life."

"But there seems no heart in it," I said, warmly. "I should like him better if he evinced a decided preference for her. She is a pretty, dainty little thing, and a man might well be proud of her."

"It is questionable taste to display much fondness in society."

"He need not be silly about it. But I have seen his eyes light up and his whole face in a glow at some other woman's coming," and then I paused, half frightened, for I seemed upon the verge of an unwise confession.

"Most young men are somewhat given to flirting," she said, with superb indifference. "In a case like this it does no harm, for their engagement is settled, and I think Mr. Graham has too much sense to give up his cousin and her fortune for any foolish passion. A man is expected to make himself agreeable in society, before he is married, at least."

"It would never do for me," I said, with a rising flush. "If a man loved me at all, I should want his entire regard. I shouldn't like to see him radiant for another, and coldly polite to me."

"That spirit is wonderfully becoming to your style," she returned, glancing at me, for she could stop anywhere to announce some grace, or special defect that she wanted remedied, just as Siebenka's wife could count the striking of the clock between her husband's kisses. "Only I should advise you not to try it too often with a husband. Women rarely gain a point by making a desperate assault, while a little skilful managing works wonders."

"I detest managing," I exclaimed. "I should be perfectly satisfied to take the truth from any one else, and I must tell it."

"Experience will teach you many things," she said, "and soften your asperities."

7

Those remarks always vexed me. Did every one invariably reach the same commonplace level in feeling? So I took refuge in silence, lest I should prove unamiable.

Among the Christmas invitations was one to Mont Argyle. It was made doubly tempting to Mrs. Lawrence from the fact that some distinguished guests had been asked to meet her, and, as it were, placed it out of her power to refuse. Hugh rode over with the note, and was to spend the night.

"I wish we were not going," I said to Mr. St. John.

"So your enthusiastic penchant for Miss Keith has ended? About the duration of a woman's fancy," and he gave that light, irritating laugh.

"I like and admire Miss Keith exceedingly."

"But the whim has taken you! I doubt if my sister will consent to your staying home alone."

I wonder, if I had said my say, woman fashion, whether it would have made any difference! My delicacy *did* shrink from parading this man's regard before other eyes. It seemed like an insult to offer such attentions to me.

And yet that evening I found Hugh very gentlemanly and deferential. Had I misjudged him?

As we were to remain several days, Thirza had to look over the finery, and pack a trunk full. Just before we started, a letter came from Laura Hastings, enclosing wedding cards. The missive was eminently characteristic.

"You see," she wrote, "that, in spite of your sage counsel and advice, I am about to take the fatal step. The brown-stone mansion on Fifth Avenue, and the prospect of queening it royally, have proved too much for me. I am about to commit the unpardonable sin of marrying a man old enough to be my father, and trust to my wisdom to make a most amiable husband of him. He adores me (my dear, old men are always foolish), and I have persuaded him to take me to Europe. He is indulgent and not given to jealousy; and I fancy we shall be as happy as most people. Think of me in diamonds and point lace, and confess your love in a cottage looks shabby by comparison."

Laura's destiny was settled, then. Mrs. Lawrence considered her prospects very brilliant. Was the whole world given to the worship of Mammon?

There had been a heavy fall of snow, and our journey to Mont Argyle was very delightful to me; perhaps the more so because Mr. St. John was so bright and companionable. When we came in sight of the place it looked picturesque in the extreme. Doubtless great offences had been committed against the rules of architecture, but with all the points and angles hooded in snow it was a veritable fairy palace. Great evergreens were draped in ermine, clustering vines made sparkling snow wreaths, tipped with whitest blossoms. It was quite a luxury, and the country people were making the most of it.

As to interior, Mont Argyle looked most inviting. Cosy rooms, warm and light, deep windows, little nooks and corners, and a fragrant perfume from the Christmas decorations, the spicy odor brought out by contact with the heat, clusters of bright berries interspersed, and vases of cut flowers, giving a kind of summery suggestion.

I felt quite well acquainted with Miss Keith, from our frequent meetings, and yet I hesitated a little in making advances.

"I am so glad to have you here," she said, as I came down stairs. I always made my toilet operations brief when left to myself; and I was anxious to gain a few moments before dinner.

"Are you, really?" and I glanced at her pure, sweet face.

"Yes; I have been counting upon a visit for so long — since that night of the ball. What a lovely time it was! And Laurelwood is so perfect in itself! I don't blame you for wanting to stay there. And then such hosts of engagements as you must have!"

"I do live in a whirl," I said, laughingly.

"But it must be very charming to have people like you so well; though I don't know how one could help paying you homage."

"So you think the royal road to my heart is flattery?"

"No; and that isn't flattery, either. But if I *could* find the royal road —"

"Well, what would you do?"

"Besiege the castle."

Her frank eyes touched me with their pleading light.

"It capitulates;" and I stooped to give her the kiss I had held in my heart for her a long while.

Hugh sauntered up to us, and began to talk to me. I watched them both narrowly. They certainly were *not* in love with each other. If there had ever been any flame of passion, it had burned itself out.

Dinner was announced, and from that till bed-time I hardly said ten words to Miss Keith; for at the table the conversation was general, and led by General Graham, who proved an admirable host. Afterwards I sang a little, and woke an admiring chord in the general's heart. He had volumes of old ballads, and kept making selections so continually, that his niece interfered.

"I am afraid we shall tire Miss Adriance," she said, gently.

"O, no," I replied; "music is one of my luxuries, and I like to make it afford pleasure to others."

"Your singing is a part of yourself," Hugh whispered; "it is connected with my first sweet memories of you."

I would not even raise my eyes to his, but an uncomfortable flush crept over my face.

Mrs. Lawrence and Mrs. Graham settled to a harmless, high-bred gossip about laces, and jewels, and silks. Mr. St. John looked over a book of Italian engravings with Miss Keith — Ellen her name was. Their conversation had a look of animation, for her eyes brightened, and a faint peach-blossom tint fluttered over her face. Now and then a murmur of his voice floated to me in soft deliciousness that stirred me strangely. He *did* admire her.

Hugh Graham and his father were stationed one upon each side of me, and I studiously averted the glances that annoyed me. *Would* no one see? Were they all blind? Or was this harmless flirting?

"There," General Graham said, at length, "you have given me a rare treat, and I will not be unreasonable. Few young ladies would entertain an old man so pleasantly. Ellen often sings to me; but she is our own."

He uttered the last two words with a lingering fondness.

"You are to come to me for music while I stay, since you can compliment so prettily," I returned, with a smile; and then I ensconced myself beside Mrs. Lawrence, keeping Hugh at bay. We retired quite early, in view of the next night's dissipation.

The Christmas dinner at Mont Argyle was different from most of the festivities I had shared; a select but really delightful party, with some old Scotch traits and preferences; an evening of dancing and other entertainments, and a veritable mistletoe bough, under which there was no little amusement.

I had been waltzing with Hugh — perhaps a not very prudent movement, when I had been rather curt and cold all day; but it was one of those events which seemed quite out of my power to prevent. Being warm and tired, I declared that I should dance no more, and drew my hand away, with a petulant gesture.

A moment before I had seen Ellen enter the conservatory, and, as some one called Hugh, I followed thither.

She was not there; but I sat down on a low bench and glanced out of the window at the moonlight — frosty, it appeared, as the snow. How strangely cold and still all that great world looked in its garb of ermine.

There was a step beside me, and a form bent over, clasping me with unmistakable fervor.

"My darling! my darling!" was breathed through passionate lips.

I tried to raise myself, but the branches caught my dress.

"You *must* hear me now. All day you have shunned me and treated me coldly, because you knew —"

"Hush, Mr. Graham," I said, at last, confronting him in the shady light made by the branches; "you have no right to say such words to me."

"I have the right of a man who has just learned what love is; who snaps the green withes that bound him, and dares to think for himself. And I believe you *do* care. I have seen the color come and go in your face. You have kept outwardly tranquil because you were proud and honorable; but that is no longer necessary. I shall not hesitate to acknowledge my mistake — mistake indeed! I never knew what love was until I met you last summer; and Heaven can bear me witness that I have been true to that one thought."

All this had been uttered in a rapid breath — a resistless torrent that I could not check.

"Mr. Graham," I said, coldly, "your truth and honor are due to another woman."

"She shall no longer stand between. I will tell her this very hour. If I have been weak in waiting—"

"You were weakest when you loved me. Listen while I say that I do not, cannot love you."

"Because you think of my cousin, and the bond between. I did not know, when I drifted into that compact, that the world held such a glorious woman; that I should see her, hear her speak, clasp her soft fingers in such a tender touch."

"This is a wild, unreasoning passion. It humbles me to be made the recipient of it. Let me go, Mr. Graham!"

"No; you shall not leave me until you have said one little word—that I am dear to you. I can wait for love. I can earn forgiveness by devotion."

If I had loved him, I must have yielded to that imploring face. But instead of a simple liking, I began to experience an aversion.

"Shall I call for assistance? A guest in your own house!"

My tones were haughty, and I believe my eyes literally flashed fire.

"My darling, you are cruel;" and he stood apart, with folded arms.

I passed out, meeting Ellen in the hall.

"What is the matter?" she asked. "Your face is in a glow, and your hands are like ice. Where have you been?"

Before I could answer, some one joined us. I was glad to see a movement among the guests for departure. We returned to the drawing-room, where General Graham was wishing a party good night. Mr. St. John stood by the mantel, an impassible statue. There could be no going to him for counsel.

I saw no more of Hugh that night, but I took Ellen up to my room.

"What a curious mood you are in," she said, presently; "or do you always grow handsome at midnight, when other people begin to fade? For you are so brilliant, you look quite uncanny."

"Ellen," I began, "are you satisfied with having me here? Would you not be happier if we had never met?"

She looked wonderingly at me an instant, then the soft eyes drooped.

"No," she said; "do not think of that. If you will only let me love you. But you have such a strange, weird charm that I sometimes feel almost afraid."

"How much do you love your cousin?"

After I had asked the abrupt question, I felt abashed.

"O," she said, with a little cry, "don't think of me. I guessed it all long ago. Our engagement was a childish affair — better broken than kept. And if you can make him happier — "

"He has been mistaken," I returned, with a rising flush. "You may feel that I have led him on but to mock him at the last; yet it is not so. I have tried to make him understand that his attentions were not only wrong, but distasteful to me. I have endeavored to lead him to think of you — "

"There is no reason, now," she said, almost joyfully. "Do not think I shall be heart-broken."

"My dear Ellen, if you *can* comprehend," I exclaimed, impatiently, "I do not love your cousin."

She looked blankly at me. I believe she suffered deeply for his disappointment.

"Don't hate me," was my imploring petition. "If you *could* know how honorable I have tried to be, even if these black facts do stare me in the face. And I have not one friend to pity or comfort."

She kissed me tenderly. I fancied there were some

tears upon her face. Yet she was not throbbing nor trembling, as I did, in every pulse.

"Dear," she said, "it is late, and you are over excited. Rest assured that I do not blame you. I had only hoped—" and her pale lips quivered.

"And you did not love him? Tell me that again."

"I did not love him, though I should have spent my life in trying to make him happy."

There was no mistaking that calm tone.

"Ellen, do you know what love is?"

I enclosed the little face suddenly with my hands, and turned it towards the light. It was a vivid crimson. Ashamed of having thus rudely wrested her secret from her, I let her go. We kissed again in silence, and parted. I hugged to my heart the consciousness that there was some real love in the world. But did it ever meet with a just reward?

CHAPTER VIII.

" We twain have met, like ships upon the sea,
   To hold an hour's converse, so short, so sweet.
   One little hour! And then away they speed
   On lonely paths, through mist, and cloud, and foam,
   Perchance to meet no more."   ALEX. SMITH.

I SLEPT very little that night, and kept revolving the
problem of destiny in my mind. How oddly we all get
linked together and confused by a tangle of circumstances!
Could I have done differently, and would it have been
best? Would Ellen have been happy in marrying her
cousin ?

I was still in bed when Thirza came, although the sun
was shining in at every window. I felt languid and apprehensive, and wished I could be transported back to
Laurelwood. Instead, I must go through not only this
day, but one or two more, keeping my serenity undisturbed,
outwardly, at least.

I found Ellen waiting for me in the hall, and appreciated
the act of delicacy on her part. We were the last to enter
the breakfast-room. Hugh's color deepened as I gave him
a furtive glance, but, the conversation being general, all
awkwardness soon passed away. Our host was planning a
drive for the morning's enjoyment, though Mrs. Graham
insisted we had much better stay at home and rest. When
I found the general had decided to take me in his party I
was ready to go; for at present I did not desire to risk
another interview with Hugh. But this gave me no

opportunity to see Ellen; for after lunch there was music, and a few calls, which occupied the time until dinner. However, we all dispersed early in the evening. I caught a glimpse of the wistful eyes following me, and said, in a low tone,—

"Will you come to my room, Ellen?"

"With pleasure," was the response.

So, after Thirza had brushed out my hair, I dismissed her. A moment after, I answered the low tap at my door.

Ellen seated herself on the hassock, and leaned her arms upon my knee. What a simple, lovely child she seemed.

"I have had a long talk with Hugh to-day," she began. "We are both better satisfied to give up the engagement. It will disappoint uncle sadly; but I do think it will be wiser for Hugh. I should never have been strong enough to rouse his ambition or pride. It would have proved another wasted life, idled away in ease and indolence. The right chord has been touched, although —" and as she paused, I saw a tear glittering on her long lashes.

"I am afraid I have made a good deal of trouble for you all," I returned. "I cannot tell you how much I regret it."

"Is there *no* hope for Hugh? Miss Adriance, you don't know what he is capable of. And if there was some high aim to lead him on, I know he could and would strive to render himself worthy of such a woman."

"My darling, you rate me too highly. I cannot even solve the difficulties in my own path; and I should be a poor guide for any other human soul. Love might inspire a woman; but I have not even that. We could never be anything beyond the most ordinary friends."

"Then it is useless to try?"

"Is not the richest love spontaneous? Why have you failed in learning to love him?"

The fair face flushed, and the eyes were downcast.

"I want to be honest with you," she said, presently. "I fancied in the earlier years that I did love him. My nature is quiet, and to a certain extent passive; he was stronger, and swayed me by the force of his impressions; but he was young, and there was no occasion for hurrying our marriage. So it has gone on. Last summer we were staying at Sulphur Springs, uncle's favorite resort. I met a stranger, and formed one of those transient acquaintances that generally leave behind only a pleasant memory. But this man had a soul that spoke to mine, moved it as nothing else ever had. I did not dream of danger. On the last evening of his stay we walked together for an hour or two, and drifted out on the swift current of love. It was told in looks and a clasp of the hand, for he knew I was engaged to my cousin, and he waited for a sign from me. I was brave enough then to put by the tempting cup not meant for my lips. Heaven knew what it cost me, but I did it. And if Hugh had loved me, I should have striven hard to banish that remembrance."

"Would it have been right?"

"Yes. I cannot argue, I can only understand that strength and courage are meant for just these emergencies. It is when one wants to do a wrong thing that one must pray to be kept from temptation. My duty was here."

"And yet Hugh had failed you before that!"

"I did not know it. He talked of you; still it is only recently that I felt the bond was irksome to him."

"If you had been aware last summer —"

"Don't," she said, with a sudden quiver through her frame. "I acted up to the light I had. I wanted above all things to do right, and I was bound by ties of affection to uncle and aunt."

"But you see Hugh didn't stop to think of what was

right, or whether he would give you pain. What if you had loved him?"

"Dear, is it wise to suffer over things that can never happen? There is enough pain in our daily lives."

"I think a man should be just as honorable, and true, and brave as a woman," I said, warmly.

"I am glad to have known one man who dared to thrust self behind him, who chose to suffer in silence, rather than pain the woman he loved by useless persuasions, and who was grand enough not to tempt her to break her word."

"Very few men are such heroes," I said, feeling the bitter truth.

"But now and then one stands like a Saul above his fellows. It keeps our faith in human nature from dying utterly."

"And now are your souls to remain forever apart?" I asked, eagerly.

"As God wills. If he means that I shall attain to so high a bliss he will bring it to me."

"I could never be so patient. What if Hugh should return to his allegiance?"

"He never will. It is like opening the eyes of the blind."

"What strange lives we women lead," I said, impulsively. "We are flattered into thinking ourselves nearly omnipotent, and if we cry for the moon, are told that all these things are above our comprehension. Men can find a proud existence in action; they can rear a grand future. Science, and art, and employment open to them golden doors, while women sit at home dawdling over idle dreams, their hungry lips stopped with a few trifling, flavorless kisses, and then they are expected to be high-minded, lofty of soul, and clear of brain. We are fed upon stones or chaff."

"I think all lives may hold in them something good and

useful. We too often disdain the common round of duties in longing for some great thing."

"And you mean to take up the 'common round'?" I said, with a half smile. "You have gone nearly through the octave for women. I can't make it seem right that one should suffer a good deal and enjoy a very little. I shall not be content to die until I have one long, delicious draught of joy."

"No fear but that it will be yours. I think you can win every good gift fate has to bestow."

"And you? Is there nothing but neutral tints left?"

"Don't pity me with your great, sorrowful eyes, but help me to be strong. I did not mean any one should ever see that grave. Whether there will be a resurrection morning for the buried hope, I cannot tell, but I have no right to brood over it. And now, dearest friend, you know all."

There was a great fire of logs blazing in the wide chimney, and she sat between me and it. The impression that I had seen her somewhere before came over me strongly again. Small, dainty as a sprite, yet exquisitely human, loose curls of palest brown, two or three removes from flaxen, and those soft, heavenly blue eyes. What a strange, dim remembrance it was! Ah—and I gave a sudden start, then laughed as I said,—

"Did I alarm you?" It was suddenly coming to a pause in a train of thought.

"No," she replied, "but you are nervous and tired, and must go to bed."

"Make a compact of friendship with me for all time," I exclaimed, as she rose. "I may try you, for I'm impulsive, impatient, and unlike most people, I fancy. But I want the assurance that some one loves me."

"I do, indeed." Then our lips met in the quivering radiance of the fire glow, and she stole softly away.

I was content to let her go. I hardly dared believe that first hasty thought right, and yet she was the impersonation of Philip Westervelt's "Ellen." I seemed to understand the key to all his moods that had impressed me vaguely at the time. He had spent part of his summer in Virginia, and it was not at all improbable that they had met. I could satisfy myself easily, and then — why not bring these two souls together without a long and weary probation?

I was convinced the next morning, when I happened to mention him. It was in a conversation with Mrs. Graham, and I dared to expatiate upon the delights of the pleasant home that I had shared for a brief while. The fair face flushed suddenly, and she listened with eager, secret attention, but made no mention of it afterwards. I believe I liked her the better for this womanly pride and reserve.

How could I resist a little castle-building with such tempting materials?

My own trials were not yet over. Hugh sought me, and insisted that I should listen once more to the tale he had to tell. I felt that it would be better to end the matter positively, and yet I own his devotion *did* touch me to the heart's core. He was willing to wait, anxious to undertake any task that would render him more worthy or raise him in my estimation. Any hope, however distant.

I could not make him understand how absolutely hopeless the case was. If I refused him love, he begged for friendship — a doubly dangerous boon. Exhorting him to a more stirring and manly life roused anew his passion. I could have cried from very despair.

"Hugh," I said at length, "you will make me hate the day on which I first saw you. It is black enough now."

"A day of days to me," he answered, sorrowfully.

Ellen promised me a speedy visit, and the rest were

warm in their demonstrations of regard. But I was glad when we were leaving Mont Argyle behind in the distance.

I was afraid Mr. St. John suspected that matters were not in the most tranquil state. He was a little sharp and cynical for several days, but we settled to our olden life, and I was beginning to breathe comfortably, when one morning we were surprised by a call from General Graham. He had brought Ellen, but that was not his real errand, for he was in the library a long while with Mr. St. John. Ellen purposed remaining a week, so I carried her off in triumph, although I trembled for my plans. I intended that Philip should be here when she came.

Mr. St. John sent for me after General Graham had gone. Something in his eyes warned me of danger.

"I have a proposal of marriage for you," he announced, in a biting tone, veiling his displeasure with a peculiar suavity of manner.

I colored violently, and felt that I hated Hugh for his pertinacity.

"As your guardian it is my duty to lay it before you," he said, with lofty courtesy.

"It was made and answered a fortnight ago," I returned, angrily.

"May I ask if you accepted?"

He must have known, but his face was imperturbably calm.

"I did not."

"Ah. It seems that Mr. Hugh Graham, lured from his allegiance to his cousin by a more powerful attraction, has broken his engagement on the strength of some encouragement."

"It is untrue!" I exclaimed, indignantly. "I never gave him the slightest hope."

" A man should be wise enough to distinguish, but since women think it no sin to display false lights as it suits a whim or pleasure, we must have a little pity for the unwary."

There was a fine irony in his tones that exasperated me.

" You are unjust, Mr. St. John," I said ; " I may have been unwise last summer because I was ignorant, but since then, I have been most guarded towards Mr. Graham. I can only say that I am sorry he should have considered it necessary to make any application to you. And if he were to ask me every day, my answer would remain the same."

" Then you decline the honor?" He uttered this with the most profound indifference.

" Should you advise me to accept? Will a man who fails in his first faith be one of the prizes in life's lottery ?"

There was a little quiver of the eyelids, and the faintest color rising in his cheeks.

" Remember the temptation," he said, ignoring my question.

" Since men are so weak, perhaps strict seclusion would be better for women. They do not like to be held answerable for the faults of others."

" Miss Adriance, what woman would be willing to thus martyr herself?" and he gave a scornful little laugh.

" Well," I returned, roused to resistance, " if they choose to dare the flame, let them pay the penalty. My conscience acquits me."

" A fashionable woman's conscience is a convenient article."

If one could only sting him, give him back pain for pain ! but I believe the man is invulnerable.

" If you will please inform Mr. Graham that a marriage between us is quite impossible, and that I wish to hear

8

nothing further on the subject, I shall be obliged," I said, sweeping loftily from the room.

From Ellen I learned the state of affairs at Mont Argyle. Hugh had taken upon himself the whole blame, and confessed that his love for me would henceforth be the ruling passion of his life. He had begged his father to intercede for him, thinking Mr. St. John might have some power over me. If he had, he was certainly chary of using it. She pleaded with her eyes and her low, faltering voice, but uttered no entreaty.

Before I retired that night I wrote a little note to Philip, telling him that I was unhappy, and desired to see him, which was true, for I did not wish to wound the delicacy of either. It was a mere chance whether he would get it and be able to come in time, but I resolved to risk it.

Then we had some quiet, pleasant days, in spite of a few small annoyances. Mr. St. John was a delightful attendant when we were together, but if I chanced upon him alone, he made me feel there was a gulf between us that had not been satisfactorily bridged over; as if in some way I had mortally offended him. Did he think I ought to have told him before? He surely was not a man to invite confidence.

Perhaps I wrong him there. Ellen thinks him the incarnation of manly goodness and nobility. She never wearies of talking about him. Once I said, "Is he at all like your hero?" and she answered, —

"He seems different from all other men. I believe a woman would be afraid to love him. My hero, as you call him, is more intensely human."

Would a woman be afraid? I once fancied —

No matter. I know now that it was a mistake.

I waited in nervous anticipation for Philip. One evening he dropped in upon us, to the surprise of Mr. St. John.

I had asked him to keep my secret, and he did it excellently. There was a momentary confusion in welcoming him, and then Miss Keith was introduced. She was pale as a lily, and kept in the shade of Mrs. Lawrence's flowing robes, but the hand she extended trembled visibly to watchful eyes.

"This is an unexpected pleasure," Philip exclaimed. "Miss Keith and I are old friends."

"I did not know that," — and St. John looked puzzled.

"We met last summer at Sulphur Springs." Then he paused and turned away, as if moved by a sudden consciousness. She was silent, too, and presently went to the table and took up a book she had been reading.

I did not design to have him remain long in doubt; but nothing ever happens as one plans it. Mr. St. John kept him engrossed the whole evening. I could absolutely have cried with vexation.

But I came down early the next morning, and found him in the library. The happy face was grave and clouded, but he smiled at my entrance. A few commonplaces passed between us.

"You don't look as if you had been very deeply troubled," he began. "If it would not sound like flattery, I should feel tempted to tell you what I think."

I held up my hands deprecatingly, and said, —

"I have found beauty a rather perilous dower."

"So soon?"

"Don't laugh at me. Be kind and tender and impartial, and help me to decide whether I have committed a great crime or not; for I do need a friend."

"My best is at your service, as you well know."

I told him the story of Hugh Graham's ill-fated passion, and could hardly repress my delight at the interest he displayed, all the deeper for another woman's sake; yet I had no selfish feeling about it. And then I spoke of Mr. St. John's comments.

"I do not see where you were to blame," he said, with sweet seriousness. "But I am sorry you and St. John disagree. Since you cannot help being beautiful, I suppose we must pity your misfortunes. And it *has* been productive of some good, for it will save two people from an ill-assorted, loveless marriage, and give to another— Sydnie, I must tell you. I met Ellen Keith, and loved her unwittingly. If I had known *all* then, I might have spoken; but I believed I had no right. To hear that she is free — free," and he lingered softly over the word. "Yet how cold and shy she was last night."

"She would not flaunt her love in any man's face," I said, warmly.

"No. She is purity and delicacy itself; and heroic, too. Last summer she put away the tempting cup with firm hand. God only could know the anguish of her soul. It shall be repaid a thousand fold. So you see I cannot blame you."

The others were in the hall, and we went to breakfast. Ellen was pale, as if she had scarcely slept. Mr. St. John remarked it.

"You are losing your roses," he said, with kindly solicitude. "As the morning promises to be fine, I think we must have a brisk canter over the hills. You will not mind the cold."

Her eyes brightened at that.

"It will be different from the lazy rides we used to have when you were in New York," Philip said to me. "I second the proposal with all my heart."

We waited until the sun was making rapid strides in the blue arch overhead. It was a really delightful winter day, with a crisp but not unpleasant air. Mr. St. John tacitly gave Philip his choice of a companion, and I fell to his share.

We had some odd, sharp skirmishing. I was in a splendid humor, too happy to be irritated by anything he could say. And somewhere on the road Ellen found her roses.

I fancied that Mr. St. John suspected Philip's penchant. They were left a good deal to themselves the remainder of the day and evening. Ellen ran into my room the last thing at night, blushing and happy, yet timid as a fawn.

"And so the prince won the princess?" I exclaimed, laughingly.

"O, Sydnie! did you guess?" and the sweet face was pressed against mine.

"At Christmas, darling. Philip had unwittingly betrayed his part of the secret before. And, since I had made one miserable, I longed to bring the other to happiness. Don't blush so pitifully, little white daisy, and keep my secret from Philip until your wedding day."

"I wonder if it is wrong to be so happy?"

"Wrong, child? What are you dreaming of? When God brings the love of a brave, sweet, generous heart to you, would it not be ungrateful to mope and sadden over it? I love Philip so well that I shall be jealous if you don't give him every atom of your soul."

"Poor Hugh!" She uttered the words with a soft sigh.

"Hugh isn't to be compared to Philip. I'm glad some one has come out right, for I began to fancy the world was in quite a jumble, every man and woman going the wrong way. What shall I wish for you, sweet?"

"You have given me everything. Do you know I never blamed Hugh for loving you? I could not help it myself; and Philip says —"

"No treason from Philip. I'm glad you are not jealous, and love to hear his praises. Mamma Westervelt dotes on him. Now to bed, lest your castle disappears."

She kissed me, and went away. Hitherto I had lived much within myself; but now that I had admitted guests, and given a feast, my sympathies widened, and joy became a tangible thing.

How very happy they would be! She would suit Philip so perfectly; and his great, manful soul would give her a worship that but few women ever gain. I thought of Laura and her golden fetters, a mockery on marriage. Henceforward I should have some faith.

Ellen had arranged to return to Mont Argyle on the following morning. Mr. St. John was to accompany her, and he extended an invitation to Philip, who was to go on to Washington afterwards.

"I've hardly been civil to you," he said, as we stood waiting in the reception room for Ellen to come down. "I have left a host of things yet unsaid. Are you working out your own life problem satisfactorily?"

"Pray, do not demand too much of me," I said, gayly; "I have been studying ball-room philosophy."

"You have a brain for better things."

"Does it matter much? One day follows another in purposeless confusion, and thus they go."

"Pursuing shadows. Will you recognize the great truths of life when you come to them? For if you passed them by and took the shadows, you would make an irremediable wreck."

"Do you see that in my face? Are we not sufficiently friends for you to redeem your promise?"

He thought a moment, giving me a peculiar, scrutinizing glance.

"Yes," he rejoined; "and if I vex, you must be merciful

and forgive. You have a strong, sweet, but haughty nature, intolerant of restraint, impatient, singularly reserved
at times. Many people go through life scarcely taking a
lasting impression, because all feelings are so easily effaced.
It will not be so with you. You have an ardent temperament, tropical fire and passion in your veins; but you are
proud to the last degree, and would endure what might
kill another woman. With your affluent nature and mani-
fold charms, there will be much temptation to use your
power; but O, be careful. When you love —"

"What then?" for he made a long pause.

"I could almost pity the man you will love. You haven't
much faith; you will try him sorely at times. Heaven
grant that he may not be too weak for his destiny."

"Not very flattering, I must confess."

"But I do give you credit for power beyond what most
women possess. You absorb all impressions rapidly, and
therein lies the greater danger. You will the sooner ex-
haust pleasures and enjoyments, and then must come continual restlessness or discontented stagnation. It is a
strange, daring, yet delightful nature to rule. If I could
place you in the hands of a strong, patient, generous
friend —"

"I think I shall prove sufficient for myself. I suppose I
shall presently come to the level of other women."

"Heaven forbid!" he said, earnestly.

"Peculiar people are always a trial," I returned, with
some feeling.

"You must learn not to be a trial. My dear friend, the
grace of a patient spirit is worth striving for."

"I am not patient; I never could be."

"On the contrary, you *can* be. There, I have sermonized you and teased you, but I want you to know that no

brother would ever be more ready to defend you than I. It is because I see great possibilities that I tremble."

There were steps in the hall, and tender farewells.   Mr. St. John glanced back once, questioning me with his eyes, all aglow with bewildering lights.

CHAPTER IX.

"The good want power, but to weep barren tears,
The powerful goodness want, worse need for them;
The wise want love, and those who love want wisdom,
And all best things are thus confused to ill." SHELLEY.

AFTER Philip and Ellen had gone, we settled into comparative quiet. Holiday festivities were over, and we had been so gay that it was good to have a little rest. At least it seemed rest not to have more than one or two balls or dinner-parties where we had counted them by dozens. Mrs. Lawrence was lovely and placid as ever; Mr. St. John changeable and puzzling. I knew he was glad to have his friend happy, and yet he appeared to hold a curious grudge against me on Hugh Graham's account. I could not seem to learn what course would have met with his approbation. I confess I did sometimes enjoy ruffling his lordly plumes. If other people found me entertaining and thought me handsome, why should I not bask in the golden sunshine of youth and pleasure?

Ellen wrote to me that their affairs had been brought to a satisfactory conclusion. Hugh was going to Scotland to visit some relatives, and her engagement was approved of by her aunt and uncle. The only trouble now would be leaving them. Philip was anxious for a speedy marriage, but she meant to wait until another fall, at least. They had been acquainted but such a little while; and, somehow, she dreaded to make so important a change. I believe she would actually have given up her happiness, even

then; and I was glad that Philip possessed just the kind
of frank, resolute nature to sway hers. He had such a
cheerful fashion of finding his way through difficulties.
Doubting Castle would not long be an abode for him.

And so the spring came to us:—long, lovely days,
touched with faint fragrance, murmurous winds chanting
ballads from orient shores, and that tender suggestiveness
the world always presents when waking from its long
sleep; hardy blossoms, nodding in early beauty, budding
trees, and birds twittering softly, or cleaving the air with
their swift, glittering wings.

One day I received an epistle from the only schoolmate
I had really loved, though we had not been very fervent
correspondents. She reminded me of a promised visit,
and begged its fulfilment now, as she was about to be married. If I would only be her bridesmaid! There were
several reasons why she wished this; and in any event,
she *must* have the visit. Did I remember our long talks
at school, which had been the wonder of the other girls?
She had never found just such a friend, and longed for
me more than she could express.

Something in the letter roused my curiosity. No tender
mention of her betrothed, no girlish hopes nor fears, not
even hesitation. I cannot tell why, but I had always fancied Anne Sutherland one of the girls who would never
marry. Not that she was unattractive or in any degree
morbid, and she certainly was worthy of a happy destiny.
Had she gained the prize?

I went to consult Mrs. Lawrence. The fact of the Sutherlands living in an aristocratic part of the city won an
amiable hearing for Anne, yet I believe she would rather
it had not happened.

"Really," she said, with her sweet, half-indifferent smile,
"you seem to be the centre of romance. Promise that you
will not commit any folly yourself."

"The girls at school used to call Anne and myself 'old maids,'" I returned, laughingly. "I think I am in no great danger."

"O, I expect you to marry some time. Only it is well to exercise a little judgment."

"Which means, that I am not to fall in love with a poor man!"

"You still seem to consider the love a necessity;" and her tones were as cold and as near to sarcasm as hers ever came.

"It *is* to me. I could never content myself with gilded shams; feast my material senses while my soul starved. I *must* have something real."

"My dear Sydnie, your feelings are too strong. Many of the so-called love-marriages are extremely unsatisfactory. Do not wreck your all on this fluttering phantom. It is as likely to be a sham as some of those things you protest against so vehemently."

"At least, Philip and Ellen found it," I said triumphantly.

"Yet, you see, they were not governed simply by fancy."

"Do you suppose," I said, warmly, "that Philip considered whether Ellen was rich or poor? She might have been altogether dependent upon her uncle, for aught he knew; or he might have had nothing besides his health and energy."

"Society is a kind of protection and voucher for these things. If one pays heed to its wise restrictions, one will never go very far astray."

Her dignified tone and air of superior wisdom amused me.

"Mrs. Lawrence, did you never experience any temptation to love?" I asked.

"My mother committed that folly. She chose to be

disinherited for the sake of the man she married. My grandfather overlooked it far enough to adopt Stuart. The other children, except myself, died young. I do not think my home was particularly happy; and when Mr. Lawrence, a wealthy West India merchant, made me a proposal of marriage, I accepted it, with no regret, though he was forty and I but sixteen. He was proud of my beauty, kind and indulgent; and we lived together most comfortably."

Certainly she was neither faded nor worn. No trials or cares had dimmed the fair face. But could *I* endure such a life? The volcano at the bottom of my soul would find vent and scatter widespread desolation.

I took her pleasant cautions and advice in good part, and decided to go at the earliest date Anne mentioned, which would give me a fortnight still at Laurelwood.

Mr. St. John was very unreasonable and captious about it. Our winter calm was breaking up into a March torrent. He sneered at love as a school-girl's folly, and seemed to delight in vexing me when no one was by.

"You'll come back with your head so full of romance that we shall seem dismally tame and prosaic people to you," he said.

"I haven't complained of the tameness yet. On the contrary, Laurelwood has been very gay, to my thinking; more so than it will be with the Sutherlands. Judging from my friend, they are a quiet household."

"I have not been quite correct in my selection of a word, perhaps. It was not exactly amusement that I meant. You and your friend will be up in the seventh heaven of rhapsody when you come to renew the vows made in your moonlight walks. I wonder she has not occupied more of your attention, Miss Adriance."

"We never made vows," I retorted, angrily. "You draw too largely upon your imagination."

"Could any school-girl pass through such an ordeal un-fettered? You surprise me more and more."

He lifted his level eyebrows with an incredulous expres-sion that roused me to a white heat.

"If you had been a woman, you would not misjudge us so abominably. Since you are incapable of forming a true estimate of women's regard for each other —"

"It is a pity," he interrupted, with his mocking smile. "I should have made you so much more desirable a com-panion, as I could then have understood all these little feminine virtues we men are so apt to consider absurdities."

"Doubtless the sex would receive a charming addition. Personally I am not in want of companions."

There was a pause, and I began to congratulate myself inwardly. He turned as if to leave me, then said, in that imperturbable manner, and a low, cutting tone, —

"I am fully aware that friendship can do nothing for Miss Adriance."

"Not unless it brought those within my range who could be kind and courteous without considering it derogatory to their manhood," I retorted, bitterly.

"You have been most unfortunate, we will admit. Youth is not always the wisest season of life."

"It is owing to circumstances, *not* choice." I was angry enough to say anything.

"Allow me to congratulate you that events are likely to place you among more congenial companions. You have my best wishes;" and, with a haughty bow, he sauntered through the hall.

I believe he takes delight in annoying me, making me the target for his satirical shafts. If I did not know that he could be gracious and tender, I could the more easily forgive him. And then why does he sometimes take such pains to please me? He is a mystery, a book wherein the reader no sooner fancies he understands one page before the leaf flies over and leaves him astonished at the change : the attractive and the repellent forces are so great in him, and he affects those with whom he comes in contact so differently. There are times when I positively hate him; then again I am drawn to him by a power that I cannot resist, and find him all gentleness. If he would always be thus!

The morning of my departure he met me coming down the stairs, and paused in the hall.

"You will return in a radiant mood, doubtless. Believe that I shall take great interest in watching for the day."

"I am not given to sudden or wonderful changes of temperament," I said, curtly.

"Only of *temper*."

"As you like."

I would have passed him then, but he turned and crossed the hall with me.

"I've proved your stability, I think. At all events, come back good-humored. I have almost forgotten how you look when you smile."

"It can be of little consequence, then."

I kept my eyes on the marble tiles, and would not glance up.

"One likes to live in peace and charity with all men and *some* women."

That soft, peculiar sound in his voice! It sped through my nerves, but I would not allow it to move me outwardly.

"How cruel you are! At least, let us part friends;" and he held out his hand. The deep eyes radiated crystals of light — for now I could not keep them from meeting mine.

It was my turn, however; and, coolly ignoring the

power that I was aware I could contest only for a moment or two, I said, —

"I did not know we were enemies. I have not been considering the subject."

His face gloomed over with a strange expression. I could not understand whether he was pained or angry, and must have yielded in another instant, but Mrs. Lawrence came fluttering down, heralded by the scent of some rare perfume. She was to accompany me to the station.

"Good by," Mr. St. John said, with gay carelessness. "I dare say you will be a convert to matrimony when you return."

I glanced back once after we were in the carriage. He was leaning against one of the fluted columns, twining a slender creeper over a trellis. There was a look of prideful longing and melancholy in the face, that haunted me for hours afterwards.

My journey was both rapid and comfortable; though, having no companion, I found plenty of time to speculate upon my friend. We had been room mates, and drawn together by similar tastes and feeling. The clique headed by Laura Hastings never had possessed any attractions for her; indeed, she was a thoughtful, studious girl, with that rare self-reliance that kept her from exacting much from those with whom she was brought in contact. Neat, orderly, and quiet, I found her really delightful for constant company.

Her mother had been an invalid many years. And Anne's ambition, it appeared to me, was to render herself capable of supplying her mother's place as far as possible. She had talked of the children and their domestic *ménage* until I seemed to know them all, and experienced none of the awkwardness of going among strangers. But why she should have decided to marry so suddenly, and why she had made no mention of a lover in her previous letters, puzzled me not a little.

It was late at night when I arrived at Baltimore. Anne and her father came for me. Mr. Sutherland was one of those tall, quiet, aristocratic-looking men that carry generations of refinement in their faces. He gave me a cordial, high-bred welcome, and proved himself no less a gentleman than Mr. St. John, except that he was more formal. Anne resembled him in many respects. She, too, was tall, slender, and fair. Animation always rendered her pretty; but ordinarily she was too grave. It seemed to me that daily duties and events only touched the outer surface of her soul, and that the fire deep within had never been kindled.

I knew by her bright smile how glad she was to see me. She questioned me a little about my life, and how I had enjoyed it since our parting at school; spoke of Laura, and two or three others.

"It seems a century since then," she remarked, slowly.

I longed to ask about herself, but delicacy withheld me. There would be time enough for all explanations.

"Mamma and the children have retired," she said, half in apology, "so you will not be able to make their acquaintance until to-morrow; and I know you must be weary, so you shall have a cup of tea and then go to your room. Mamma left strict injunctions that you should not be kept up a moment longer than was necessary."

Her voice was soft and cheerful; and I could guess nothing from the calm face. Patience, I said to myself; but as I gave her a good-night kiss, I held her in a tender and reassuring clasp.

"You have forgotten nothing," she exclaimed, with a sudden impulse. "I was almost afraid I should find my friend changed."

"Not to you," I responded.

I soon fell asleep, and it was late when I rose the next morning. I gave a thought to Laurelwood and its inmates, and missed Thirza's swift fingers. Anne soon made her appearance, charmingly neat in a morning dress of French cambric. The house was astir with children's flying footsteps and pleasant voices — rather new sounds to me.

Mrs. Sutherland awaited us in the breakfast-room; she, too, was very fair, but small and fragile looking. A sweet, patient face, bearing traces of much suffering, but not peevish or melancholy. Walter, four years younger than Anne, inherited this slender constitution, blond, blue-veined complexion, drooping eyes, nervous, susceptible temperament, and was subject to a spinal malady that would incapacitate him for the severe struggles of life: four younger ones, healthy, frolicsome children, to whom Anne was a second mother. She appeared to comprehend their wants at a glance, and her quiet ministry subdued and harmonized them completely. It was indeed a happy group.

When the children were despatched to school, and Anne's household tasks completed, we found ourselves at last together in the cosy sitting-room. Mr. Sutherland went to his business early in the morning, and did not return until the late dinner hour. We were not likely to be interrupted for some time.

"Anne," I began, "I am all impatience to hear about the lover whose fascinations have proved sufficiently potent to win you from this home. Take a little pity upon me."

"There is no romance about it," she returned, slowly. "It is to be just a plain, unpretending, matter-of-fact marriage."

"And the love? I must confess to you that I have developed an insatiable thirst for love matters."

9

She turned her eyes away absently. "He has loved me for years," she said, "and is content to take me, trusting to the future."

"Then you don't love him?" There was a good deal of disappointment in my tone.

"Yes," she replied; "I think I *do* love him; only it isn't the passion that girls talk about. He is noble, generous, thoroughly good and trustworthy, but a quiet man, like papa. Some people may feel deeply, yet never put it into words."

"I like the outward sign as well," I said, with a smile. "But how reticent you were at school! I don't seem to understand you at all, and I used to fancy that I did. I am sure you left this marriage quite out of your plans."

She flushed warmly as she answered, —

"We have been engaged since Christmas, only. Before that I never dreamed — Will it tire you if I tell you the story?"

"Tire me! I am wild to hear it; and I suspect there is considerable romance about it after all."

It was a moment or two before she began, but her voice was clear and smooth, and she evinced no agitation.

"Papa and Mr. Otis have been friends a long while. Two years ago last summer, just before I went to Madame W——'s and met you at school, he used to be here a good deal, though I was shy and took very little notice of him. Papa was making some new business arrangements, into which Mr. Otis put considerable money. He was going to Europe, and, having a large fortune, needed to use but a small part of it. For a while papa was very successful. Last fall he met with some heavy losses. Business was exceedingly dull, and as it went on into winter he grew alarmed. At this juncture Mr. Otis returned.

"Papa had said nothing until then, for he did not want

to distress poor mamma. Indeed, he told me first. He
had barely enough to meet all his liabilities if he gave
up then; but it was sacrificing everything — this house,
to which mamma had come as a bride, all our little luxuries, our servants, our hopes of the future — for papa had
contemplated giving Walter an art education, as he evinces
a great genius for it. I felt stunned at the prospect. For
myself, I could have borne poverty and toil; but when I
thought of the rest, my heart grew heavy within me. I
knew papa had a fine, honorable pride, that could not endure a suspicion of wrong dealing, and that, hard as it
was, he would rather give up all than go on involving himself. So he announced his misfortunes to mamma. We
had a sad, sad time, I assure you. I tried to comfort them
both, and planned for the new life, how I could take charge
of the house and the education of the younger children.
I was really glad to devôte my life to them.

"One day papa came home looking so bright and relieved that I uttered an involuntary cry of joy, and begged
him to tell me what had occurred. One of those marvellous incidents that happen to some people, and sound
like a fairy tale. He had gone to Mr. Otis and laid a
plain statement of the case before him, explaining what
he purposed to do; and, upon looking into the business,
Mr. Otis concluded to advance the necessary capital to
place everything in good working order, and become a
partner. He would not even listen to papa's idea of
mortgaging the house. And so we had but a fortnight
of sorrow after all, and no change would be necessary.
Then Mr. Otis came to visit us. Walter took an extravagant fancy to him; he had brought such hosts of curi-
osities home with him, and seen nearly everything of note.
His rooms were a perfect study: Walter used to spend
all his leisure time there; and Mr. Otis insisted that it was

time for him to begin his true education — for he means
to be an artist; but with his health it will be slow work."

She made quite a pause.

"Well," I said, "and then he fell in love. Anne, I
am quite interested in your hero. And you fancied that
you must marry him."

"I like to hear him talk: his pleasant voice sounds like
a stream flowing through grassy meadows. Do you remember how the girls at school used to discuss spiritual
influences, positives and negatives, natures that attracted
and swayed, and others that were impressed and yielded?
Here was a mysterious agency for me. Mr. Otis seldom
conversed with me, yet I felt that he always wanted me to
be present. I could tell when his eyes were following me.
I had an intuitive perception of the kind of music he liked,
the flowers and books he was fond of; in short, I could
not rid myself of an impression that some irresistible
power was linking us together. And when papa told me
he had proposed for me, I scarcely felt surprised."

"You should have summoned all your strength to resist,"
I said, suddenly.

"I don't know that I wanted to. I felt that papa was
pleased, and expected me to marry him. Mamma thought
him tender, generous, and loyal hearted; and when he told
me that since he first knew me I had hardly been out of
his mind, and that on his return, if he had found me gay,
and drinking eagerly of pleasure's cup, he should never
have had the courage to speak, my heart went out to him
strangely. His had been a lonely life, with no near relatives; and he is not the kind of man to make friends readily.
I understood that this would be the one love of his
soul, and, somehow, I couldn't blight it. But I told him
that I did not believe I was really in love. He turned to
me quickly, his face pale, his eyes filled with apprehension,

and asked me if there was any one I fancied or liked better. Though he meant to devote his life to making me happy, he would not have me sacrifice even a thought."

I looked at her steadily. A faint color wandered over her face, but the brightness and hope that should have been its glory were not there.

"Well?" I questioned.

"There was no one in whom I had as much confidence, no one for whom I cared specially. Of course we always have friends, but friends are not lovers."

She turned away, though her tones were very distinct and untrembling.

"I don't like it," I exclaimed, impulsively. "It is almost as if Mr. Otis bought you."

"No, Sydnie; don't say that. I was quite free. He made me understand *that* in a most delicate fashion."

"Are you *glad* to marry him?"

"I never thought of marrying any one. I used to plan to stay here with mamma, and watch the others growing up. The idea was so new to me that I hesitated a little."

I remembered Ellen, and her sweet, delicious hopes. This was but a paltry imitation.

"Anne," I said, "you are cheating your own soul. When it is too late you will awake to the truth. You don't *love* Mr. Otis at all. Gratitude and pity have swayed you."

"And yet I like to think of depending upon him. He gives me such a sense of rest and security. I fancy that I must be different from other women. Those wonderful, extravagant loves frighten me: I seem to shrink from them. Something quiet and grave suits me best. And then —" taking up the thread of her story as if we had not made this digression — "we glided into an engagement. It did not appear a bit strange to me. Papa, mamma, and Walter were delighted. Mr. Otis bought a house only a little distance from this, and we are to go to housekeeping immediately. The engagement has been short, but I think it quite as well. I am nervous, and want it all over. I fancied it would be so pleasant to have you to help me select furniture, dresses, and all that, for mamma can go out so little."

"I wish you had not made this engagement. Suppose, instead, I help you to break it?"

"No." She turned suddenly pale. "I believe I am right. I mean to go on." Then, in a changed tone, "You see now, dear, why I have not written about it. I could not have explained all."

"I don't wonder, surely. When can I see Mr. Otis? I shall make up my mind then whether it is best to forbid the banns or not."

"He is in every day or evening. I think he is rather nervous and shy before strangers; but it soon wears off. I want you to like him. And, Sydnie, please don't talk this way before mamma; she believes that I am going to be very happy."

"And I *know* you are not: is that it?"

"No, you don't; you can't know what is alone in God's keeping."

She uttered this with a curious, latent energy. Just then we were called to lunch.

I sat at the table, revolving Anne's story in my mind. It was so odd that she, of all other girls, should tell it. Looking in some women's faces you seem to read that they were born for a happy, contented love, to be the centre of a cheerful home, and have children growing up around them. She, with her pretty, motherly ways, her delicate tastes, fine, sensitive feelings, but not high or wide range of intellect, appeared just the one for such a life. Would not coldness freeze her into a stiff formalism, crush her tender, yearning soul, that needed bluest skies for its blossoming?

The children came home presently: they were just the kind of little ones to make friends with. I was electrifying them with some rather noisy selections from Trovatore, when Anne summoned me to the drawing-room. Mr. Otis had come, and wished her to go with him and select some paper for the new house, if she and her friend were not too tired. So I went in for a brief introduction. Such things are invariably awkward, and I forgave him for being stiff. He certainly looked old for his years, as he was but little beyond thirty. Not prepossessing; merely a plain, quiet gentleman, the kind of person one might suppose would make a good, trusty friend, but not an enthusiastic lover.

His taste was certainly fine, and he paid little regard to expense. He was so desirous of pleasing Anne, that he would have purchased half the warehouse, and had his walls adorned every week in a different style. She hesitated; in fact, I suspected she took no great interest in the matter. She was *not* happy.

What a strange world it is! so very few coming to the highest enjoyment. Some lives full of straining effort and self-denial, and yet never attaining the peace that crowns unconscious love, that should come as a birthright to all earnest souls.

CHAPTER X.

"I never
Could tread a single pleasure under foot."
ROBERT BROWNING.

ANNE was really bright and gay at the dinner-table. A sense of relief seemed to pervade her. There was a little talk about the new house, and her face flushed to a pretty and becoming color. I half fancied her happy, after all.

I was playing for Walter in the drawing-room, when we were both startled by the entrance of a visitor. Walter did the honors of the introduction — a Mr. Channing, who attracted me at the very first glance — a handsome man of five and twenty, who recalled to one the statue of Antinöus. He reminded me curiously enough of Mrs. Lawrence. The same slender, subtile grace; the light, airy motion; the silken, soft, glittering hair, and summery blue eyes, large lidded and languid. His features were exquisitely cut; a straight, Grecian nose, a beautifully-rounded chin, and mouth as perfect as an infant's. The full, scarlet lips were curved and smiling, and if there was any defect in his face, it was that the upper lip looked too short and too weak for a man; but this one would hardly cavil at.

He glanced at me after the introduction, and I could not help experiencing a peculiar thrill of power; as if he were paying unconscious homage, and so delicately done withal, that one could not be offended.

Anne entered. He rose and shook hands with her, calling a bright flush to her cheek.

"I am positively disappointed," she said. "I wanted the pleasure of presenting you to Miss Adriance."

"Well, suppose we have it over again," and he laughed. A string of tiny bells put in motion could not have been more musical.

"And we have been so much engaged to-day that I have not told her a word about you."

"Then I must be judged upon my own merits. Miss Adriance, please be merciful."

"O!" Anne said, with a little impatient gesture. "But a few evenings ago I learned that Mr. Channing and Mr. St. John —"

She paused, for there flitted across Mr. Channing's face such a comical, half-deprecating expression.

"Were connections. I'll finish the sentence, Miss Sutherland, and Miss Adriance must judge who is to be commiserated."

This air of gay audacity sat wonderfully well upon him.

"I confess you brought Mrs. Lawrence to my mind," I said, feeling pleased and interested.

"Thank you. I don't aspire to the gloomily grand, as does my magnificent cousin Stuart. Isabelle is a charming woman, but she displayed a good deal of courage when she undertook to humanize her brother. Miss Anne said he was your guardian."

"Isn't it odd?" Anne exclaimed. "I was quite startled when I made the discovery, for I have been acquainted with Mr. Channing a long while, and known you so intimately, too." Then she colored afresh, and looked strangely conscious.

"And you are really relatives?" I said, recovering from my surprise.

"Honestly and truly, on our mother's side. Though I suspect St. John long ago disowned all relationship with

such a gay fellow; he's so miserably grave and severe.
Doesn't he sometimes threaten to shut you up in a dark
closet?"

"No," I answered, laughingly. "I have found Laurelwood a very enjoyable place."

"Perhaps he comes down from his pedestal occasionally.
I made them a visit when Isabelle first went there, and I
assure you I was glad to escape. I cannot endure those
morose and bitter people who shroud themselves continually in sackcloth, and will not be content unless they
see their neighbors sitting in ashes. Life is such a delightful thing to me! If there is a stray gleam of sunshine I
want to be in it. I enjoy summer bloom and beauty,
without bewailing the fact that it must fade when winter
comes."

His voice was so purely musical, and his face summer in
itself. One listened as to chords played perfectly.

I had found Mr. St. John bitter, but I was half ashamed
to confess it; so I said, —

"We have been rather gay and dissipated all winter."

"Then a change has certainly come over Giant Despair.
Miss Adriance, you amaze me! Doesn't St. John preach
you homilies upon the waste of time spent in such frivol-
ities?"

"I haven't been sermonized very seriously as yet."

"Wonders will never cease. And though I wouldn't
shadow your bright visions, I am afraid I have little faith
in his conversion."

Presently we rambled on to something else. He never
wore out a theme, or allowed his listeners to weary of it.
He was at home everywhere. Any trivial subject blossomed
in grace and beauty at his touch. Choice bits of sentiment
floated out on the wave of conversation, sparkling like the
changeful sea in a midday sunshine. Poetry, music, art,

nothing came amiss to him. One could not pause to ana-lyze, but enjoyed without cavilling, as one does the richness of tropical scenery. It gave me a curious sensation, as if I had remained too long in an over-fragrant conservatory.

Before he went away he made an engagement to take us to visit a gallery of paintings then on exhibition. All the evening Anne had been bright and winsome, treating him with the familiarity of a brother.

After he had gone, I lingered by the piano while she collected stray sheets of music.

"You like him," she began, in a confident tone.

"How could any one help it?" I said, honestly.

"I'm so glad. He is to stand with you."

"What an odd circumstance! He ought to stand in another capacity, Anne. You have been a different being this evening."

"There's something inspiriting about him, like wine. Perhaps I am too easily impressed."

I took her face between my hands. "Confess, Anne," I said, "that you could have loved this man."

She struggled to free herself. "If I had met him now for the first time, I don't know what effect he might have upon me; but I have known him from childhood."

"And how have you escaped loving him?"

"I do not think he ever loved me." She said it very simply and honestly.

"But women do not always wait for that."

"I don't know that I quite understand it myself, only I can *feel* that we should never do for each other."

"Why?" I asked in astonishment.

"It seems as if he would need a strong and powerful charm to hold him. He would want something rare and startling, a bud one day, a blossom the next, and ever after a different kind of fruit. I am gráve by nature, and have

but little variety. I should give all at first, and though it
might grow more precious to some, I can fancy others
tiring of it."

"What an odd girl! Do you think him fickle?"

"He has not proved fickle in friendship." Her eyes
wandered from mine as she uttered this.

"There's some mystery about you two people. I can't
imagine how you *could* consent to marry that unattractive
Mr. Otis when you contrasted him with Mr. Channing."

"I didn't contrast them. Mr. Channing has been away
nearly all winter. I cannot make you understand just the
kind of friends we have been. He is distantly connected
with some cousins of mine, whom I used to visit frequently.
I think from the very first we accepted the fact that we
were to be nothing but friends."

"And how did he take your engagement?"

"Calmly enough. Don't fill your head with foolish fancies, Sydnie. It is a matter of indifference to Mr. Channing
whom I marry."

I thought there was a dash of bitterness in this. "It is
of more importance to me," I said, warmly. "I cannot
endure the thought that you are going to make yourself
miserable. It would be better even now to break this engagement. There is nothing but a paltry feeling of gratitude concerned in it. Love is shamed by such a mockery."

"Hush, you wound me. Let me go my own way — it is
best for me. Come, we are staying up unconscionably,"
and shutting the piano almost violently, she drew me into
the hall.

I went to bed with a head full of vague ideas. It seemed
to me that Anne ought not to be allowed to take such a
desperate step. Were her parents blind?

I watched her and Mr. Channing narrowly the next day,
and confess to a secret mortification in finding him polite

and devoted in the most gentlemanly manner, but not in the slightest degree lover-like. Indeed he paid me the more exclusive attention. Anne was by far too generous to be suspected of anything like jealousy.

It was singular, but in a week's time I accepted the fact, even if I could not be quite satisfied with it. I found, too, that Mr. Channing was no great favorite with Mr. Sutherland, while he did admire Mr. Otis warmly. Sometimes the latter thawed a little when we were alone with him, but Mr. Channing's presence made him awkward and reserved. I was forced to admit that Mr. Otis possessed many fine characteristics, and a delicacy that one would hardly have expected.

We were kept pretty busy. Shopping, ordering furniture for the new house, being subject to the nod of the dressmaker, and entertaining callers, occupied us incessantly. Anne seemed to enjoy the excitement, and I no longer attempted to dissuade her, or discourage her in any manner. But I had a fancy that if Mr. Otis had given less lavishly, and demanded more in return, claimed Anne as a right, and not taken little crumbs and odd moments of leisure, it would have been better for both. She was so rarely alone with him. Indeed she seemed to shrink from intimate personal contact, while she really had no aversion to him.

Mr. Channing pleased me wonderfully. His beauty did not pall as one became accustomed to it. Every emotion brought a change to his features, a new light in his soft, deep eyes. His was a remarkably expressive face. Another charm was his reading. With his exquisite intonation this was drowsy, lulling music, that lingered in one's brain long after the sound had ceased.

I wrote to Mrs. Lawrence about meeting him; indeed he begged to send a message. What was my surprise to

find a note from Mr. St. John enclosed in hers, a few
words that angered me in an instant. Its contents were
these : —

"Miss Adriance : I regret extremely that you should
have met Mr. Channing under such peculiar circumstances.
While he is agreeable to the verge of fascination, he is not
a man I should select for intimate companionship. Be
careful in your acquaintance with him.   St. John."

It was mean and cowardly thus to attempt to bias my
opinion of Mr. Channing — his own relative too! — as if I
were a child that had to be warned at every step, and he a
person dangerous to any woman's peace. I smiled scornfully over the advice, resolving that it should not interfere
with my enjoyment of his pleasant society in the slightest
degree. Mr. Channing was not lacking in moral principles,
or addicted to any small vices. Refined to the verge of
fastidiousness, elegant in all his tastes without being fop-
pish or sentimental, what was there to annoy or distress
one? St. John was manifestly unjust and unreasonable.

If he did not admire Mr. Channing, I must confess there
was but little love lost between them. The latter was not
bitter nor satirical, and yet he had a keen appreciation of
the ridiculous, and a trick of drawing exaggerated pictures
that was most amusing. One day he was enlarging upon
Mr. St. John's habits of seclusion and distaste for society.

"No one is quite good enough for his magnificence," he
said. "I should think you two women would be a daily
trial to him. Perhaps he takes you upon the Romish principle of penance. I don't see how he can resist the opportunity of calling you up every night, and reading you a
solemn lecture."

There was a touch of reality in this that disturbed me.

"Perhaps *you* have converted him," Mr. Channing went
on, in a peculiar tone, seeing that I did not reply.

"O, no; I have not the courage for such an under-
taking;" and I unwittingly told the truth.

"He prides himself immensely upon his apathy and im-
penetrability; as if marble could possibly experience a sensation! Do you know what I should be tempted to do if I
were a handsome woman, Miss Adriance?"

"What?"

"Besiege the citadel, and when it capitulated, march off
with the utmost indifference; for you women do occasionally play with hearts, and this would be only a petrified
semblance. Wouldn't he chafe and fret? Fancy a tiger
with the toothache! Ah, your eyes say that is wicked, but
I would like to see him conquered."

"You are cruel."

"O, Miss Adriance, he seems such a great, useless, mis-
anthropical fellow, full of quips and quirks, and sneers and
bitterness. Does he make any one happy? Commend me
to the sweet humanity that is not too proud to smile, or
weep, or love."

"Yet he has some friends who admire him extravagantly," I said, thinking of Philip Westervelt.

"What taste they must have!" and he made a grimace
at which I could not forbear smiling.

How differently he had affected the two men! Philip
loved and revered him, while he and Aylmer Channing
could not meet on the plane of ordinary friendship. The
latter had a ready sympathy, quick understanding, was
most generous of his powers, lavishing his gems on every
side, indifferent as to their ultimate fate. He had lost his
mother when a mere child, and a gay young step-mother
had been the companion of his dawning manhood. He
would not have resembled Philip under any training, and
yet in his way he was equally charming. We do not hew
a Hercules out of every block of marble.

Mrs. Lawrence sent a very cordial invitation for Mr. Channing to accompany me home. I confess I rather regretted arraying myself in such decided opposition to Mr. St. John's advice. But there was no help. I gave it as requested.

It was only a few days before the wedding. We two were alone in the drawing-room.

Mr. Channing glanced up, his face in a radiant glow. "How exceedingly kind of her," he said; then colored a little, and added, timidly, "Shall you like it? Will it be pleasant for you?"

I was sorry to have him make it a personal matter, and answered, rather confusedly, "that it would be very agreeable."

"I'm glad not to have to part with you so soon;" and the low key into which his voice dropped gave me a most uncomfortable feeling. "Laurelwood is so lovely that I shall enjoy it beyond everything with you. And May is the most beautiful month of the year. How any one can exist, and not thrill with delight at the sweet voices of Nature, but go groping along, dumb and blind, seeing no stars overhead, no greenness on the earth, is a mystery to me. These great throbs of fragrant, awakening life, kindle in me a fervent enthusiasm."

He looked so charming as he uttered this, his fine eyes aglow with dreamy passion, and wondering smiles curving his scarlet lips, that I forgot my momentary uneasiness, and answered him warmly.

"St. John and I never agree on these subjects," he continued. "He has a horror of romance, and thinks sentiment of all kinds only fit for a parcel of school-girls. With him the world is false and illusive, men are shams, women dolls, who can understand nothing higher than dressing and dancing; you are wrong from the beginning, and, do your best, you can never get right; yet in some incomprehensible manner, you are to work out an excellent destiny from these incongruous elements. Has he never treated you to his sublime theories?"

I could not help smiling. I had hardly been able to make more than this out of my guardian's disquisitions. Yet after a moment I felt condemned, and said, —

"I think you do Mr. St. John some injustice. I have seen him appreciate the noble and grand in Nature, and he has proved a kind friend to several who have come in his way. I believe he is not a man that one would understand readily;" then I paused, for I felt my color rising under these strangely soft and luminous eyes.

"He has a lenient judge in you. But confess, Miss Adriance, hasn't he a way of making one feel weak, aimless, and inferior, while he goes up to his Titan heights, looking coldly down, and offering no one a helping hand? He isn't a broad, genial, generous man."

It was true.

"However, we will not allow it to spoil our delight. I count on having such an enjoyable time. And yet you alone give me courage to enter those Dantean portals."

These personal allusions made me nervous. Perhaps it was merely his complimentary way as a man of the world.

Anne kept wonderfully calm, sustained by the inward strength that she called her duty. Once I ventured to ask if she were happy, for, somehow, in this time of confusion, we had drifted apart.

"Do I act as if I were miserable?" and she gave a tremulous little laugh.

"I don't feel at all satisfied about you. I find myself constantly wishing that some one else stood in Mr. Otis's place."

"Hush! That is a forbidden subject, you know,"

10

"Are you afraid to hear Mr. Channing mentioned in such a connection?"

"Are you not convinced by this time that I possess no strong attraction for him? Do I shun him any way as if I were pained or wounded?"

I confessed that she did not.

"I have chosen Mr. Otis; I shall endeavor to make him happy: and in ministering to another, one cannot fail to reap some reward. Dear Sydnie, never feel distressed about me."

She smiled away some tears.

Then we went on with the wedding preparations. The children were wild over Anne's beautiful dresses; friends came with bridal gifts; and, amid all that was pleasant and sweet, the marriage day dawned, one of those marvellous April mornings bordering so closely upon the espousal of May that two voices seemed blending in every waft of fragrant air. Tiny, detached drifts of frost-white clouds sailed through a sky of peerless blue, and the broad sheets of sunshine were radiant with beauty. I felt inspirited.

Mr. Channing was like the most devoted of brothers; he kept the bridegroom from being unnecessarily awkward, put everybody in the right place, laughed, jested, and made it as gay as possible. We went to church, and walked up the aisle, with curious eyes staring at us from both sides; the ceremony began, responses were given in a low tone, and the hand I ungloved was cold and trembling, but the eyes were turned steadily forward, as if looking at the new path. What strange courage we women sometimes display! Then they knelt down to receive the benediction that was to crown their lives.

It was all done, past recall. Another had been added to the list of happy or miserable lives.

The reception, tiresome as it was, interested me greatly. The bride was pale and quiet, but looked lovely in her soft white silk and flowing veil. Mr. Otis acquitted himself very creditably; Mr. Channing was charming beyond description; and when we had laughed and talked, shaken hands, eaten bride-cake, and smiled over our wineglasses for the appointed time, Anne and I made our exit. I helped her change her dress for a travelling costume, kissed her tenderly, and wished her a happiness I feared would never come; and then she went to her mother for a few last words.

She had preserved a remarkable composure, I thought; but it gave way then. The other farewells were brief, and they drove away on the pilgrimage that had fallen to their lot. For how many of these things come from absolute and unbiassed election?

We had a gay time after they were gone. Quite a party remained, and the evening ended with a little dancing. Mr. Channing lingered until the very last, and left with a promise of seeing me early the next day. He had added a great charm to the visit for me. Not but what I could have enjoyed myself very well with so pleasant a family under other circumstances; indeed, the children made a great outcry when they found my departure so near at hand. Walter endeavored to persuade me to remain until Anne's return. It was odd, I thought, that they should seem to count upon her being just as much to them as before.

"I don't know that I could have parted with her if she were not going to live so near," Mrs. Sutherland said.

How would Mr. Otis like these constant claims? Perhaps his boundless generosity took in the whole family.

The wreck and ruins of the wedding feast seemed everywhere visible; and the house wore a listless, disconsolate look the next day. Anne was missed in every trifling event. Her sweet and yielding nature must have possessed some strong points thus to make her influence felt and needed.

With my good by I gave a promise of repeating the visit. Then I turned my face homeward, speculating not a little on my reception. Mr. Channing proved a delightful escort; I liked him exceedingly, yet Mr. St. John was hardly out of my mind a moment. Would he deem himself aggrieved by the presence of his cousin, and the fact that I had not heeded his suggestion? I did not well see how I could have helped it.

What a strange tangle most lives are! I wonder if we choose anything. Rather it appears to me that we take the events as they come along, and use them as the present moment dictates, and afterwards bewail mistakes, helpless to relieve them.

Two of my companions had decided their destinies. I was not much better satisfied with Anne's marriage than with Laura's, and half convinced that the latter would enjoy more real happiness. She would not try to make pure and high motives harmonize with the position in which she would be placed, and know none of the wearying struggles of fruitless endeavor.

I thanked God for the bright promise of Ellen's love. Yet how narrowly that had escaped going down into darkness.

CHAPTER XI.

" The heart
Oft grows inconstant in its own despite,
And most in love ; because of cruel gods,
Who envy man's obtaining that, the which
They deem their own."   SIR WALTER RALEIGH.

" Still, when we purpose to enjoy ourselves,
    To try our valor fortune sends a foe ;
    To try our equanimity, a friend."   GOETHE'S TASSO.

THE fragrant breath of a glorious May morning greeted me as I opened my eyes after a night's sleep at Laurel-wood. There had been a shower in the night, and the distant fields were a glittering sheet of emeralds and diamonds; every tree was a haze of sunshine; spring gusts went wandering through the pines, sweet with the promised luxuriance of coming summer.

A warm glow quivered through my frame. I pushed the heavy hair back from my forehead, and drew long breaths of this bewildering air. I thought of the time when I had first come here, and a quick rush of feeling overpowered me for an instant.

But I was forced to return to common daily life. Our welcome of the night before had been warm and cordial from Mrs. Lawrence, and very courteous from Mr. St. John. I was anxious to know how it would prove by daylight. Perhaps, after all, there was no real antagonism on Mr. St. John's part. Natures like his, strongly marked by positive qualities, generally prove severe in their requirements, and

impatient with what they consider mental inferiority. But
are they any happier or capable of higher enjoyments than
the others?

Thirza came to assist me. Mrs. Lawrence had already
gone down; so I begged her to be expeditious, and soon
joined the family. They were all in the breakfast room,
the two gentlemen talking amicably; so there had been no
instant declaration of war. In fact, I thought Mr. St. John
unusually gay and brilliant. He inquired about the journey, the visit, and hoped our newly-married friends had
behaved quite to our satisfaction, and were as happy as it
was possible to be. Mr. Channing made most of the re-
plies. Whatever had appeared incongruous in the union
he very delicately kept in the background. Indeed, listening to him, I began to fancy that Anne had been a rather
fortunate girl, and stood a fair chance for a pleasant life.

I could not help contrasting the two men. Aylmer
Channing bore out the resemblance to Mrs. Lawrence in
many particulars, and especially in that peculiar appearance of youth and gracefulness. He had the beauty of
some old god; you could hardly disconnect him from
Grecian groves and festivals that legends have brought
down to us. The comparison made St. John appear really
plainer — gave him a force and ruggedness: the massive
brow and head were indicative of power and sternness,
where the other's displayed an elegant ease and languor;
his face was sharply cut, cold, indrawn, while Mr. Channing carried in his a continual glow of enjoyment.

Mrs. Lawrence was really delighted to have me back
again, and I yielded to the charm of her welcome.

"So you like cousin Aylmer," she said, when we were
alone. "I wonder that I didn't think of inviting him in
the winter, though I don't believe you suffered for lack
of society."

"Indeed, we had our hands full," I rejoined, with a smile.

"Aylmer is one of the most finished gentlemen I have ever met. The Channing estate is large, too, and there are no children by this second marriage. I wonder that your friend did not choose him instead of looking farther. He tells me they have been acquainted for years."

"Her husband was an old friend, also," I said, rather coldly.

"What a picture you two people must have made!" she went on, presently, in the tones whose melody was sweet to fascination, even if the theme was deficient in charm. There was something in her manner that gave me an uncomfortable feeling. Why must people look at every ordinary acquaintance or friendship with a view to matrimony? It vexes me.

For several days all went on smoothly enough. Mr. St. John took very little notice of my return, and made no reference whatever to his unlucky note. No one would have supposed he entertained the slightest objection to his cousin. Not that he acted hypocritically: he made no show of affection for Aylmer, but treated him with the nicest courtesy. The circle of neighbors around Laurelwood greeted my return with a most cordial warmth, and we were in continual demand. I had observed before this the peculiar reserve with which most people treated Mr. St. John, or rather which he demanded of them. He was not a man one would be likely to take liberties with. Mrs. Lawrence they drew into their gayeties as if quite by right, and in this pleasant social atmosphere Mr. Channing was instantly included. Invitations poured in upon us as thick as at Christmas tide. It was such lovely weather for rides and drives and little parties!

"You have worked a wonderful change in my august

cousin," Mr. Channing said to me. "Why, he is quite a civilized being."

"You overrate my influence," I returned. "I have found no change in him since my arrival."

"Ah, you didn't know him before. And Isabelle told me a day or two ago that he had gone into much more society since Miss Adriance came."

I colored a little at this.

"He would be stock or stone if he did not pay some tribute to your charms," was the rejoinder, to which I made no reply.

But that evening Mr. St. John departed from his usual serene mood. We had been talking of a book which had interested us all a good deal, when he demolished our favorite characters with some of his sweeping assertions, very unjust, I thought, and the two had a rather sharp skirmish.

Aylmer went to the window, presently, complaining of the heat, when Mr. St. John remarked, in a sarcastic tone, that he did not perceive any change in the temperature.

I was near by, and could not resist the temptation of saying, purposely for his ear, —

"Marble generally *is* impervious to heat or cold."

"Thanks," he returned, with a scornful little smile. "Perhaps it would be well to congratulate you on the same principle."

"I haven't been in this atmosphere long enough to become petrified; but it probably would occur if I had no alternative beyond remaining," I answered, sharply.

"How fortunate that a summer sea awaits you! Of course there are no such evils as tempests under your bland sky."

Aylmer called me to watch the curious effect of some distant light. What a hard, haughty face I encountered as I passed!

I begin to understand what Aylmer meant when he said they did not agree. The war between them has been fairly inaugurated. There are bitter retorts passing to and fro, veiled by politeness to be sure, but sheathed in sarcasm. Mr. St. John acts as if he thought his cousin's fine qualities put on for effect. Aylmer has a quick eye for beauty, and glowing descriptive powers that in some men would savor of affectation, but with him are perfectly natural. St. John points these with irony or ridicule; and if Aylmer's temper were not the sweetest in the world, he would certainly be vexed.

I stood on the balcony in my riding habit one morning, waiting for the horses. Mr. St. John rose up out of the vines.

"I suppose you are going to discover another smile or dimple in the face of your beautiful nature," he said, with an irritating curl of the lip. "You have a rare interpreter in your attendant."

"He certainly is," I returned, roused to warmth; "a worshipper whom not the slightest touch of grace escapes."

"Whether it be in a pretty woman or a pretty landscape, a well-shaped hand, or an harmoniously colored tulip."

His comparisons vexed me as much as his tone. "At least he is your cousin," I said, pointedly, turning my eyes full upon him.

"I am at a loss to know whether that is intended as a compliment for him or myself."

"It was not meant for a compliment at all, merely a reminder."

"That I should take a few lessons of my charming cousin? become a regular Jemmy Jessamy, flatter and flirt, carry fans and perfumed handkerchiefs?"

"I fancy he possesses some virtues not *quite* above your comprehension."

"Indeed, I thought I enumerated the prominent traits."

"You are determined to see nothing that is good; to pervert and ridicule what others admire."

"I have been aware for some time of the direction your approval has taken, and that you would hardly admit calm reason to make a statement."

"Make as many statements as you like," I said, angrily, my face in a blaze at his imputation.

"At least, Miss Adriance, you will allow that the acquaintance of a lifetime is better worth judging from than that of a few weeks. Not that I expect to have the slightest influence over you. I am aware that one hour in Mr. Channing's fascinating society would eradicate any other impression."

"Women are more easily impressed by gentleness and generosity," I said, turning coldly aside.

"Women are impressed by any idle, conceited coxcomb, who chooses to appeal to their vanity, pay them homage, and dangle after them continually. Tell them the truth, and they will hate you — it is like them the world over. A little glitter and show is all they ask."

"Your experience in women must have been rather unfortunate," I said, in a sweet, irritating tone, that I knew would exasperate him.

He flushed and frowned, and some lightning rays of passion shot out of his eyes. His lips quivered, but made no sound, for just then the horses were led around, headed by Aylmer, who had been superintending some changes in the equipment of mine.

I ran down the steps in triumph, flinging back a disdainful smile.

"Don't you envy us, Stuart?" Aylmer asked, gayly.

"Nature is in holiday apparel; her heavens are blue, touched with floating drifts of silver; her earth an enchanter's realm, and the air is rosemary and thyme."

Mr. St. John vouchsafed no reply. We mounted, and rode quickly down the long avenue. Presently Aylmer said, —

"So Memnon has gone back to his voiceless marble! What have you been doing, enchantress?"

"Nothing to make him so rude."

"How majestically sullen he was! Do you know I half suspect he *did* envy me?"

"Not on my account," I said, shortly.

"I am not so sure of that. He cannot be so widely different from all created beings. I half expected to hear him order you to your room, and dismiss me on the spot. Every morning when I rise I look on my dressing-table to find a paper duly attested, wherein he disowns all relationship to one Aylmer Channing, late his loving cousin, and requests that he shall be no more troubled with such delectable society."

"Not quite so bad as that;" and I laughed. I liked this ridiculous exaggeration much better than sentiment, and therefore used every effort to keep him gay.

I confess he does have a singular effect upon me. Every one admires him; and I can see that Mrs. Lawrence puts us in each other's way continually. Mr. St. John does this also. It piques me to be given to him in this positive manner, as if I had no other resource. Mr. St. John seems to shun me. We might as well be at the antipodes for any real interest or pleasure we are to each other. He is hard, icy, and impenetrable.

I believe I am coming to a serious part of my life. The open sea seems to divide; and, looking down one stream, I see a clear, sunny, rippling tide, whose music lulls one to a restful calm. No promise of storms or tempest, no matter how distant. The other is full of frowning rocks, disturbed and unquiet shores, where it would require all one's strength and wisdom to guide the helm, to shun the dangerous ledges, and keep the bark in a safe channel.

I wonder why it is, but I have a misgiving that this sweetness would pall upon me at length — grow utterly wearisome. And yet it is what most women like. It is in my path, and I have only to reach out my hand and accept; for Mr. Channing has shown his love in many ways, and has evinced such a tender consideration for my happiness. He has youth, rare personal endowments, wealth, and a certain winsomeness that attracts friends on every side. Few would fail of being perfectly happy with him. Why does it not satisfy me?

Ah, why? Heart, what have you done? Why this wandering in gloomy places for a glance from perverse eyes that freeze me with their coldness? Why sip this draught of bitter rue while the goblet of life's sweetest wine stands untasted? Weak and unwomanly as it may be, I can confess here to myself, with no other eyes to witness my humiliation, that I do care for one to whom I am as nothing.

He has attracted me strongly from the very sense of invincible power that is generous only as a conqueror; and if he had striven to subdue, I think I must have yielded eventually, even if I had resisted at first. Once or twice he has carried me along the current of his impetuous desires, and I have learned how sweet it was to yield to so superior a force. But does he care? He has been unjust, impatient, cruel; and that a man can never be to the woman he loves. Ah, dream too sweet for me; the thought tortures my very being!

I can never decide with any certainty upon Mr. St. John. A short time ago he threw me constantly in Aylmer Channing's society, never accompanied us anywhere, pleaded urgent business, letters to write, or persons to see; and now he has changed inexplicably. I have a consciousness that he follows me everywhere. I catch a glimpse of fierce, restless eyes when I least expect; and now and then he confronts me in a manner so peculiar that it startles me.

Mrs. Lawrence has had the house full of company, though I believe he first proposed inviting some guests. We have had outdoor amusements; and within, music, charades, tableaux, and the like. It has been quite a gala time; and Aylmer has proved a strong attraction. Mrs. Lawrence admires him exceedingly.

I think he remarked this curious surveillance, for one morning, as we were rambling in the grounds, he spoke of it. I laughed at first.

"He means to frighten away any possible lover by those portentous looks, and keep you here in his castle until you consent to become humble Esther to his magnificence."

"A remarkably distant event," I replied, rather curtly.

"I should hope so. I cannot imagine a woman loving him. His haughty pride, imperious will, and cold, disdainful nature, his lack of tenderness, and his utter inability to enjoy the highest and keenest happiness, would repel any true woman."

"Are you quite just?" I ventured to say, under a passionate heart throb.

"Just? Haven't you used your own eyes? Ah, Miss Adriance, you cannot lead me very far astray in regard to yourself. He *is* barbarous to you sometimes, and you suffer from it as any high-toned, sensitive nature would.

I know him so well that his sharp-pointed shafts never wound me. I forgive for relation's sake."

Was it really his dainty, generous philosophy? I did not want to misjudge one so amiable, and yet I wondered how deeply he could be wounded. His bright, exuberant nature seemed akin to a summer day with its great waves of sunshine, singing birds, and wafts of fragrance. How would it be in winter — in trouble or sorrow?

"Of all things wonderful! My amiable cousin coming to meet us! He has certainly developed a phase of jealousy;" and Aylmer gave a light, rippling laugh.

I turned suddenly in a half incredulous mood. Mr. St. John had caught the sound. O, that bitter gesture of contempt, as if he could have struck some one to the earth; those scornful eyes dilated and sparkling! What unseen fire fed them — jealousy or hate?

Aylmer opened the conversation in a most courteous manner. I debated how I could escape from them both, for I knew this covert peace would prove of short duration. But when I would have left them, Mr. St. John said, pointedly, —

"Pardon my intrusion, Miss Adriance, and remain. I am the unlucky third."

"My dear cousin, allow me to appease your tender conscience. Our ramble was most unimportant, and you were no interruption whatever."

I fancy he did not like the tone, for Aylmer gave it a peculiar sound, and his reply was sharp. He must have been strangely out of humor. I was really glad when a turn in the walk brought us in sight of the house.

Most of the guests had left us, and he showed a disposition to retire into his former impassibility, but Aylmer was really tormenting with his light ridicule. St. John's ready wit seemed to have deserted him, for, though he was bitter, his adversary gained all the triumphs. It was excessively wicked; but I really enjoyed seeing him vanquished. What was in those deep, mysterious eyes? Great waves of something, that kept coming and going with phosphorescent light, showing depths and heights, but giving no clew to the translation thereof.

Quite late in the evening I remember I was lingering over the piano, when Aylmer asked him a question about some musical composer. He had been making a pretence of reading, but did not progress very rapidly, if one might judge from the slowness with which the leaves were turned. He sat now quite unconscious, his face compressed with some strange, strong purpose.

"Stuart, are you in love?" and Aylmer's dainty lips gave out their musical ripple.

He started up nervously, and shot a rapid glance around.

"What foolish trifles amuse you," he said, haughtily.

"I have asked one question half a dozen times at least. I know of nothing else that can render a man so oblivious — do you, Miss Adriance?"

"I am not experienced in such matters," I returned, confusedly.

"You are, at least. A man who has a new love every month, *must* be a competent judge!" and St. John glanced at him scathingly.

"What says your poet?" replied the other.

> "'Tis better to have loved and lost,
> Than never to have loved at all;'

and then it doesn't affect one so powerfully as to take away one's senses."

"Some people never would suffer in that respect."

"Stuart, you have been in a most unamiable mood all

day. Something must certainly be weighing upon your mind."

"What weak, womanish nonsense!" St. John declared, loftily. "Since love and its accessories suit you so admirably, keep to your own sphere. You will find sufficient attraction in it."

The look, as he strode out of the room, was for me. Scorn, anger, and derisive pity, quite as if he despised me. My heart was under my feet in a moment, and I know I repaid him glance for glance.

"The tiger has been caught in the toils. Bravo, Miss Adriance!" Aylmer said, gayly; but I turned away, humiliated and pained to my inmost soul.

CHAPTER XII.

"Ere such a heart regains its peaceful state,
How often must it love, how often hate;
How often hope, despair, resent, regret,
Conceal, disdain — do all things but forget."

POPE.

MR. ST. JOHN subsided again into his lofty reserve. He began to·treat me with a studied indifference, as if I was altogether beneath any friendly concern. And yet it was singular how attentive he was in any point of duty. Much as he and Aylmer bickered, he never for an instant forgot his position as host, or made his guest feel that he was an unwelcome visitor.

I wished that Aylmer had not been quite so ready to tease. Mrs. Lawrence looked upon the warfare between them as a matter of mere amusement, and oftener hastened to the rescue of her cousin than that of her brother, though their bitterest encounters had generally occurred in my presence. But one morning, at the breakfast table, when he appeared unusually distraught, Aylmer said, gayly, —

"Cousin Isabelle, I made a discovery a few evenings ago."

"What was it, pray?" and she smiled.

"That Stuart is in love. He has grown most melancholy of late."

"Like other diseases, I suppose, the older one is, the more severe the malady. You are not past hope," and she glanced at him with a glimmer of amusement.

"As if there was nothing to a man's life but this insane

11

folly!" he retorted, in a sharp, bitter tone. "I believe the world runs mad on the subject. When you find me committing such a stupendous blunder it will be time to laugh; at present I have no such intentions."

There was an awkward silence for a moment, but Mrs. Lawrence covered it with her usual ready tact.

I sat still, chilled in some inexplicable way. I knew she had never considered him a marrying man, or likely to be attracted by any woman. O, what wild, fatal dreams I had been indulging in!—dashed to a pitiless ruin at a word. How was I to recover, to retrieve my pride, to cast off this influence that had begun to envelop me so closely? I rose slowly, every pulse filled with keenest anguish. As I passed him, he turned his cold eyes full upon me. Not a ray of light or tenderness—I must find my way alone out of this labyrinth, endure my tortures without a moan.

Well, I *would* conquer. No one should ever penetrate the depths of my soul for this secret. I would uproot it to the uttermost fibre. More than all, I would make myself happy. I plunged into a brilliant mood, and for the remainder of the day was extravagantly gay, but this did not escape his bitter comments. They touched me to the very soul, and as he sauntered majestically away, tears of passionate pain sprang to my eyes.

"My darling, what has my barbarous cousin been saying to you?" and the soft, sweet voice fell on my strained and tortured nerves like fragrant balm, softer and sweeter than ever before. "Sydnie, I *must* say it now—I love you with the tenderest affection of a man's heart. Day after day I have lingered in the hope of finding some moment when you would listen. You must have fancied—"

My breath came in gasps.

"Hush!" I said. "Your pity has been stirred—your sympathy aroused—"

"But I loved from the first moment that I saw you. Nay, I shall take no refusal, my darling. I will wait, but I feel that you *must* be mine at last. In my love you shall be shielded from the slightest cloud or shadow; not a harsh word or a frown shall ever invade the sacred precincts of our affection. I have longed to say this so often, so often! I have dared to dream, to hope. Must it go for nothing? I have treasured looks and tones, and believed that you of all others could not be insincere; could not betray with so dear a smile."

I felt the rain of kisses on hair and brow, and experienced a thrill of delight at the thought of being so precious to one fond heart; and like a flash all my wants and desires were unveiled to my own soul. I seemed to look at myself in this extremity with sad, powerless eyes and nerveless hands. Why not drift with the current? Would the salvation be worth the struggle?

Once in a hundred times perhaps a woman might attain to Pisgah heights through the influence of a soul strong enough to master hers and take it into guidance. This could never be my happy lot. I had missed the destiny that might have moulded me into the completeness I knew I was capable of attaining. So what matter?

I knew there was one side of my nature that Aylmer Channing's grace, and beauty, and tender winsomeness could never touch. In some moods I should be forever alone. I could never rise to any great heights; but was that absolutely necessary for a woman? This continual straining after unknown good produced dissatisfaction, impatience, weariness. Why not enjoy the bright portion of life, and let these puzzling speculations become food for essayists and reformers? I *did* like him; might it not reach the heaven of love at last?

"Be patient with me," I said at length. "I cannot answer you now."

"My darling, if you *would* only find rest in my heart. Every pulse of it beats for you alone. I will wait; but I *must* hope. Do not forbid that."

The lustrous eyes, suffused with tenderest passion, won me against myself. The smooth flowery stream was destined to be mine.

I slept but little that night, so engrossed was I with the events that seemed to press upon me with their momentous importance. If I could only shift the responsibility, if I dared ask counsel of one in whom I had a curious, absolute faith, in spite of our utter lack of agreement. That was quite impossible, however.

After all, how quietly the greatest difficulties settle themselves! Before noon of the next day Aylmer had made Mrs. Lawrence his confidant, and she came to congratulate me.

"I am not actually engaged," I said.

She was persistently sweet and persuasive. Aylmer's graces lost nothing at her hands, and his love was set forth with an eloquence of which I had hardly deemed her capable. She made it appear the very thing I had desired, the great good and blessing of my future life. Listening to her, my scruples grew weaker, my wearied brain and heart lapsed into peace, thankful for a resting-place at last; and when I found how deeply Aylmer's heart was engrossed, I had not the courage to array an army of paltry objections.

A strange, sweet atmosphere surrounded me for a day or two, then the tempest broke forth. I was alone in the library when Mr. St. John entered, his face pale, but his eyes glittering with half-suppressed passion.

I glanced up from my book with the presentiment of a crisis.

"May I command your attention for a few moments?" he asked, rather loftily.

"*Command!*" The word stung me. My lip curled with resentment as I replied, coldly, "I await your pleasure."

" Am I to understand that Mr. Channing is authorized *by you* to ask my consent to an engagement between you and himself? "

" He is," I said, haughtily; and I felt my eyes kindling.

" If not too impertinent a question, I should like to know how long he has been your favorite lover? "

There was a little sneer in this that roused me, but I kept my temper.

" We have been engaged a few days, if that is what you mean," I said; and then I glanced out of the window, with an indifferent air.

" I preferred hearing this from you, that I might know in what light to consider it."

" Had you any doubt? " I asked, scornfully.

" I did not know how far an undue susceptibility and a large share of vanity might lead a young man who makes fascination a study."

" You had no right to question it. It is like your usual generosity."

He made an angry gesture, and frowned in a sharp, imperious manner.

" And this absurd child's play was with your consent? "

" If you mean by that," I returned, burning with indignation, " that children only can understand and appreciate the best gifts of life, love, and tenderness, I hope we shall never attain to your cold, narrow, selfish ideal."

" Children! Love! Miss Adriance, it takes a man's heart to receive the impression of this indelible tenderness and ardent affection, akin to the infinite; and it requires the purely developed soul of a woman to appreciate and return *such* love."

" Indeed. Have you been studying the subject? "

"I am aware that with many, a man is simply a fashion-able butterfly, who dances elegantly, has his mind well stored with small talk, vapid as his own brain, and makes his body a walking advertisement of the latest fashions. I cannot comprehend the purpose of such men's lives, unless it be to flatter foolish women and flirt."

"Your knowledge of the world is varied as well as ex-tensive."

"Of late I have seen some interesting subjects for study."

"I hope they have repaid your profound attention."

There was a pause, in which we both took breath. Every moment I seemed to hate him more bitterly, and yet how magnificent he looked, his arms folded upon his broad chest, his brow white with passion, and his eyes fairly blazing. How he could temper and control himself! He fairly extorted my admiration.

"Am I to believe you sufficiently infatuated to think Aylmer honestly desires this engagement?"

"Call it infatuation, or any name you choose, it cannot make the love less a fact."

"*His* love a fact! I gave you credit for better sense!"

O, the withering contempt in the tone! It roused me to white heat.

"Because I am not misanthropic enough to doubt, be-cause I know the reality of this feeling in hearts still human, and accept the offering, you taunt me with a lack of sense. What have you to say against his love? What can you say?"

"What can I say? One important truth. He has flirted from heart to heart, loved dozens with the same passionate admiration that he offers you, bowed at every shrine that came in his way. In six months he will weary of you."

"It is false!" I said, passionately. "You are unjust,

suspicions, and prejudiced. Because your cousin is not cast in your narrow mould, you are resolved to see no virtue in him. All we ask of you is a simple assent."

"Suppose I refuse for the present?"

"We can wait. I have no fear, although you are so doubtful."

"Very well," he said, coolly. "The matter may remain in abeyance for some time. Perhaps your eyes will grow clearer."

I sprang up, roused in every pulse. Did he dare to display his fancied power over me in that fashion?

"I ought to be flattered by this solicitude, seeing what excellent reasons you can give for your unmanly vigilance."

"Miss Adriance, be calm, I beg of you. Just now you have been caught by a little glitter and show, and you have not had sufficient experience to distinguish between the false and the true. In three months you will weary of the bond yourself. You really do not know what love is."

The cool contempt stung me. His piercing eyes were turned full upon me, and I felt mine shrink from the glance. *Could* he read my heart, see how I had wavered between love and pride and resentment? Even now I felt myself in his power, and longed to free my soul from the unworthy bondage — for it *was* unworthy. What did he care whether I was happy or miserable? He would not so much as raise his finger to add to my comfort; but instead, torture me by cruel words and unjust suspicions. I tried to steady my voice, which I hardly dared trust, and said, with cold calmness, —

"Very well, we will wait."

A strange expression flitted over his face. It seemed to me that he was almost disappointed at my resolve.

I took up my book again, and presently he left the room. Not too soon, indeed, for my eyes were full of bitter, passionate tears. The life I wanted to make so happy and complete, so worthy of true existence, stretched out before me a miserable failure. Not the conclusion that I most desired; and yet I must take it up and make it my sole earthly good.

When I recovered my self-possession, I went to Mrs. Lawrence's room to learn the meaning of Mr. St. John's resolve. I found her flushed and nervous also.

"My dear Sydnie," she began, with a forced smile, "this has been a rather awkward and unfortunate explanation. Aylmer feels dreadfully about it. The truth is, Stuart indulges in some strange notions about his right of guardianship; and when he takes a freak in his head he *is* queer and unreasonable. As if a girl of nineteen did not know her own mind! I am absolutely vexed. And his objections to Aylmer are so trifling — so unjust. He never was a great favorite with my brother."

"Well," I said, haughtily, "we can wait. Time will prove who is right."

"Aylmer has been quite gay, to be sure," she went on, rather deprecatingly; "and young men with his attractions can hardly help flirting a little. I have no doubt about his regard for you, and he will convince Stuart of its truth. This is carrying animosity too far."

"He expresses some solicitude for me, also," I returned, scornfully.

"My dear, don't let this distress you;" and there was a tenderness in her tone that sounded like real affection. "Above all things, do not distrust Aylmer. You possess so many charms that you appeal to both sense and soul. I have been talking with him, and he certainly is a most enraptured lover, quite up to your ideal," and she smiled.

"I shall not doubt him, unless he gives me just cause," I answered, gravely, with a consciousness that he was not exactly my ideal, and a certain forlorn sense of being astray in the path where it was of the highest importance to be right.

"Stuart was brought up in such an odd, hermit fashion, that he hardly understands the real world. His opinions of love and marriage are crude and unreasonable; indeed, he hasn't much faith in any one's regard. He can be very good and generous, but the softer graces of life never seem to cling to him. We agree very well, because we go our separate ways, and never seek to convert the other to any particular opinion. But in this matter I found him unusually perverse. He has not a particle of sympathy with lovers. I wish he had married like any ordinary mortal."

"You do not think he will?"

I uttered this with a kind of breathless pang, and waited for her answer, as though it might be of momentous import.

"O, no, my dear. He is looking for impossibilities in a woman. He will never find the right union of strength and pliancy, self-dependence and tender, yielding grace, wisdom, intelligence, beauty, — in short, perfection. Then he thinks all women more or less mercenary, and actuated by selfish motives. As if it was not proper to do the best one could with one's life! Men always consider this point."

"But men do often love disinterestedly," I said, slowly. "And if we made ourselves better companions for them, were not so continually filled with trifles and excitements, and convinced them that we *were* capable of reaching a high point of excellence —"

"I thought you had outgrown this foolish romance;" and she laughed lightly. "You will generally find that these studious, speculative men worship a high ideal in their brain, and end by marrying some silly doll who has hardly the taste to dress well. I am glad you have chosen so wisely; for I used to have a little fear about you. I know you cannot fail of being happy with so charming and genial a nature."

"I still think that I do not desire to trifle away my whole life. Holidays are well enough, but one does not want them forever. We are censured for being vapid and superficial, and accomplishing no real good in the world."

"Men must ridicule something, and sneer a little, or they would hardly be men. But they all like laces better than Latin in a lady's boudoir, and enjoy flounces more than philosophy. It is best to leave these grave matters to clergymen and essayists. The world must have something to talk about."

She always treated serious endeavors in this light, indifferent fashion. In one sense her life had been a perfect success: she had hosts of warm friends, a splendid position, was admired, and could have won lovers by the score had she so chosen. Men of intellect and genius always paid her marked attention — I had noticed that. She could converse well and gracefully, but hers was not a high order of mind. And then I thought of Laura's triumphs. Was there any real discrimination in the world?

She was summoned to the drawing-room by the advent of some visitors. Passing me, she kissed my forehead, and begged me not to be unhappy.

"Stuart will soon be aware of his folly and unreasonableness."

That did not comfort me. I was in a state of dissatisfaction and tumult. My anger against Mr. St. John seemed to be dying out. What if he *should* be right?

O, what was I doing? Since I had allowed myself to drift into this engagement, pride, at least, demanded that

I should be true. I said decisively that I would learn to love; my heart should yield its sweet meed to the one who deserved the treasure.

Mr. St. John insisted that there should be no announcement of the engagement before autumn, and that we should both consider ourselves perfectly free. I acquiesced with a haughty silence; Aylmer was very indignant, and Mrs. Lawrence annoyed.

I believe I did enjoy Aylmer's devotion for the next few days. He claimed his right of possessorship with a certain hesitancy that I did not like as well as a more masterful resolution. Is there an instinctive desire in most women to have the power taken out of their hands, to please themselves by chafing against a chain that in their inmost hearts they acknowledge to be a precious bond?

I had no sense of this: I was free, too free. Generosity and principle must sway me henceforth.

Two months ago I had met Aylmer Channing, little dreaming then how intimately he was to be concerned in my destiny. We parted tenderly — fondly; and when he was gone I felt lost and solitary in the extreme.

I had heard from my friend Anne : her short tour ended, they had returned and taken possession of their new home, and everything was most pleasant. Mr. Otis had decided to assume the charge of Walter's education, which was exceedingly generous. Mamma would be relieved of much care : the old home ties were evidently the strongest. I fancied she was making an effort to be happy — playing with shadows; but I could no longer blame.

We went back to the old routine, and began to make plans for the summer. I was not anxious for Newport, and, as there was no husband to win, Mrs. Lawrence proposed short journeys to several points of interest, which appeared very pleasant to me. I began to experience a

strange craving for excitement. Sulphur Springs, Old
Point Comfort, and Cape May were laid down in our
route.

In September Philip was to be married. I cannot con-
ceive of a lovelier picture than Ellen in her radiant contentment. I was forced to confess that there was something
I lacked, and it gave me a pang of anguish. Would I ever
learn my lesson?

Mr. St. John treated me to a sort of satirical patronage.
I had been wild indeed to fancy his regard anything beyond the considerate care he believed he owed me. And
yet there had been moments of madness when flushing
cheek and kindling eye stirred every pulse of my being:
some words that I could never forget; had they any
meaning? Cold as marble he seemed now, superbly indifferent to any pain or joy that I could give.

There was one day on which these remembrances thronged
about me with a peculiar force. Just one year before I
had come to Laurelwood. Mr. St. John went away in the
morning; Mrs. Lawrence was busy selecting her dresses,
and pointing out alterations to be made; and I, having
nothing to do, roamed through the shady walks and lingered by the sparkling fountains. A soft, droning murmur filled the air, and steeped one in delicious languor.
How heavenly beautiful the place was! I recalled so distinctly my first sensations, and the pleasure they had af-
forded Mr. St. John. We had not harmonized, and he
would be glad to have me go, doubtless. But how could
I leave this Paradise? Ah, he would never guess the
pang.

I felt ashamed of myself for the weakness. It had been
my misfortune to meet a man whom, if fate had been
kinder, I could have loved with my whole soul. I told
my heart the truth this day. But a gulf divided us. In

the Babel-like confusion that had intervened, our languages had changed, and we were never to understand one another again. The tower that might have gone skyward with sweetest hopes and anticipations, lay a mass of ruins at my feet. From the fragments I must construct a new temple, alas! of the earth, earthy. The dim aspirations that had whispered to my soul of its better portion were to be hushed — thrust out as phantoms of the past. A long, wearisome march lay before me : if I could brighten it with love, well; if not, then Heaven help me!

I clasped my hands in a cry of supplication — longing to do, yet vexed and hindered by all about me. This was the record of a year.

All along my future life, at intervals, there would rise a white stone, a monument for a lost hope. The glad joy of the old days stood apart. I was walking lonesomely along between doubt and fear, the solemn music of the deep sea rolling between, the shores widening.

CHAPTER XIII.

"The eyes will not see when the heart wishes them to be blind. Desire con-
ceals truth as darkness does the earth."   SENECA.

WE had a very pleasant summer. The Grahams were
at the Springs, their usual resort. It was so different from
Newport. A quaint, old-fashioned courtesy was noticeable
in most of the gentlemen, the majority of them middle-
aged and heads of families; in the younger ones a certain
chivalrous spirit, not formalized to the rigorous requirements of fashion.

Then the jaunting around strange places interested me:
dreamy sails on the beautiful bay, winding around low,
velvety shores, or sand barrens that sparkled in the summer sunlight; foliage, rich and deep, vivid in color, and
varied by a thousand blooms; and the broad ocean, that
one never wearies of; the same, and yet ever changing.

At Cape May we found quite a host of notabilities. I
was more than ever struck with Mrs. Lawrence's tact and
power to please. She reminds me of old tales of those
wonderful French queens of society, who ruled with a
smile and a nod. And yet it seems singular that a woman
should care so little for love. I cannot understand it. I
wonder if I am weak to long for it so intensely! Life
would become an utter failure to me without some satisfying happiness.

Aylmer was a constant correspondent. His letters were
glowing with love and expectation, and I felt myself in-

sensibly drawn towards him. The Channings had gone
north, and made a brief sojourn at Newport: while there
Aylmer had met Miss Gertrude Hastings, who was turning
every one's head with her loveliness. Mrs. Varick was still
abroad.

Mr. St. John had been kind and companionable, but I
had shunned him considerably; I cannot tell exactly why,
only that he seemed always studying me, and I came to
have a nervous, apprehensive feeling regarding him. His
eyes go down to the depths of one's nature in those swift,
lightning glances, and I hardly felt sure enough of myself
to thus tolerate another's inspection.

We had barely reached Laurelwood and resumed our
accustomed state, when Mrs. Westervelt and Philip presented themselves. What a rush of old memories flooded
my heart at the sight of that sweet face! She was so happy
in her son's joy, so fond, so thoroughly comfortable, that I
half envied Ellen the mother she was to find.

At Mont Argyle they had become quite reconciled to
Ellen's departure. Some news greeted me on my first visit
there that gave me a sudden start of astonishment. Hugh
had comforted himself with a bonnie Scotch lassie, and
would bring home his wife by Christmas tide. Ellen rejoiced in this, and I was unfeignedly glad. Yet a peculiar
feeling blended with the satisfaction. In this brief while
he had forgotten his love for me — that he thought of the
unchangeable — and his ambition. He had been found
worthy. of some other woman's affection, and there his
quest ended.

It was right, of course. I had not held out the slightest
hope, and the old dreams of me could be fraught with
pain only. Was love anything beyond a present satisfaction? Out of story-books did it last, remaining more
faithful to a dead hope than a living pleasure? I felt like

asking, with Wallenstein, "What pang is permanent with
man?"

It is well that we can deck the old grave with new roses.
Are we not all creatures of transient emotions? So I gave
Hugh a sister's benediction.

They were decidedly gay at Mont Argyle. Troops of
young people, three bridesmaids elect and their attendants,
for Mrs. Graham desired that everything should be done
in a manner befitting their position. Ellen was grave,
but sweet. Mrs. Westervelt thought her charming. I
compared this with my one experience, and felt that here
was promise of happiness indeed.

There was a good deal of going backwards and for-
wards. Philip was my attendant, generally. We took up
our old social intimacy, and I found very much to enjoy.
Even Mr. St. John thawed in this rich and genial atmosphere.

Philip and I were riding one afternoon — his last day
of grace, I called it, for on the morrow he was to go to
Mont Argyle, and emerge from thence a Benedict. He
had been unusually silent for some time, watching me
closely. I confess my spirits were rather riotous.

"What is there so peculiar about me?" I asked, at
length.

He suffered his rein to fall loosely over his horse's neck,
and glanced up, with a sorrowful light in his clear, hazel eyes.

"There is always something peculiar about you — different from other women."

"I hate those compliments," I said, shortly. "I have
not the vanity to consider myself better, so the comparison
is equivocal."

"I fancied once that I held the clew to your nature.
Some maze has been too tortuous for me. St. John said
something this morning that astonished me greatly."

I felt my face crimson. What right had Mr. St. John to discuss me with his friend?

"Don't be vexed," he returned, as if he understood the feeling which actuated me. "I half guessed, and made him speak against his will. About this fancy —"

"You must have been vastly amused by the description of a young woman's love affairs," I interrupted, with a bitter smile. "Mr. St. John has displayed a fine sense of honor!"

"I will not have you blame him. The fault was as much mine. And we discussed nothing. He spoke of this fancy —"

"Since it hurts his tender conscience, I will call it by its right name. Early last summer I became engaged to his cousin, Mr. Channing; but as he did not approve sufficiently, we are waiting with the utmost patience."

"And you love this Mr. Channing?"

"I will not submit to be questioned or dictated to," I returned, angrily. "Whatever choice I make is for myself alone."

"Sydnie!"

"Am I incapable of judging what is proper for myself? Do I understand my own feelings at all?"

"Do you?" The grave, tender face was turned towards me, with an appealing expression that smote me bitterly.

"You may have judged from false premises," he went on, in a softer tone. "We all make mistakes sometimes."

"I believe Mr. Channing is a gentleman. Mrs. Lawrence approves my choice."

"And you confess that Mr. St. John does not?"

"He is unreasonable, and blinded by foolish prejudices."

"I met Mr. Channing in August. I will concede that he is a most elegant and accomplished gentleman, a per-

12

fect man of fashion, and admitted to be fascinating. His attention appeared to be equally divided between the two belles of the day, — Miss Hastings, who, by the way, is wonderfully beautiful, and a Miss Raynor."

" Well," I said, with a provoking smile, " I am not at all jealous. Mr. St. John stipulated that we should consider ourselves entirely free. I am afraid if you bring him to the strict letter of the law, I must plead guilty also to indulging in sundry flirtations at Cape May."

" O, Sydnie, it pains me to see you so hard and cold. Have you not enough confidence in your friends to believe that they desire your happiness above all other considerations ? "

" When I seek it in their fashion, perhaps; but I dare to believe that I can judge the most wisely for myself."

" My dear friend, you are standing on the threshold of that sweetest of all lives — a woman's. With your peculiar organization, your capability for intense emotions, you have great power for joy or sorrow. There is such a heavenly influence in a true, earnest life. How will you answer to your own soul if you pervert your good gifts to inferior uses ? "

" I fancied you, of all others, thought love a woman's highest glory, her purest spiritual development."

" When it *is* love ;" and he gave me a sad, furtive glance. " Are you satisfied to accept the gay world as your portion ? "

" I find it pleasant while one is young. When I tire of it, I can take up the graver matters of life," I said, carelessly.

" It, may be too late for happiness. I cannot bear to have you trifle with these most sacred things. I want to see the sweetness of your heart expand and ripen in choicest fruitage. It is worthy of better sustenance than these poor mockeries you thrust upon it. When I see you yielding your life wholly to pleasure, bearing restraint and truth so impatiently, I tremble for you."

"I do not feel it an imperative duty to fulfil every one's extravagant desires concerning me," I said, coldly.

"How you have changed! Forgive my preaching. I know it has annoyed you; but I feel for you a most profound and sacred friendship. O, if you could realize what true and fervent hearts are interested in your welfare, you would pause and hesitate ere you took any irremediable step! for with you a wreck would be terrible."

My blood seemed to falter slowly through my veins. I was more deeply moved than I cared to show. Indeed there was but one step to take to convince these two men that I was not rushing madly to destruction. There was a time when Mr. St. John might have saved me; but he had not cared. Even now his face rose before me in all its mocking pride and masterly strength. Confess to him that I had been in the wrong! Take his censures meekly! No; I could not swallow so bitter a draught.

"I suspect I am merely a commonplace woman after all, since ordinary people and events have the power to satisfy me. I am quite content to take life as it comes. I began with some Utopian ideas, but I have found them of little account, and grown wiser."

"Quite satisfied — you can say that?"

We had been ambling slowly along, and now he laid his hand on the mane of my horse, looking steadily into my eyes, his own torturing in the infinite depth of their pathos.

"Satisfied;" and I gave a gay nod.

"You have disappointed me bitterly, bitterly; and not only me —"

I could bear no more, and, touching Selim, bounded

away. Why did they all conspire to drive me wild, to make me do all manner of reckless deeds? I longed to plunge into the cool, green forest, and shut them out of my sight. Why had I ever come here to be tormented with visions of bliss, and know they could never be mine, to stretch forth my hand for the golden fruit, and receive only an empty husk? Whose fault was it? The tide of circumstances had proved too strong for me.

As if to make amends, Philip was most gracious and gentle that evening. Every look, every act, told me that his friendship would remain mine until the latest moment. If another had been thus kind in some of my desperate needs!

The marriage was perfect, the party delightful. Philip and Ellen started on their life journey amid showers of congratulations and good wishes. The rest had a gala time, the country element giving it a peculiar zest. What dances and merriment! General Graham was the most charming of hosts. It was with no little pride that he announced his expectations of doing this over again for his son in a few months. I was pleased to be as great a favorite as ever, to find that in the general joy no one recurred to my unfortunate episode.

We were in quite a reasonable state of existence when Aylmer made his appearance. I had been looking forward to this with an inexplicable dread, but it vanished speedily. Did I really love him more than I knew?

"I have counted the days of my banishment," he said, with his rapturous fervor. "Each one brought me nearer to you, my darling. How wearisome they have been to me, filled up with trifles, the one great joy always missed, you can never know.' But I have you again, my own, my own!"

Was there anything to doubt here? The kindling eye,

the glowing cheek, and tender voice gave no room for distrust. And then, I never could make myself mistrustful of him, no matter what others said. Was it the result of overwhelming faith, or lack of that intense love which is so easily tortured and depressed?

The season was at the height of its glory. I believe the sights and sounds of nature touched me more keenly than any link connecting me with humanity. Laurelwood was like a brilliant picture. Knolls of richest shrubbery, burnished by the umber-softened sunshine of autumn; the emerald tint of the lawns, broken by clusters of bright, nodding blossoms; the drowsy babble of stream and fountain, and over all skies of such royal loveliness! I just wanted to ride and ramble continually, to live in the present, and take no thought of the future.

"My darling, I have the most delightful tidings for you," Aylmer said, one morning, drawing me out on the balcony, his own face suffused with joy and hope. "St. John has consented to a marriage at any time we may appoint."

I hid my face on his shoulder, rejecting the kisses so freely proffered. A bolt of destiny seemed to strike and transfix me. The sunshine fell at my feet with a cold glitter; the very loveliness of the earth mocked me, chilled me.

"The barrier between us and complete happiness no longer exists. We are blest beyond compare. Why do you not rejoice with me, dearest?" And he strove to read the secret I was thrusting into a nameless grave.

"It is so sudden," I murmured.

"O, my love, forgive my abruptness. One can hardly come from such waiting to bliss at a bound."

"No," I said; "I cannot make it real."

"It has been cruel in St. John to subject you to such a trial. He is convinced at last of the truth of our regard."

"Yes." It was a knell of hope to me.

"But you haven't told me how happy it renders you."

"Do you need words?" I asked, slowly.

"No, I can believe. I am not one of those miserable, suspicious people who have no faith. You will find me generous there, my darling."

Too generous. If he had demanded a fuller confession, if he had made me feel the sacredness of the trust I was accepting, it would have been much better for me. Was it because the love was so tender, or the heart so easily satisfied?

"Let us take a turn in the grounds," I said, for I felt if I stood another instant in his careless embrace, I must break away from it, or utter some wild cry — motion, change, anything!

"You don't feel this as I do," he went on. "Why, I am all in a quiver of joyous excitement. The very trees seem to dance before my vision, and the birds never sang such marvellous songs."

"I suppose I take matters more quietly. I wonder if we are really suited to each other?" I said, with an effort.

"I shall not allow you to think treason;" and he gave me a bright, winsome smile.

"It is well to consider —"

"I will not have you growing grave when I have reached the summit of earthly hope. St. John has sulked, and been morose as a bear, considering; so we really have no hard work to do. I am glad he at last consents to be decently gracious; and now, my darling, you have only to name the day. I am most anxious to take you into my keeping."

Unconsciously I had been making this very consent a sort of test. I asked myself, as I had many times before, if it was at all probable that I should meet with the very

destiny that I desired above all others? I would marry
some time, the most of women did; and since this had
come to me, since I could render Aylmer supremely happy
and have a charming life myself, why go on waiting for
impossible events?

"It takes you a long while to think of the day," he said,
playfully.

"There is no need of haste," I returned, almost coldly.

"But listen, love. It was May when we were first engaged, now it is September. Surely you do not need to
test my affection after this probation! I do not see any
necessity for delay."

"We will not attempt too much in one day," I said,
with a poor effort at gayety. "I must have a talk with
Mrs. Lawrence."

"And she is my strongest ally. I shrewdly suspect she
converted St. John to our mode of thinking."

We rambled through the walks, he so engrossed with
his own feelings that he never sought to fathom mine. I
could illy have borne the scrutiny; and yet, so unreasonable are we, the very leniency annoyed me.

"I cannot spare you a moment," he said, as I made a
motion to go indoors. "If you knew how much I longed
for you, you would make the delay brief as possible. Be
merciful!"

My heart smote me for my waywardness and want of
faith. I made a new resolve that I would give him the
love I owed, the duty our promise demanded.

"So it is all settled," Mrs. Lawrence exclaimed, as I
entered her room. "My dear, I congratulate you. Such
a brilliant marriage, too! I expended my utmost eloquence upon Stuart last night, and convinced him that he
was seriously interfering with your happiness; and this
morning I was delighted to find him in a more amiable

frame of mind. Why he should ever have acted so foolishly I cannot divine."

Was there any cause underlying his solicitude for me?

"Aylmer is wild with delight. I don't believe I could
have found a happier destiny for you. And it will make
no rupture in our friendship. I have really grown attached
to you, and feel perfectly satisfied with your prospects."

When the bell rang for lunch, I found Aylmer waiting
in the hall. His manner had acquired something quite
new, a certain air of possession that gave him the position he had lacked before as a lover. I was not sure but
the majority would consider him more attractive than Mr.
St. John in all his gloomy dignity.

I felt a little awkward and confused, but Mrs. Lawrence's
fine tact covered this admirably. Aylmer showed no disposition to triumph, and in my heart I thanked him for the
generosity.

Mr. St. John took no notice of me until evening, then
he did deign to congratulate me in a formal manner, and
assure me of his interest in my welfare. I could see that
it was a mere matter of duty.

The next day we fell into some dispute, trifling enough
at first, but he soon exasperated me by his cool, satirical
sentences. He talked at me rather than to me — something of high aims forsaken, noble purposes perverted, the
great trust of life betrayed. He made such bitter, sweeping assertions, he was so manifestly unjust, that I absolutely shrunk from the hard, narrow soul, whose glamour
had once so nearly conquered mine. Where had I found
anything lovable in him? What tenderness or generosity
could a woman expect who ventured to disagree with him
in never so slight a particular? Aylmer was right — no
one could be happy with such a tyrant.

I believe I should have been well satisfied but for the

talk of marriage. Aylmer's plan caught Mrs. Lawrence's attention at once — that immediately after our wedding we were to go to Washington. The winter promised to be unusually gay. In that case Mrs. Lawrence would spend a month or two there also.

"A most auspicious debut," Mrs. Lawrence declared. "The fates seem to place everything desirable in your way. Next summer you can go abroad and win triumphs."

As if I was to consider only the attention I excited! Did this homage ever satisfy a woman's heart?

"I believe you like cross, sullen, and uncomfortable people," Aylmer said one day, "or you would be glad to marry and go away, just to escape the glowering looks of St. John. He cannot endure the sight of happiness."

Did ever a woman like taunts better than love?

Every day the net seemed drawing more closely around me. What was I waiting for — hope of escape?

Now and then I examined my heart. I *did* desire to love Aylmer Channing, and I felt comparatively satisfied. Why should a stray glance of Mr. St. John's have power to disturb me?

"Stuart," Aylmer said, at length, "I want you to assure Miss Adriance that you feel perfectly satisfied to yield your claim as her guardian in my behalf. She cannot resolve to decide upon the exact period when I may take her into my keeping."

"You are mistaken when you suppose that anything I could say would influence Miss Adriance," Mr. St. John replied, with a little hauteur.

"You will say it, at least?"

Aylmer's voice was boyishly pleading, and his lustrous eyes glanced up with infinite entreaty.

"Miss Adriance knows that if I had not been entirely

convinced of the fact that her happiness depended upon this marriage, I should not have consented."

"There, you hear, Sydnie! When everything and everybody conspire to make you happy, why will you resist?" and he turned in triumph.

"You are all in such urgent haste;" and I tried to laugh.

"I've settled upon Christmas, Stuart."

"I don't see what objection Miss Adriance can make to the time, if she means to marry at all."

Mr. St. John's face was calm as he spoke, but his eyes shrouded in impenetrable reticence. Yet something warned me that I was at the very verge of a volcano.

"Have it as you like," I said, carelessly.

"O, thank you a thousand times! Isabelle, I have won!" and Aylmer's voice trembled with the deep excitement of satisfaction.

I took half a dozen steps towards him, and laid my hand in his, saying, in a tone of emotion, —

"God willing, I consent to become your wife that day."

Awful words, that bound me irrevocably! I fancied that I had made the last struggle then, and was at peace.

Aylmer snatched my hand and pressed it to his lips rapturously. But another revelation greeted my astonished vision: St. John's hands met in a passionate, nervous clasp, and his intense eyes settled upon Aylmer as if he could have hurled him to the uttermost part of the earth, — so fierce and terrible that I stood positively magnetized, my very breath chilled. And then glance encountered glance. Was it love, or hate, or disdain, or revenge, that we read in each other's eyes?

"Heaven help us both," I felt tempted to cry.

He walked carelessly out of the room.

CHAPTER XIV.

"What miracle
Can work me into hope? Heaven here is bankrupt—
The wondering gods blush at their want of power,
And, quite abashed, confess they cannot help me."

NAT LEE.

"My dear Sydnie, you have come to your senses at last," Mrs. Lawrence commenced, with a smile. "I am thoroughly glad. But there are only three months in which to prepare; so we must be expeditious."

"Three months! Why, one could be married a hundred times in that period."

"I suppose so, if the ceremony were all. The engagement had better be announced immediately."

"Announced!" I exclaimed, aghast.

"A very short time, I assure you. You will be busy shopping and having sewing done, and go very little into society."

"I don't expect to begin wedding dresses until December at least," I said, positively; "and I do hate to be gossiped about. Three weeks will be the utmost limit of my endurance."

"What are you thinking of?" And her soft eyes opened in unbounded astonishment.

"Thinking that no announcement or wedding dresses will be made for the next two months. Aylmer goes home to-morrow, and we shall return to our usual life."

"This is most unreasonable."

"Most reasonable, it appears to me. Twenty things may

occur — death, disagreement, changes. I don't want to
hear one word of the matter outside of Laurelwood. I
mean to take all the comfort and pleasure that belong to
Miss Adriance proper; and the first of December I promise
to deliver myself into your hands, and become the most
pliable young woman you ever saw."

"What a singular girl!"

"Yes, I *am* singular. It is the last gasp of expiring
liberty."

"One would think you did not wish to be married."

"I believe I don't: but it's a woman's destiny; and what
matters a few years, sooner or later?"

"You *do* love Aylmer?"

"As well, perhaps, as I am capable of loving any one.
I've almost become a convert to your faith. He will make
a charming husband, fond, indulgent, and all that, and I
shall, no doubt, settle into a sensible wife. The old belief
was all a farce — the chimera of a school-girl's brain."

She glanced at me in silence.

"Dear Mrs. Lawrence," and my tone softened, "be patient with me this brief while. Only, I don't want the
talk and the congratulations until the latest moment."

"We shall have to do something, though. We couldn't
more than make the dresses in three weeks."

"Do all that can be done quietly, then. Save the fuss
and the tumult to the very last."

With this we compromised.

Aylmer and I parted tenderly, after the fashion of lovers. Was I hypocritical and insincere? Heaven knows
that I was honest in my resolve — that I meant to use my
utmost endeavors to make this man happy, when he laid
"his sleeping life within my hands." But this restless mood
tortured me into strange phantasies.

Mr. St. John was polite, interested in all that demanded

his concern; but cold and withdrawn into self—abstracted. He might have experienced a momentary twinge of jealousy concerning Aylmer, but he had not been moved thereto by any love for me. Every day I realized this more and more. No betrayal, no weak moment of tenderness, no longing. A great gulf was between.

And yet I lived through the two months very comfortably. The old gayeties seemed to have a fresh zest for me. I was brilliant, attractive, and glittering, like an ice-peak in the sun of a mid-winter noon. Nothing seemed to warm me — to touch me with that enkindling spark of humanity which brings all souls to a level. So the days sped along.

With the first of December came Aylmer.

"My darling," he said, "how wonderfully beautiful you have grown! but there's a look about it that almost frightens one."

"Do you fancy that I shall melt into a shadow — etherialize?"

"No, not that: the Scotch have a good word for it — uncanny."

I laughed.

"You'll set all Washington to raving about you this winter."

"Well, if I soar too high, you can clip my wings, you know."

"I shall never want to do that, my darling. Believe that I shall be proud of all the admiration you win."

So generous, so delighted in the success of another. I tried to make him feel that I appreciated his tenderness.

Mrs. Lawrence was in her element. I verily believe she and Aylmer were much more concerned about the respective elegance of silks, laces, and jewels than I. The whole thing seemed incongruous to me. That one should care

so much for the adornment of the body, so little for the
aliment of the soul! After the excitement was over, what
then? After one wearied of dresses and revels and idle
compliments, what could appease this restless, gnawing
hunger?

Matters went on to everybody's satisfaction, except that
it rained continually and kept us indoors.

"Do you realize the date, and how fast the month is
going?" Mrs. Lawrence asked, one morning.

"Why? Are you counting on the moon to make a
change in the weather?" and Aylmer yawned. "I verily
believe the sun has forgotten how to shine?"

"It is the tenth, and not an invitation directed."

"There's plenty of time," I said, quickly.

"None to spare, at least."

"I wish people could get married without all this foolish
fuss and talk," I exclaimed, petulantly.

Aylmer glanced up. "I believe this vile weather affects
you, too. The first respectable morning we will take a good
long gallop, and bring ourselves back to serenity."

"Well," I said, with an effort, "let us amuse ourselves
counting up our dear five hundred friends."

With that we adjourned to the library. Aylmer was
quite out of spirits, more so than I had ever seen him.
There might be many rainy days to life — what then?

Moralizing over one's wedding cards was not quite the
thing.

Presently we all became interested. The lists were gone
over by each one, all the additions made, and St. John offered to direct them. Aylmer amused himself writing a
few, then sauntered up and down the room. A sky of
hopeless gray, drooping so low that it seemed to envelop
the tree tops; a drizzling, uncomfortable rain, and a melancholy wail through the distant pines. More than once the

vision of Aunt Mildred's death crossed my mind. How strange that I should think of it now!

We lingered over our lunch, we strolled through drawing-room and conservatory, counted the flowers we might expect to blossom in time, went to dinner without any appetites, dawdled through the dessert, and at last lights were brought in.

"What a musty old hermit St. John is!" Aylmer said, pettishly. "If he had not gone off to his den, we might have had a game of whist."

"I will send for him," Mrs. Lawrence rejoined.

"No, don't; his high mightiness would only feel bored. Commend me to a city in rainy weather, say I. Sydnie, suppose you sing."

I went to the piano, mistrusting my voice, but I determined to make the effort. It was a failure, and he nervously critical on this evening.

"You are dreadfully out of tune," he commented, presently.

I rose angrily: my first impulse was to leave the room; then I reconsidered, and crossed over to the sofa. What a handsome face this was, thrown into clear relief by the crimson pillow! An exterior merely: the soul was narrow, dark, ill-governed, with no resources in itself. Could I minister to it, could I *endure* it for years and years?

"How dull you are to night."

This time I was wounded. I stood irresolute, every pulse within me mutinous, and rising to a white heat.

"My darling," he said, with sudden softness, and drew me to a seat beside him. "When we get to Washington we shall be as gay as larks. I only wish Christmas came sooner."

The fondness had lost its flavor. Kisses were weak and insipid. There were no true and fervent depths in him to be roused by love. All that I had been trying to make myself believe vanished in an instant and left a hideous blank. Already we had come to the dregs. In time, when utterly wearied with his vapidness and trifles, I might even hate him. I shivered at the thought.

"You're not well," he said. "This miserable weather has given you a cold. Isabelle, I can't have her looking like a fright on her wedding day."

"Never fear," I answered, bravely, and with a touch of scorn.

"I think it would be as sensible to retire as sitting up here playing stupid," Mrs. Lawrence remarked; and we accordingly dispersed.

I went to my own room, and in a burst of passionate emotion buried my face in the pillow of the lounge. The wild wind blew tempestuous gusts of rain against the windows, and then moaned off down to the hollows with a desolate wail. I pressed my hands to my burning, throbbing temples. Not a tear came, but a long, hysteric sob tore its way up from my very soul.

Circumstances had betrayed me into this engagement, but *must* I go on and consummate my misery? Was there no strong hand to snatch me from this fateful destiny? Did I dare pray to God?

O, I had trifled so with life, with myself! I had perverted the holiest desires of my woman's heart, stooped to gather shining sand that the next wave might wash away. With great capacities for happiness I had wrought evil only, and now I was whirled helplessly along the great stream of life, no one caring for the wreck. The time foretold by my one best friend had come upon me, and I was overwhelmed.

Something rose above the storm without and within. My tense nerves caught the sound — a low, sweet strain, such as a summer wind sings in the lap of greenest meadows; flower wreaths shaking out faintest perfumes, murmurous leaves touched by a soft south wind. Then it grew stronger, firmer, as if animated by a living soul — a child in careless play, rambling over mountain wilds, prodigal of youth and all that youth holds dear; gay, joyous, soaring on the wings of fancy, quivering with every breath, easily moved alike to joy or tears.

I forgot the storm and my own misery. I raised my face and listened with absorbing interest.

Girded with the fearlessness of youth that has courage for all things, it went gayly onward. By-ways enticed it, mountain tops glittering with brightness hurried it, beguiling voices of sirens sang their tender songs, and then the real struggle began. The storm, the strange melody, the war in my own heart — how it thrilled me with contending emotions!

There was a lull in the tempest of passion. I heard the calm, sweet voice of the earlier days imploring, then the din and wrangle of bitter strife — a strange, awesome wail as of a soul in peril. Who would gain in this mighty battle?

The gentle voice returned. It was Peace crowned as a victor. The storm of passion died away, and in its place lingered a sweet, ineffable calm.

Was that solemn chant of life prophetic? I was kneeling in the brooding silence with clasped hands and tearful eyes. Could I yet be saved?

———

There was a sky of azure and a golden sun the next morning. I felt faint, as one who has kept too long a vigil, and yet I lay in a hush of dreamy contentment, as if the crisis of my life had passed, and my heart, like the dove of old, had found rest. Had I the courage to put my latent resolve into execution?

I dressed slowly, and went down stairs. The letters detained by the storm of the preceding day had just arrived.

"I intended to see you before you went," Mrs. Lawrence was saying to the servant. "There is a great package of mail matter that must be sent immediately."

While she was speaking, Aylmer started towards me, nodding gayly, his face wreathed in sweetest smiles. My heart wavered so that its beating became audible. Could I give him a traitorous glance, promising hope?

He paused and took up a letter, breaking the seal hastily. A quick cry passed his lips.

"What?" Mrs. Lawrence was startled by the ashen brow.

"My father! Dead! Merciful heavens!"

Mr. St. John joined the group. There was no mistaking his solicitude.

"Dead!" Mrs. Lawrence repeated, raising her eyes in consternation.

He handed the note to St. John — a hasty telegram that made known only the merest facts.

"I must go immediately, you see;" and Aylmer's voice had a strange wandering sound. "The first train." Then he came around to me.

"These festivities must be delayed," I said, in a low tone.

"A bad omen;" and he smiled faintly.

"No matter now."

"It *is* best. No one would want a wedding at such a gloomy time. And then, everything will have to be changed."

"Yes."

"My darling, this is most unfortunate."

"I am inexpressibly shocked," Mrs. Lawrence said. "You have our warmest sympathies, Aylmer;" and she clasped his hand.

"I will write soon and let you know — "

"We had better give up our present arrangements," I remarked, decisively. "You can tell nothing surely as yet."

Mr. St. John's eyes met mine with a glance that thrilled and terrified.

"You have been saved," it said plainly, and I am sure mine answered, even at the risk of betraying all that was in my soul.

It was a melancholy breakfast, and the parting was sad enough. Something in Aylmer's clinging love touched me inexpressibly. Had I misjudged him the night before?

"Could anything have been more unfortunate?" bewailed Mrs. Lawrence, as she ordered the elegant dresses to be folded away. "I think with Aylmer, that it is an unlucky omen; but I hope it will end rightly."

"It will; rest assured of that," I said, confidently.

I was glad to get every reminder out of my sight. There was the wraith-like veil and orange blossoms — would they ever be needed?

Aylmer wrote as soon as he reached home. His father had been ill only a few days, not considered at all dangerous until within an hour or two of his death. He found his step-mother plunged into the deepest grief. Her sister, Miss Raynor, was with her at the time. I remembered her as one of the Newport belles mentioned by Philip.

The Christmas that was to have been my wedding day we spent very quietly. Another change had come over Mr. St. John. Instead of shunning me, he seemed to seek my society, escort me out, evinced much interest in my comfort, and was uniformly gentle.

How many events had crowded themselves into the brief space of a year! I hardly appeared to myself the same person. And now the sense of coming freedom gave me a singular buoyancy. How it was to be brought about I hardly knew, but it was a sure hope to my hitherto burdened heart.

In the evening, Mr. St. John seated himself at the organ and played Milton's grand old Hymn of the Nativity.

"Will you try it?" he asked, presently; and I sang, blending my voice with his full, deep tones. There was a light directly in front of the organ, but the far corners of the room were in a dim, twilight shade. The grand, swelling melody roused all the worship of my nature. I felt as if I could have listened and sung forever.

"How the music stirs you," he said, in a soft, pleased voice.

I thought of another night, and a most peculiar experience.

"This appeals to me in a powerful manner," I answered.

The eyes, charged with luminous light, were turned full upon me.

"You played one night some time ago —" and I paused.

"Yes. You liked it?"

"I cannot tell you how it moved me. It seemed the struggle of a human soul."

"It was. A soul in bondage freeing itself."

He uttered the words slowly. All the fascination he had ever possessed for me returned with renewed force. Something within me confessed the man my master.

He rose and faced me as if he would have spoken, then took two or three turns across the room.

"I wonder if any human soul is strong enough to force its way out to the light?" he asked, abruptly.

"I think it is," I made answer.

From that night I date a new life, as it were. I began to see my mistakes more clearly. Pride and self-love had led me far astray, and I had many tortuous paths to retrace. How little advancement I had made in any path of usefulness!

I experienced many misgivings concerning Aylmer. For a few weeks his letters were frequent and extravagantly fond. I answered them in a spirit of tenderest sympathy, because just then coldness would have seemed cruel, but I purposely refrained from positive declarations of affection. I confess to a little pang when I found they passed unremarked. No woman likes to own herself so poor in power over a lover's heart that the withdrawal of tenderness is no longer capable of giving pain. He appeared to be much engrossed with his step-mother and the business, which was rather complicated. He even ceased to make excuses about the visit, and no longer referred to the marriage.

I lacked the courage for an overt act. It was so difficult to make issue with him. I fancied that when we met it could be more easily done. Perhaps, too, I was afraid that Aylmer would prefer an appeal to his cousins, and drag me into a painful explanation, so I waited in wretched indecision, resolved upon one thing only — that I would not become Aylmer Channing's wife.

We were less gay than usual, as Mrs. Lawrence was indisposed for several weeks, yet the time passed very pleasantly, and ere I was hardly aware spring dawned upon us.

One day I was startled by a letter from Mrs. Otis, so different was it from her usual epistles. I thought they all had a strained and wearied air, as if she was striving for peace continually, and yet failed to attain that high satisfaction. But this was bright, sunny, and hopeful. She asked me to come and help her keep a new and better wedding-day on the anniversary of the old. The whole current of her life had changed.

Another sentence held me in a strange, cold grasp. It was this: " Is it selfish, dear, to rejoice that your engagement is broken? I seem to understand a woman's needs so much better than I did a year ago, that I feel now, brilliant and fascinating as Aylmer Channing is, he could never render any true, loving, and loyal woman permanently happy. To come to the dregs when one has expected a draught of clear, rich wine, would be terrible."

I had announced to her that the marriage was delayed; since then neither of us had mentioned it. She must have learned this from some other source, and in a moment I was all anxiety to know the truth. So I proposed a brief visit, in which Mrs. Lawrence acquiesced, but Mr. St. John was instantly annoyed.

"How easily you tire of Laurelwood," he said, captiously. "Women can never be satisfied unless they are in the midst of excitement."

"We shall be quiet enough," I returned. "I shall see less society than I do here."

"But more dangerous! For conscience' sake, Miss Adriance, don't bring home another lover."

That was bitter. "I assure you I am not likely to," I returned, haughtily.

"There is some sensible advice in the old couplet, —

> ' It's good to be off with the old love,
> Before you are on with the new.' "

I felt the sarcasm in his voice, but I would not allow it

to ruffle me. O, if we could but be friends, patient, true, and tender! For a moment I was tempted to confess my difficulties to him, to admit my wants and weakness. His faithless smile deterred me. There was no safe middle ground for us.

I found Anne wonderfully improved. At first I could hardly credit my senses. Bright, winsome, and girlish, in a phase that she had never exhibited before. Even at school she had always been grave.

"You must be supremely happy," I said, with a pang at my own confessed lack of such inspiration.

"Not *quite* that, but reasonably so," she answered, with a smile.

"And you have reversed the order of things — fallen in love with your own husband."

She flushed daintily.

"I believe I begin to understand some of the great truths of life. And I think —" with a little falter, "that I always cared more for him than I really knew. It has been a thorny, confused path, and sometimes I nearly lost the way; but what matter, since the end is clear and bright."

"You really love him — you are perfectly satisfied?" I asked the question with sudden curiosity. I was eager to know how complete one's belief might become.

"I can answer your question truthfully;" and the sweet eyes drooped with love's own shyness.

"I must hear the story, Anne."

We were in her sitting-room, a cosy little place, bright with sunshine, and in each window a hanging basket filled with trailing vines and some gay tropical blossoms. The home-like air impressed me. No stiff formality of arrangement, no lack of cheerful ease.

"It isn't much of a story. Who was it that said some

people wrote idyls, others lived them? I fancy I must express all truths by living them."

"The only right way;" and I sighed a little.

"You are not unhappy?" She knelt beside me, and clasped my hand in hers, looking up with fond, questioning eyes.

"I am *not* happy, or even comfortable. Like you, I have gone astray in thorny paths, though I had not your excuse. I suspect I must lay the blame upon my own waywardness."

She made no reply; and after a moment, I added, "Why did you fancy my engagement was broken, Anne?"

"Is it not?" Her bright cheek paled suddenly.

"Not a word of the kind has been spoken on either side."

"Sydnie!" Then her look of surprise gave way to one of grief. "Forgive me," she said, slowly. "I have wounded you most unconsciously. Let us forget it; only believe that I am sincerely sorry."

"What do you know?"

I held the sweet face within my hands, and fathomed the pure eyes. Some secret that she could not entirely conceal lay within their depths.

"I must know. It is of vital importance to me," and the strength of my nature overpowered hers.

"I will tell you the truth," and she made an effort to steady her trembling voice: "Mrs. Channing has a young and beautiful sister, whose fascinations, it was said, exercised a powerful influence over Aylmer last summer at Newport. Since Mr. Channing's death she has been Mrs. Channing's constant companion. Aylmer has been at home all the time, and the rumor is that as soon as propriety will admit, a marriage is to take place. And, my darling, I do not think it mere careless. gossip. It came well authenticated to me."

"And do you believe it true of *him?*" I asked.

"Must I be cruel, dear? My eyes have been opened, Sydnie, though I know women do not generally show their wounds to one another. He gave me a cruel thrust early in the battle of life, and yet it is only this winter past that I have realized the depth, the pain that might have been mine, and, thank God, was not. Don't fancy me actuated by any old soreness. To-day I should be glad to see you happy with him, but this I do not believe any woman can ever be. He lacks the grand element that hallows all love — constancy."

"And yet he was once your ideal," I said, almost reproachfully.

"Yes, he was. I will admit that, and more. There was a time when one word more would have won me irrevocably. Circumstances alone prevented it. He used all the arts so natural with him, and if I had not been restrained by a sense of my inability to hold anything so brilliant and supply its needs, I must have yielded. When we met again the charm was gone. He had satisfied himself, perhaps, and no longer cared for my feeble incense. By some strange process we became friends. He still bewildered me with his beauty and dangerous sweetness; but since I had no expectations, I lingered in the glare with a peculiar sense of security. Then came my engagement with Mr. Otis. I accepted him partly to please papa, partly because I did feel very grateful, and a good deal from the firm belief that he loved me, and would be much better satisfied with a quiet regard than none at all. I hate myself for it all now;" and she made a sudden gesture of abhorrence. "I had not seen Mr. Channing for some months, but an accidental current drifted him to my vicinity. He had heard of my engagement, and congratulated me warmly. It is his misfortune that he should always seem so earnest, so interested, for it misleads others. During the summer before, there had been some playful badinage at my cousin's about standing at our marriages, he gayly promising to perform the kind office when needed. She accepted him at once, as her bridal was at hand. He referred to this jestingly, and a sudden resolve came into my mind. I would ask you, and judge in what estimate dispassionate eyes held him. Remember that then I admired him to the utmost, and had never felt inclined to blame him for not loving me. I understood all our differences too plainly. I could never satisfy a nature that demanded such incessant variety.

"If I had possessed sufficient courage, I should have confessed the truth to Mr. Otis. It was not that I really loved any one else, but that I did not love him. I was so afraid of giving him pain. And then the explanations loomed up like a huge mountain, and terrified me. I could never undertake them. Unconsciously you touched upon the secret, sensitive chords of my nature in one of our many talks, and then I felt I must go on at all hazard."

"My poor Anne," I interrupted. "How could you conceal all this misery under such a cheerful demeanor?"

"It did not seem to require any effort then; besides, I was only negatively wretched. I had no sharp, positive pangs, such as reveal the soul. It was harder afterwards;" and her voice faltered.

"Well," I said, "after you were married? — "

"Mr. Otis was very kind and considerate. He provided every luxury, every pleasure, made me feel that I was perfectly free to spend as much time at home as I wished; in short, demanded nothing of me. Instead of drawing nearer together, the insensible breach between us widened, until it could be distinctly perceived. It gave me a thrill of nameless terror. What could I do? I felt so helpless, so lost, as if I were floating in a great unknown sea, without chart or compass.

"And then a very simple incident occurred. Mr. Otis was compelled to go east on some business. The weather being unfavorable, I did not accompany him. Ten days only, and yet it seemed interminable. I missed the tenderness, the watchful care, the sure support that I needed more and more every day. While I was in this mood, one of those fearful railroad accidents happened that shock everybody. I hardly thought of it as concerning myself, until I received a telegram from Mr. Otis. He had escaped unhurt, by a miracle, he said.

"A sudden burst of remorseful tenderness rushed over me. Are there such things in love as instant conversions? If he had been brought home dead, I hardly think it would have moved me as deeply. I experienced a most intense and agonizing desire to see him, to tell him that my soul had been kindled with some deep inward fire, and longed to answer the needs of his. I could see the loneliness of the spiritual life to which I had condemned him by my coldness and reserve. I felt then that I did love him truly, and I was wild to show it by words as well as works. Ah, I cannot tell you how I waited. I even sent the children home. For the first time in my life I wished to be alone with him, so that no indifferent eye should look upon the sacredness of our meeting. It seemed as if he would never come. The train had been detained, and it was quite late in the evening when he arrived. The servant admitted him in the hall, and then he came straight to the sitting-room. I sprang up, and was folded to his heart, but I could not speak for sobs that well nigh strangled me.

"'My precious wife,' he exclaimed, 'are these tears for me?' And there was a depth in his tone that I had never heard before. It fairly trembled, and the strong arms shook as if with an ague.

"Ah, well, one can never remember just what one does in these great straits of life. Perhaps it is as well;" and the crimson flushes deepened from brow to throat. "And all the while, Sydnie, he feared that I had loved Aylmer hopelessly. At least he began to mistrust just before our marriage."

"Yet he dared to risk the chances?"

"He loved me so, dear. I can never be sufficiently grateful for all the patient kindness. And it seems as if I had not understood Aylmer until lately. He makes a changeful holiday feast of love, forgetting that it must be a woman's daily bread, too often rendered black and bitter by man's selfishness. My dear friend, have I pained you beyond forgiveness?"

"It was right for me to know this. And now I will be equally honest, even if the confession *is* humiliating. I have *not* really loved him. Two weeks before our appointed marriage day I resolved to break the engagement. I don't know whether I should have had the courage, but he was called away by his father's sudden death. Since then I have been temporizing."

"O, my darling, I am *so* thankful;" and she raised her eyes, bright with tears that were not all sorrow. "You are worthy of a higher happiness."

"I don't know that I am worthy of any," I exclaimed, vehemently. "I have been wilfully blind, impatient, wise in my own sight, and now I reap the whirlwind that I have sown — the loss of esteem, the mortification of this position. I hate myself!"

"And I have been the cause!" she said, with poignant self-reproach.

"No, you shall not blame yourself. Mr. St. John warned me, and even withheld his consent for a time. He thought his cousin fickle, fond of change and excitement. I shall bring my unlucky engagement to an end immediately, thankful that there has been so little said about it."

How much truth was there in a man's regard? Hugh Graham was happy at Mont Argyle with his sweet young wife. He had met me with a good deal of complacence, and, after our first greeting, betrayed no embarrassment. Yet I confess that in my heart I honored him; but the treachery and faithlessness of Aylmer Channing were beyond forgiveness. I had allowed myself to be beguiled by this adoration, offered at many a shrine before, and perhaps to be laid upon others. The remembrance of every kiss stung me. The tenderness I had allowed to be paraded before Mr. St. John rushed over me with a bitter sense of humiliation. He, knowing what it was worth, had smiled over it. How *could* I endure his triumph?

I soon made Anne understand that no deep regard was concerned in the promise; and then she urged me not to delay the step so imperatively necessary. And as I glanced at her beaming face, I gave thanks that she had so soon found the grand secret of life, and was walking in pleasant ways.

CHAPTER XV.

"Meantime I seek no sympathies, nor need;
The thorns which I have reaped are of the tree
I planted;—they have torn me and I bleed;
I should have known what fruit would spring from such a seed."
                                        CHILDE HAROLD.

LOVE had certainly improved Mr. Otis. I do not mean that he had grown handsome or graceful; but there was an ease and manliness about him that was exceedingly attractive. Through much pain and many doubts, he and Anne had reached the true level of their lives. It might not be a safe precedent to follow, but in this case it had brought about admirable results. That they were really happy one could not for a moment doubt.

Now that Aylmer Channing's beguiling glamour no longer served for contrast, I found him entertaining and agreeable. He warmed curiously when Anne was present. Her love seemed to enfranchise him from any lingering awkwardness or over-sensitive feeling. Neither was he deficient in fine tastes or cultivation; and I soon found that many a woman might be satisfied with such a destiny.

Walter Sutherland was still delicate, though slowly improving. His passionate thirst for art, and his ambition to be able to distinguish himself, were dangerous aliments for such a highly-wrought organization. I smiled over the many efforts Mr. Otis made to turn his attention into other channels, and give the physique a chance with the restless brain, wondering how he could understand and minister so well.

After a few days' consideration I wrote to Aylmer. I did not make the slightest allusion to the story I had heard, but confessed my own dissatisfaction with the engagement, and proposed that it should be relinquished, as I was quite confident that I should not find my highest happiness in its consummation; — a cool, dispassionate letter, that betrayed not the slightest haste or anger, for beyond my irritation at his faithlessness and duplicity, I was not at all wounded — perhaps only too glad to have the crisis come in this manner.

Still I waited in a peculiar state of mind, wondering a little in what mood he would answer.

Was the man radically false, or was it only the result of a facile temperament, and utter want of conscience? For I believe, in his long and closely written epistle, he actually persuaded himself that he loved me, that he would suffer acutely in giving me up; but, since it was *my* desire, he could not insist upon anything that was likely to render me unhappy. He spoke of the delightful past with touching pathos — the walks, the tender conversations, the hopes we had cherished, and the void that would remain to him. Yet he did not implore me to change my mind, or threaten any deed of desperate daring. Instead, he breathed a hope that, though love between us might be dead, friendship would still remain.

Alas, when confidence had ended with me, all was over. I could meet Hugh Graham with a true and tender regard; but if this handsome face ever crossed my path, I should feel tempted to spurn it with unutterable loathing.

But even this incident did not detract from the pleasure of my visit. I felt that in Mr. and Mrs. Otis I had friends for life, friends that I could count upon in any emergency.

On my return to Laurelwood, I gathered together Aylmer's gifts, elegant and fanciful, like himself — jewels with quaint devices, books superb in their binding — and was making a package, when Mrs. Lawrence tapped lightly at the door, and then entered. My face was dyed the deepest scarlet.

" Excuse me ; " and she drew back, hesitatingly.

"I must tell you," I began, with desperate courage. "The engagement between Mr. Channing and myself has ended."

" Sydnie !" She stood pale and trembling with astonishment.

" We have decided that it would not be for our highest happiness. I believe he understands it as well as I ; " and there was a touch of scorn in my voice.

"And you allowed this nonsense to ruin such brilliant prospects ? Are you crazy ?"

" The brilliant prospects did not tempt me at all."

" They would have tempted any other woman. What else *could* you ask ? And I thought you had satisfied yourself about the love."

" I believe it was only a passing fancy with him : I find that I was quite mistaken concerning my own regard."

" He might be a little wavering, but you, of all other women, could have held him true. Your beauty that never palls, your voice, your spirit and variety would have kept him captive forever, if you had so willed. Of all folly this is the wildest."

I had never seen her so thoroughly roused.

" I should not want a husband whose affections it was necessary to retain by continuous effort," I said, haughtily.

" With all your endowments I can foresee that your life will prove an utter failure, and all on account of these romantic follies. Was ever a woman so short-sighted ? "

" The fault is not entirely mine," I returned, warmly,

"Last summer I heard that Mr. Channing had been strongly attracted by Miss Raynor, his step-mother's sister. He needed only to be brought within the circle of her influence again to have the charm completed. Knowing this, I preferred to resign him while my claim was yet undisputed."

"A false, foolish story! Miss Raynor has nothing but her beauty, and that is not to be compared to yours. You have been most hasty and unwise. Is it too late to repair the mischief?"

"Too late. Even if I could yet believe him true, which I do not, I should still refuse to marry him. I learned, before he left us in December, that he was *not* all that I had fancied him, or even what I desired."

"You will never find what you desire."

"Perhaps not."

"And these Raynors are poor, miserable schemers. What girl of eighteen would marry a man three times her age except for his money? More than once this wily step-mother has tried to entangle Aylmer. And if you had made the slightest effort — "

"I did not consider his salvation worth any effort on my part;" and I smiled disdainfully.

"So I perceive. Poor Aylmer!"

"I don't think that I *could* have helped his liking Miss Raynor," I said, rather indignantly, "and I was not anxious to be jilted — for it would have come to that. I consider that I have had a very fortunate escape in *any* event."

"What step do you propose next?" and there was some irony in her tone.

"I have not decided;" and I smiled, in spite of my irritation.

"Do you remember your age?"

"Almost twenty: quite ancient, I must confess."

14

"You will not be likely to find any better chances for marriage than those you have passed by. I think you have had everything offered you. It stamps a woman's success to marry while she is still admired and sought after. If she waits, the world throws up its hands, and says, in a tone of relief, ' Well, she's married *at last*,' as if one had tried all one's life to bring about the event."

"I don't trouble myself about the world, and certainly shall not marry for the sake of any favorable verdict it may give."

"It is not a pleasant thing to be thrust aside where you have once reigned; to find yourself superseded by younger and fairer women. I wish you could have been married without any of this nonsense."

I thought of that December night with a shiver.

"I ought never to have made the engagement," I said, with some remorse. "Aylmer attracted me wonderfully at first, but I never loved him."

"How pertinaciously you keep to that theme! You will never love, then; for he was acknowledged to be irresistible. And it is rather mortifying, when I took such pains to convince Stuart that you *did* love him. You know he insisted that you did not understand your own desires on the subject. We can hardly blame him for enjoying his triumph."

That stung me. The mocking, satirical smile flashed across my vision — the face that could torture one with a look, the voice whose tones could cut like a keen sword. Well, there was no escape.

"I really hope you will come to your senses some time," she said, sweeping out of the room.

I felt that I had seriously offended her. She had been very kind, indeed, and taken an infinite deal of trouble with my belongings. If I had married well, she would have been amply satisfied; but what if I never married at all?

I resolved, if there should be any further discomfort, that I would propose a change of abode. Then my heart gave a great gasp. To leave Laurelwood, bid it farewell for all time — could I do it?

Mr. St. John appeared to take the knowledge of the present state of affairs very coolly indeed. I despatched my package, cleared away the mental debris, and then proceeded to take a survey of my situation. Were all the years to go on like these two, appreciating no claims but those of society — dressing, visiting, dancing, and flirting? I really longed to try the world in some other guise. What *could* women do? Nothing but marry, it seemed, unless they possessed a remarkable genius, or were compelled to toil for a livelihood. Neither of these reached my case. Weariness and ennui staring me in the face, I actually envied those to whom fate had apportioned useful lives.

I took up my books with a spasmodic effort. I practised music, read French and German, and indulged in long rambles. If Mr. St. John found me thus employed, a peculiar smile would wander across his face. We had both observed a long truce, and I had a misgiving that the battle would open soon.

"How very industrious you have grown," he said, finding me on the balcony one afternoon. "What is the new aim?"

"I am not sure that I have any aim," I answered, listlessly.

"You are despondent. Miss Adriance, it will never do to take a lover's defection so seriously. It is one of the chances of the service, you know."

The hot blood rushed to my face. "I am not in the slightest degree lovelorn," I answered, shortly.

"A female Alexander, grieved that there are no more empires to conquer. You have grown discouraged early in the fray."

"I have no desire for such paltry triumphs," I returned, haughtily.

"Paltry! A man's heart thus to be contemned! You are pitiless."

"I have won no heart that could suffer in being cast aside."

"You do not hold your lovers in very high esteem. It is like a woman."

That roused me. "When one true lover sues to me, I shall respect him at least, if I cannot return his regard."

"And all the rest is most convenient pastime — flirting."

"I have *not* flirted," I rejoined, angrily.

"What do you call the episode with Mr. Channing?"

"Not *that*, at least."

"Then you *did* love him?"

There was a fierce gleam in his hard eyes, and a sudden sharp frown settled about his brow.

"I did *not* love him. I was strongly attracted, and perhaps overpersuaded by the apparent tenderness of his regard for me. I honestly tried to do my duty, and when I became convinced that I could not, asked to be released from my promise."

"And this is a woman's boasted constancy! So infatuated that she can listen to no reason, ready to throw her whole life away, and in six months' time so weary of her bond that she sues for release."

"It is possible that one can be mistaken in a person. I do not pride myself upon my penetration or infallible judgment."

"Alas, if love is held subject to idle caprices! And your mistake in Aylmer was one of wilful blindness. You were warned repeatedly."

"How was I warned?" I exclaimed, aflush with indignation. "You refused to do him even common justice. You were unreasonable, severe, and caustic. One is apt to espouse the cause of the wronged."

"You are extremely generous, Miss Adriance! Mr. Channing requited your chivalrous affection very poorly indeed. I think I did him full justice in warning you at all. If I had not considered him likely to win a woman's favor, I should have held my peace, and thereby saved an immense reputation for cruelty."

"A regard that is generous and tender always appeals powerfully," I said. "One can hardly be sufficiently suspicious to question it in the beginning."

"And these are the men who succeed!" he said, bitterly, curling his haughty lip. "They can fawn and flatter, and please a woman's fancy, while truth stands aloof, too proud to degrade itself."

"No," I returned; "what we most desire is appreciation. Occasionally we are betrayed by a semblance of it."

"If half the time and talent spent in rendering women artificial and heartless was devoted to a better purpose, there would be something to appreciate," he said, savagely.

"Why do not men offer a premium on the virtues, then? The women who succeed the most brilliantly in life are not the high-toned, truthful, and pure in soul. Half a dozen really noble, natural girls, who have not made dress and attractiveness their highest study, will be eclipsed in a room by one handsome, elegantly attired woman, who has learned to make the most of herself in the manner society approves. Educated and accomplished men single her out, and pay her marked attention. Patient wives are not infrequently neglected for her, and hearts that have been musing over happy dreams, in all the sweetness of a first unshaken trust, find themselves rudely pierced by careless-

ness on the part of the man from whom they have a right
to expect better things."

"But these are the acknowledged coquettes in society.
Men do not so often seek them in marriage."

"Pardon me. Some of these women have three chances
for marriage where others have scarcely one."

"Marriage being the great end and aim of existence,"
he said, sneeringly.

"We must confess that it is. Ordinarily we do not find
a single woman of forty the recipient of as many polite
attentions as those who are younger. She is not held in
the same esteem as if she had improved her chances for
matrimony. She may have grown nobler and richer in
many directions; more refined, capable of receiving higher
truths and obeying the dictates of loftier virtues. The
probability is that nine people out of ten will sneer a little, and remark how queer she has become."

"You have been converted to a new faith, Miss Adriance. This was not the belief of your 'salad days,' as
Cleopatra terms her unwisdom."

"I have had the world to study since that time."

"For Heaven's sake, don't become cynical. Leave that
to the sterner sex."

"Will not the armor answer equally well for both? If
men can intrench themselves behind it, and fling out
pointed arrows, indifferent as to whom they may wound,
why may it not be pastime for a woman?"

For once I had met the enemy on his own ground. He
bit his lip, and there was a moment's silence between us.

"You are making rapid strides," he said, at length.
"What do you propose to do next? I should really like
to be forewarned."

"What I do cannot be of much importance," I said,
carelessly. "A woman's scope doesn't seem to be very
extensive."

"O, you can write a book, you know. That's a *dernier resort* after being in love."

I would not let him rouse me to anger.

"Since you advise it, I may possibly try," I returned, calmly.

"No, I don't advise it. Reading German metaphysics is bad enough. But there is little danger, since you are not particularly amenable to counsel."

"No one has ever taken sufficient interest in my welfare to counsel me in any of the great emergencies of life. If a woman possesses intellect and power, why should she not use it? Must we be continually sent back to our mirrors and our dresses?"

"Inconsequent, as your sex invariably prove."

"If yours are so wise, why not instruct us?"

"O!" he exclaimed, with sudden vehemence, "if human nature was not steeped in this blind, selfish egotism! If any one dared to live a true, honest life, instead of overlaying it with detestable shams! Have not men in all ages given preference to fond, simple-hearted women, who were not too proud to glory in their birthright of pure, tender, enduring affection, that no trials blanch, no time dimmed? And when they accept this for their mission, when the strength and sweetness of their souls tend to this high spiritual elevation, there will be no need of grasping feverishly at fancied tasks."

"Will it make a woman less tender to have noble aspirations or well-developed ideas of life?"

"A dream rarely realized — but then what dreams are?" and he turned abruptly away.

What dreams are? It fell mournfully on my soul, like a strain of sad, dying music. Why did we live at all, if to be forever unsatisfied? Why were these wants pertaining to the pure and profound estates of mortal being given to us, if they were not to be realized in this land of their birth? Would it not be pitiful for a soul to drop out of the world, never having known that completeness it felt surely fitted for?

Something woke a new chord in my inmost being. I do not think I was born a poet; the glorious dawn, with its intense beauty, the silence of the purple twilight, with its mysterious charm, and the vague unrest of solitary nights, when the soul seems to brood in an unearthly atmosphere, thrilled me with speechless emotion. But there were other avenues for thought. Women had trod in these paths and found them pleasant. Even if I did not succeed brilliantly, would it not be better than this tiresome round of dressing, dancing, and admiration?

Mr. St. John was a good deal surprised at the announcement of Aylmer Channing's marriage. Mrs. Lawrence had not recovered her equanimity on the subject. I foresaw that she would have hard work to forgive me. Sweet as she was, she could show her displeasure in many ways, and occasionally made me feel quite uncomfortable.

This matter was soon forgotten in one of much more importance. Mrs. Lawrence received word that a large investment in Cuba, which had hitherto been very profitable, required immediate attention. Mr. Lawrence's sister had married a Spaniard; and the brothers-in-law had both been concerned in the same business. Mr. Carme had met with heavy losses, and there would be important changes made.

"I think I had better go at once," Mr. St. John proposed. "It is May now, and I can be back before the season of extreme heat. A person on the spot can manage so much better, as writing delays interminably."

Mrs. Lawrence was pleased, and the arrangements were speedily made. A brief absence to be sure, but I could not help thinking how odd Laurelwood would appear without Mr. St. John.

"What a happy time you will have," he said, on the last evening of his stay, sauntering down to the window where I sat in the soft twilight of the moonless night. "For the next two months you will be quite free to follow your own devices."

"Believe that I feel exceedingly grateful for all past care," I returned, with mock humility.

"No, you don't, either;" and his tone was strangely excited. "Think of the many times you have positively hated my interference. But for me you might have been a happy wife."

"You are cruel," I said, wounded to the quick.

"And you are a mystery to me. Did *he* never call forth any responsive affection? Doesn't the memory of some sweet phantom hope stir your heart with strange longings? — for you are neither ice nor marble. There is the fire of a very volcano in your eyes, and there must have been moments when it found vent and swept all before it. Great heavens! that such an offering should have been laid at a man's feet, and trampled upon!"

He was moved from his usual self-poise, and his vehemence affected me singularly. I trembled in every limb.

"I think you make some mistake in regard to Mr. Channing. He gave much and demanded little. He was engrossed with his own feelings and enjoyments, and never sought to fathom the depths of my soul. If he had, I should have known the truth sooner myself."

"And there was a place in your heart that his sweetness and beauty never touched. Some chord sacred to a master hand, that gave forth no responsive music? Yet you put on the semblance skilfully! Miss Adriance, how much truth is there in a woman?"

His mocking words and scornful manner stung me, and
I replied with some passion, —

"I was weary, heart-sick. You had shown yourself
most ungentle; ridiculed the faith I might have had, made
light of my earnest endeavors, taunted me beyond endurance! Sympathy and rest were sweet. It was my misfortune that I accepted too readily; but that being done, I
endeavored to perform my duty."

"Well, why did you give up this high notion of duty?"

"Because I found that another could be as dear to him.
Was it necessary to doom myself to misery for a strict
point of honor?"

"But you couldn't have known this when —"

"I did," I confessed with a secret mortification. "I heard
it before I had taken any positive step; but my resolve
had been made long ere that."

"I knew you never loved him. I read your secret in a
dozen different ways. But you can bear no advice, no
counsel! You would martyr yourself for pride's sake,
while love stood shivering at the door where you refused
him entrance."

His masterly bearing, and stern, cutting tones, roused
me to instant defiance.

"When did *you* counsel?" I began, springing up.
"You used to taunt me with being an undeveloped girl,
ridicule my aims, my desires, my tenderest feelings, until
I was fain to hide them from your sight. But when did
you ever speak of the rocks, the quicksands, of the tortuous path where one might go forever astray? You were
hard, and cold, and cruel!"

"As if anything could have made a difference with
you!"

How he maddened me! I was not the strong, dominant, self-willed woman he would persist in believing me.
Could he ever understand?

He took my hands in his, and said, in a tone so low that it sounded like a mere whisper, but was wonderfully distinct, —

"How many times will a woman's conscience allow her to repeat the most sacred words and endearments of love? Will they have any meaning when you utter them again?" and he made a gesture of bitter contempt.

I felt my courage yielding. What right had he to torture me thus? My eyes filled with tears of pain and shame.

"I shall never utter them but once with truth," I said, vainly trying to steady my voice. "And that time is yet to come."

Then I would have broken away, but his grasp upon me tightened. He turned me quite around so that my face came in range of the long ray of distant lamplight; I could feel that his glance was like flame, and devoured every passing emotion. Scarlet flushes stole from brow to throat, and I trembled in every limb.

"Yet to come," he repeated in a tone that thrilled me, it had softened so exquisitely. "What surety have I that other false vows may not be breathed?"

"None," I replied, impelled to the truth by his steady eye, "save that the mistakes of the past have proved so bitter that I should dread ever to renew them."

"Let the past with all its failures be forgotten;" and he drew me towards him in a tender clasp. "The present is mine to make of it what I can. We will not rush into any headlong folly, but patiently abide our fate."

Did I hear aright! Every pulse throbbed and quivered with a new and intense emotion. I felt the sweet, lingering kisses of fire upon my lips, absorbing soul and sense. O, I knew now what it was to love, to be beloved? Nothing could ever make me prove recreant to that trust.

What more might have been uttered I know not, but there was a gentle rustle in the hall, and Mrs. Lawrence entered the drawing-room.   Mr. St. John released me without any perceptible stir, bending over once and whispering — "Remember," and then we both were outwardly calm.

She had thought of another item or two, and as he was to start early in the morning, explained them now. I sat by in silence, occasionally catching a fiery gleam from the eyes that were lakes of luminous light.   I fancied there was a strange depth in his voice, and every intonation thrilled through me.   We said no more that night, or in the morning either, for though I came down to the early breakfast, we were not alone.   Perhaps he might have made an opportunity, but he carried himself with regal pride.   I felt his power in the very air I breathed, and was subdued by the subtle magnetism.   Now and then he gave me a peculiar bright, fascinating look, that was not a smile, and yet answered for both smile and words.

"He shall see that I can deserve his trust," I mentally resolved with my farewell.   And yet a chill struck to the core of my heart — how would we meet again ?

CHAPTER XVI.

"Lord of my learning and no land besides."
SHAKSPEARE.

Mrs. Lawrence began to discuss our summer arrangements presently. Where should we go? what should we
do? She left the choice of place entirely to me.

"We can hardly look for Stuart until the middle of
July," she said. "He will be rather tired out with his
jaunt, and perhaps not care to undertake another, so we
can make our arrangements without reference to him."

"Why should we go at all?" I replied. "Laurelwood
is as lovely as any place I have seen."

"There will be very little society through the summer."

"Never mind society for once. I think I should like to
have a good long restful summer here."

"Very well. We will stay until Stuart's return, at
least."

I was decidedly pleased. Not for worlds would I have
been absent then. I had a gratifying belief that he would
approve of this partial seclusion.

And now I asked myself what I should do. To brood
constantly over the beguiling visions that floated through
my brain would hardly be wise. And then I remembered
how oddly I was situated.

I could not absolutely consider myself engaged; indeed,
as for real love-making, there had been very little. Mr. St.
John *was* peculiar. Did I understand him at all? Was
I certain that our natures would assimilate — harmonize?

I wondered if any woman had ever taken destiny in such a fashion before? There was only one fact of which I did feel confident. Through the exercise of some curious power, Mr. St. John was able to sway every thought and feeling. Was this love? His approval was more to me than the opinion of the whole world besides. His very presence filled my soul with radiant delight, and yet I experienced a strange fear concerning him. The possibility of his being completely my master loomed threateningly before me. It would be sweet, indeed, to yield from a deep, tender, overpowering affection.

A year ago I should have made an ideal and an idol of him at once. I seemed to have more self-poise, more wisdom, and though I was capable of experiencing a much deeper and more absorbing passion, I likewise appeared to demand more in return. Had I grown selfish, exacting?

I left off thinking of myself, and turned to Nature. Never had she been lovelier. I indulged in long, solitary rambles and delightful communings; delicious reveries that inthralled both heart and brain. The fires of youth lost their fierceness, seeming more like the perfect golden glow of sunset.

Mr. St. John wrote that the business was much more complicated than he supposed, and that he was unable to fix upon any period of return, but that it would be as speedy as circumstances would permit. We were rather quiet, for Mrs. Lawrence left me much to my own devices. In this mood of brooding repose a tiny flame of ambition sprang up. Mr. St. John had satirically said — write a book. Have we not all a thread of romance within us? And so I began.

How the days passed I scarcely remember. They were like dreams perfected by sweetest music. I neither looked forward nor backward, but simply waited.

Suddenly the music ceased; the spell was broken.

My eyes were wandering carelessly over the paper- one morning as we still lingered in the breakfast-room, when my attention was suddenly arrested by the announcement of the failure of a large New York and Baltimore house, and the suicide of one of the partners. My fortune was swept away at a single blow!

I sat there in silence. When the fire has burned to ashes, one does not look for a torch to rekindle it. There must be wood to sustain a new flame. The old has perished beyond recall.

"What is the matter, Sydnie?" and I saw Mrs. Lawrence making a sudden movement towards me. "You are as pale as a ghost."

"A poor way to bear misfortune;" and my lip quivered, failing miserably in an attempt at a smile.

"Misfortune?" Her tone was incredulous.

I handed her the paper.

"An utter failure! O, it cannot be *quite* true. These things are always abominably exaggerated. How unfortunate that Stuart is away! I will send for Mr. Northrup —he may know how to advise;" and she did despatch a servant immediately for the county lawyer.

We walked slowly through the hall. It was a warm morning; but the fragrant air revived me.

"My poor child, I cannot express my sorrow nor my sympathy. I only hope we shall not find it as bad as we expect."

What did I expect? Literally nothing. I felt crushed and overwhelmed. I cannot say that I had ever experienced any strong love for poverty, and now I shrank from the crisis with a trembling in every nerve. Very weak and ignoble perhaps, but I could not help it.

Mr. Northrup was not at home; and two days elapsed

before he made his appearance. By this time the first
accounts had become well authenticated. The old story
of extravagant living, speculation, inevitable disgrace, and
death. My sympathies were strangely interested in behalf
of the family so suddenly plunged into deepest gloom.

"My dear," Mrs. Lawrence said, in her sweetest tone,
"if you only *had* married Aylmer. He would never have
thought twice of the loss."

My lip curled involuntarily.

"I think it would be best to take a little trip north.
Your outfit of last winter can be made beautifully available with very little expense; and few will know of the
misfortune. You still have your beauty."

"No," I said, decisively, "I cannot take part in such a
farce."

"What will you do then?"

"Give music lessons or teach school," I answered, reck-
lessly.

"Sydnie, I beg you will not do anything rash nor foolish. You have many friends, and sufficient attraction yet
to make a good marriage. Look at the matter sensibly,
now, I implore you. I have decided to go to Washington
next winter, and I want you to feel that you would be
most welcome to my care. I am sure that you can not
only retrieve your fortune, but make yourself happy. You
will marry sometime."

She did not in the least suspect Mr. St. John of caring
for me. But in her opinion poverty was a kind of pesti-
lence that it was proper to take any method to be rid of.
I felt proud and defiant. Would Mr. St. John deem me
capable of mercenary motives?

Mr. Northrup found affairs in the wildest confusion.
The first reports were but too true.

"It is not worth while to worry Stuart with it," Mrs.

Lawrence said. "He will be home soon, and then his hearing cannot mend matters. He will regret the unfortunate occurrence deeply."

I hardly knew how I felt about Mr. St. John. Pride and delicacy revolted from making the slightest appeal to him. All the little tendernesses I had planned, and the ready compliance I was to show, looked too much like interest. He could make my path very smooth in the manner pointed out by Mrs. Lawrence. The thought gave me an uncomfortable shiver.

To please her I had gone on as usual. We had received an invitation to a birthnight party of a young lady, one of our neighbors, and a person I really admired. When I found that she expected me to accompany her, I made no demur; indeed, I anticipated much pleasure. Mrs. Darrell, the girl's mother, had been extremely sympathetic and cordial to me; and I felt that no loss of fortune would ever change her regard for one she liked.

The preparations roused me a little, brought me back to a more human state. I resolved to enjoy the gayeties with as much of the old zest as possible.

"How bright and lovely you look!" Mrs. Lawrence said; and I felt pleased with her commendation.

It was indeed a gala scene; the lawn hung with colored lanterns, and everywhere a profusion of fragrant flowers. Great wreaths of roses swaying in the soft June air, and the walks lined with blossoming shrubs of every variety, the porches covered, and the rooms decorated. How lovely it appeared! and to make the enchantment more complete, musicians had been stationed in different parts of the ground, and sweet melodies went wandering through many a woodland path.

I felt my spirits rising. I knew I looked well. Why should I be shut out of enjoyment through a loss brought

15

about by no fault of my own? Was I not the same? and did I not possess capabilities that had been mine a month ago? My fortune had taken away no integral part of myself.

They danced, chatted, laughed, and made themselves merry. The evening was half spent, perhaps, when I sauntered down a path, attracted by a strain of sweet melody the flutes and French horns were blowing out in tremulous summer gales. Then a voice near me said,—

"So Miss Adriance has lost her fortune. What will she do?"

"Mrs. Lawrence is very fond of her. I suppose she will remain at Laurelwood, as she has no relatives," a voice that I recognized made answer.

"And marry Mr. St. John." The sentence ended with a laugh.

"Mr. St. John isn't considered a marrying man."

"O, she will manage it. Beauty in tears is irresistible. Of course she will go to him for comfort and advice, and he being her guardian will feel moved in her behalf. You may count upon her being mistress of Laurelwood in six months."

And then followed another mocking laugh that was like a stab to me. I had heard enough. Blinded by a sudden rush of emotion I could hardly find my way back to the brilliant lawn and the dancers.

I had endured some petty slights before, but this stung me to the very heart. If I should marry Mr. St. John, how many would believe me actuated by purest affection, as I should be? I was hurt, angry, and my enjoyment of the evening came to a sudden end.

The next day I wrote to Mrs. Otis. Already she had shown me that I had one steadfast friend, at least, and invited me to visit her; indeed, she wished now that I would consider her home as my own. I should always be a most welcome guest. I had thanked her for this kindness when I was too deeply agitated to form any plans for the future. Indeed, I did not know as I had any right. But now some wild motive urged me on. I said frankly that henceforth I should be compelled to earn my own livelihood. There was but one avenue open to me at present — teaching school. My musical abilities were of a high order, and I believed that I could take care of myself. Since the effort must be made some time, it would be as well, I thought, to start about it at once. But I seemed quite at loss to know to whom an application might better be made. If she could hear and advise me immediately, it would be of great assistance.

I would show Mr. St. John and his sister that I dared brave the evils of poverty. He should not find me helpless, or positively in want of aught that he could give. I would not even make an indirect appeal for counsel. Whether it was pride that swayed me, or a just selfrespect, I would not stop to consider. To be armed was all I cared for just now.

Probably no reverse of fortune was ever pleasant. During these weeks I was in a measure shielded from gossip, because a large portion of the community had already started on their phantom chase for summer pleasures. But now and then a sentence fell upon some bare, shrinking nerve, and gave me a momentary torture. I really did not dare to propose leaving Laurelwood, yet the days had lost all brightness and beauty. I grew morbidly sensitive, and longed to reach my true level, for I knew that in losing my fortune I had lost caste.

Anne enclosed three advertisements in her reply — two for a school, and one for a governess in one of the eastern counties of Maryland, where music was made a special requirement. This one attracted my fancy strongly, and I answered it immediately, telling as much of my story as was necessary, in order to account for my temerity in seeking a situation without reference, though I sent the name of Madame W., my former preceptress. What a flood of emotion this brought over me! I remembered the day on which I had waited for Mr. St. John to come, the strange journey, the welcome here. *Could* I go away? Why, it would be like leaving my soul behind.

I need not. I felt certain that Mr. St. John would consider himself bound by those few words spoken the night before his departure. What I wanted was not sympathy or sense of obligation, but love. Unless he could give me *all* that I desired, I would take nothing at his hands. If I must hunger, it should be in a desert, not in a land of plenty.

By one of those odd circumstances that occasionally decide a fate, my application met with a fortunate reception. Mrs. Ingalls had been pleased with it — consulted her husband, who advised her to accept. There were two girls nearly grown and five younger children. The salary was very fair, although it seemed a pitifully small sum to me. My duties would commence on the first of September. That I might decline hardly appeared to enter the mind of Mrs. Ingalls.

I was not prepared for so rapid a termination, and felt rather startled at my own haste and assurance. On the same morning a letter came from Mr. St. John, announcing that he should start in the next steamer. Then he would soon be home! I owed him some duty, certainly. I had not a perfect right to dispose of myself without a slight consultation at least. He was my guardian, if no more.

I decided to wait until I saw him before I took any positive step. The ease with which I had found this situation gave me courage to believe that if it failed, I should be able to secure something else without much difficulty. I felt armed, as it were, to fight any battle now.

Such interminable days as these were! I was very quiet outwardly, but within reigned chaos — resolves, prejudices, and events vibrating and influencing one another, until I felt strangely irresolute. Even the thought of love ceased to charm.

The breach between Mrs. Lawrence and myself widened perceptibly. There was nothing tangible in her demeanor; indeed, she sometimes appeared more solicitous; but I had a consciousness that these phases were not real, and that she assumed them from a sense of duty. Disliking the senior Mrs. Channing, she could not approve Aylmer's marriage cordially, and held me in some degree answerable for it. Besides this, she experienced a pang of secret mortification that, with my many advantages, I was *not* married.

The weather was growing intensely warm. A great cloud appeared to envelop me, full of slumbrous magnetic influences, not sufficiently charged for a crisis. I had a sensation of being cut off from the rest of the world. The very air about me grew stifling, and I drew my breath with great gasps of apprehension. And in this mood I counted up the days, until one morning, when I heard a stir among the servants.

The master of Laurelwood had come!

There were joyous greetings in the hall, the sweet voice of Mrs. Lawrence murmuring a pleasant welcome. Had I any part or lot in the matter? Should I thrust myself upon his attention in this first moment of his return? Pride held me back. If he was very desirous of my presence, he might signify it. But I waited in vain for any summons. What little events change the purposes of our lives! Any time during that morning I could have been convinced by a word or a look of the great fact of his love;

when the bell rang for luncheon, the hour of grace had passed. I felt calm, but bitter and cold.

I hurried down, hoping to enter the dining-room first. He intercepted me in the hall. Somehow, I shall always remember the picture he made. The voyage had completed the work of the tropical sun, and left him almost swarthy. His hair had been cut quite closely, displaying his broad forehead, and leaving a few stray curls at the temple. His eyes had a set look, that was fairly stern, while the flowing beard, with its peculiar bronze glitter, gave him a weird, foreign appearance.

He flushed deeply in spite of the olive hue, and appeared at the first moment absolutely disconcerted.

"You seem in no haste to welcome me," he said, rather sharply. "I had been counting on *that*, at least."

"Your sister had the first right, I am sure," I answered, gravely.

"And you none?" This was uttered in a tone of inquiry.

"None," I repeated.

"At least you might ask if I were well;" and he laughed rather nervously.

"The fact is apparent. Allow me to congratulate you upon your safe return."

At this juncture Mrs. Lawrence joined us. She looked somewhat discomposed, and glanced curiously at me. My sensitive pride took alarm at once. Did she fear that her brother would foolishly rush to the rescue, and marry me?

Each one made an effort, and the meal passed most pleasantly, though the conversation was all upon Mr. St. John's journey. He was really delighted to be at home again; that I could plainly see. We lingered over our dessert of fruit a long while, and as we rose he said, turning to me, —

"May I see you in the library, Miss Adriance?"

I crossed the hall with him, and then went over to the window. Just here we discussed my foolish engagement with such bitterness. How vividly it all came back!

"Miss Adriance," he began presently, "my sister has informed me of your misfortune. I am most sorry that I should be absent at such a time; but I doubt if it is as bad, as she thinks. You are not quite disheartened."

"I have sufficient courage to bear a reverse of fortune," I said, proudly.

"You have both been looking at the darkest side. Such things alarm Isabelle a good deal. She knows so little about business."

Then, after a pause, seeing that I made no reply, —

"I think I understand the matter perfectly, and can assure you that your fortune is not all gone. Have you no faith in my assertion, that you look so incredulous?"

"Besides the lawyer's statement, I have heard from my friends at Baltimore, who were anxious to soften the blow as much as possible. There may be a few thousands saved, but even that is doubtful."

"Half at least," he said, walking down the room, his face turned partly from me.

I imagined his motive in an instant, and though it gave me a quick thrill, I could not endure to be the recipient of his generosity.

"Mr. St. John," I said, trying to keep the touch of excitement out of my voice, "I can understand that you consider yourself in some manner answerable for this misfortune; but I do not hold you so. It was Mr. Anthon's investment, and one cannot always guard against losses. I am satisfied that it is nearly all gone, and have made some arrangements for the future."

He paused suddenly. "What arrangements?" he asked, in a sharp tone.

"I have already obtained a situation as governess. It is necessary that I should depend upon my own exertions, and this offer came to me with a very little trouble."

"Governess!" He accompanied the word with such a disdainful gesture that it angered me.

"You are in haste, I think, Miss Adriance. "It is paying a poor compliment to your friends," he went on, with a scornful inflection.

"I do not propose to test friendship that far," I said, haughtily. "Dependence would not be pleasant for me."

"O, you are strong-minded! It will not harm you to air your theories occasionally; but you have forgotten one important fact. I am still your guardian."

"There is no longer a necessity for supervision. When people are at work, they seldom fall into mischief."

"It is still *my* duty to provide you a home, and yours to remain there," he said, not attempting to disguise the power in his tone.

"You can insist upon this for some time longer," I returned, coldly; "but it would not be an agreeable experiment. I question if a young lady with no fortune would be considered a valuable acquisition to Laurelwood society."

"That is pure pride."

"I *am* proud; I confess it."

"And willing to make everything bow to this demon!" His tone was bitter, unjust, I thought.

"The demon, as you style it, will not have many worshippers. There is nothing to be rendered subservient."

"Nothing!"

He strode up and down the room, his face clouded, his lips compressed, and his eyes coming to points of flame. Had I gone too far? At all events, I could not be a suppliant for his love, and, truth to tell, he seemed in no haste to offer it.

"This governessing is an absurd idea," he flung out angrily.

"I see nothing so absurd in a woman having courage to meet any exigency, and a desire not to become a burden to her friends."

"I believe friends never were very weighty considerations with you."

The taunt was too bitter. A scarlet heat flamed up in my face.

"I have consulted some friends, in whom I have confidence," and my breath as well as my words came slowly, for I knew this was a cruel thrust.

As if it had not touched him at all, he came nearer. "Can nothing induce you to give up this wild idea? You will find the routine very different from your fancy concerning it."

"I do not expect a path of roses. I have some sense, at least," I returned, with warmth and passion.

"And fortitude equal to any emergency," he retorted, with caustic dryness.

Could this man ever have loved me? Love was kind and tender, shielding its object from every chilling blast, but he was more bitter and cutting than storm itself. I felt sick at heart.

"It is not necessary to discuss the matter any farther," I said, rising.

"I shall make a strict examination into this unfortunate business, and until then — "

He paused. I was so near that our hands almost clasped of their own accord. What invisible barrier kept us apart?

He made a sudden gesture, then he let me go without another word.

I went directly to my room and answered Mrs. Ingalls's

letter, promising to be at my post at the appointed time. It had been folly to delay it. What sweet, wild dreams I had indulged in for a brief space! Gone, to the faintest shadow. I had always idealized Mr. St. John. He was not as grand and tender as the hero of my imagination, nay, he had never loved me as I wished to be loved. At times he had swayed me by his immense personal power, but the woman who won him must be a slave, and content to yield every atom of her own individuality. This did not *quite* satisfy me.

I despatched my note at once. Passing through the hall, Mrs. Lawrence called me to ask about some trifle, but with more real kindliness in her manner than had been apparent of late.

"Stuart told you, I suppose, that he believes the loss involved in the failure has been exaggerated. I am really glad for your sake. It's delightful to have some one inspire us with a little courage."

"I think he is mistaken," I answered, gravely.

"At all events we can hope for the best. I've been a poor comforter, but bad news of any kind always has a depressing effect upon my nerves;" and she ended with a faint, sweet smile.

I had learned my lesson to some purpose, and was not to be beguiled by this small display of graciousness. Perhaps I was hard and faithless, but my wound was bitter also.

That night I found a note on my dressing-table. I recognized the writing instantly. What could Mr. St. John wish to say to me in this manner? Some neighbors had been in to spend the evening, and Mr. St. John had proved most entertaining.

I broke the seal with no little trepidation, and then, drawing up the nearest chair, sat down to read.

It was — not the passionate declaration of love one might expect from such a man, but a rather stately offer of his hand, fortune, Laurelwood, the place I had professed to hold in such high regard. It was kind and exquisitely worded, but the heart seemed left out, as if he were more desirous of saving me from hardship and making my outer life luxurious and pleasant, than aiming to reach any true and high soul existence. For a long while I sat in deep thought. The world would believe that I considered this the best means of retrieving my fallen fortunes, but what would he think? He had not made one appeal to my regard for himself. Did he really hold that women were always swayed by mercenary considerations, and that to satisfy these was the royal road to their hearts?

To live with him and not be allowed the fullest liberty to love, and to express it, would be simply torture. With me the regard must soon become a passion, and repression would be harder to endure than total loss and absence.

I will not deny that pride was strongly concerned. I thought he had not treated me fairly, justly. I had a right to expect something better at his hands.

I had somewhere read of a little boat floating over the sea, holding a slumbering lady, whose string of pearls had become unfastened, and the gems were slowly dropping into the water. She woke and grasped it, terrified at seeing her precious pearls slip away. I had been a traveller drifting down a sunny stream, gathering priceless pearls — human hearts. Now they began to drop away. Should I reach out my hand to save any?

Mr. St. John was calm and inscrutable at breakfast the next morning. No look or gesture on his part betrayed the slightest concern. I believe his very self-possession roused all the angry strength of my soul. I should never be able to decide whether he loved me, and must take my step in the darkness of unbelief.

I intended to answer him in his own fashion, and yet dreaded to say the fatal words, to cut myself off from hope. So I rambled about the grounds, lingering in shady nooks that I loved so well. It *would* be hard to go.

I came suddenly upon him at a turn in the path. For a moment we faced each other.

"Miss Adriance," he said, in a strange, husky tone, yet with a touch of fierce impatience, "you must have read my note. Answer me now — I cannot wait."

The old imperious manner. There was no instinct of serfdom in me. I would not be forced into fetters. Every drop of blood in my veins revolted.

"It is easily said. No man's gold can buy my heart."

"*Easily!*"

It was an ill-chosen word. One bitter lightning glance, that seemed to scorch the very springs of life, and he turned — was lost to me. Should I utter a cry of agony, and bring him back?

When I could rouse myself from this stupor, I continued my walk. An interposing fate had settled all my perplexity. I was quite free to go. But Eve's wail of desolation seemed borne to me on every breath of the summer air. It would be rending body and soul asunder.

CHAPTER XVII.

"I see the curse on gestures proud and cold,
And looks of proud defiance and calm hate,
And such despair as mocks itself with smiles."

                                    SHELLEY.

A QUICK step crossed the wide balcony, and a cheery voice fell upon my ear. I turned to behold Philip Westervelt.

"What a ghostly face!" he exclaimed. "Isn't St. John home? I saw his name amongst the arrivals, and flew down from Washington to have a look at our travelled hero. Don't disappoint me by any evil tidings."

"Mr. St. John came home yesterday, and is very well," I returned; and in another instant the master's voice sounded from the library.

Philip vaulted into the open window. I ran away to my room, and took one glimpse of myself in the long mirror that had told me so many flattering tales. I fancied that I could see suffering already written in my face.

"This will never do," I said to myself. "It is cowardly to take the marks of the first evil blow fate gives."

So I summoned my resolution, and sought to bury the dead hopes out of my sight. One dream too bright, too perfect for earthly realization. There are many trials and crosses before one enters the promised land. I might have known that so fair a prospect was but a mirage, and that my life could be no more perfect than any other human lot. Yet had I not bereft it of all hope? Would it ever blossom with the promise of golden fruitage?

I resigned myself to fate. Struggling was vain and futile. I would not ask what the future held, but go on, no matter how thorny the path might prove.

Philip's arrival was certainly well timed, though the accident of a sudden whim. When we all met at luncheon, Mr. St. John was quite in his usual mood, and met me without the slightest awkwardness. Indeed, so serene and gracious seemed he, that I wondered if the man had any soul that could be touched. Philip was in the gayest of spirits, but somehow his happiness jarred upon me. Was·it because my own desolation became the more apparent?

I had been resolving in my own mind that I would propose a visit to Mrs. Otis as the easiest way of leaving Laurelwood. I had an opportunity of announcing this at the dinner-table, and felt that I was safely over one difficult step.

Quite late in the evening, when I was meditating a retreat to my own room, Philip asked me to walk a little while with him. It was a glorious night,.with the moon nearly at its full. The wandering air brought faint voices from the distant groves — a tender, suggestive sound that touched the heart.

"How can you leave this?" Philip asked, suddenly. "Sydnie, how much soul have you? I seem to have gone widely astray in my estimate of you."

"Your estimate may have been wrong. I don't know as I am answerable to *all* my friends."

"Why do you go?"

"Because I do not choose to stay and be dependent."

"St. John said you were going out as a governess."

"I find some kind of employment necessary. You seem to forget that I am no longer an heiress."

"St. John thinks something can be saved from the wreck."

"This is folly," I said, half vexed at Mr. St. John's pertinacity. "He is generous enough to replace a part of it; but I would not accept such a favor from any man, least of all him."

"Don't intrench yourself so strongly in your own might. Do you think so lightly of friends that you can discard them with ease?"

"We are hardly friends when it comes to that," I said, with a scornful inflection.

"And you might have been so much more! O, Sydnie, are women born blind and wilful, that they should thus throw away the great prizes of life? I felt so sure that you would end by loving Stuart. I do not see how a woman could fail to be won by his strength, that is like a resistless tide, and his sweetness that can find a way to any but the most obdurate heart. It amazes me to think that you have been insensible to all the finer traits in his character, and most of all, his love."

"Did he send you to plead his cause?"

"Sydnie!"

I felt the involuntary movement of his arm, almost as if he would have spurned me.

"We shall never agree about Mr. St. John," I returned. "To you he has been one of the dearest and tenderest friends, while with me it has proved widely different. Your romance about us has misled you. We are *not* congenial in scarcely any sense. He does not understand my most ordinary moods; and I confess he has always been a puzzle to me."

"You are proud and impatient. Forgive the truth, and believe that no sister could have a larger share in a brother's heart than you have in mine. If you will accept of our sympathy and love, our home shall be yours, freely proffered by Ellen as well as myself, and any word of dis-

satisfaction that I utter comes from a heart sore and
pained because I am grieved to see one dear friend suffer
who might be made happy by love."

"You may set your heart at rest. Mr. St. John does
not love me as you imagine."

"It is your pride that blinds you. O, pause and consider ere you throw away the sweetest gift of life, and
wreck your own soul."

"Convincing you would be a hopeless task. But I see
my way clearly, and there are no thorns that a resolute
step cannot crush."

"You are too strong and cruel for a woman. Look
down the future, and see if the path is fair! Are there no
places marked by tears? no shrine where hope despoiled
still clings to some stray fragment of what it once might
have held with a tender clasp? no day of loneliness, regret,
or despair?"

I would not own to any.

"I used to think you, of all others, would be keenly susceptible to love. I fancied it would be no light passion,
but a perfect, overwhelming tide that would regenerate
you into new being. How have you thrust out that low-
voiced angel?"

Ah, he little guessed how madly I had loved, how my
heart throbbed now in its torturing throes of anguish!
That both these men should deem me cold and heartless
was bitter indeed. But I could never make them see me
as I truly was. Therefore I vouchsafed no answer.

Presently Philip said, "You are quite resolved, then?"

"I shall not shrink from the duties that I see before me."

He faced me suddenly; but I was prepared. I felt that
not a feature would betray me, and perhaps exulted a little
in my strength.

"How beautiful you are," he went on; "like this idea of Milton's —

> ' What though the field be lost — all is not lost;
> The unconquerable will ————
> ———— and courage never to submit
> Or yield; and what is else not to be overcome — ' "

"I feel like it," I replied. I could have found it in my heart to repeat the rest.

"But the fiercest flames burn out, and then the ashes of desolation! Will you never weary on this great highway, and long for shade where none may ever come?"

"Whether it be shade or sun, I am content."

"And this is the result of a life that promised so much. O, Sydnie!"

His tone seemed to strike a knell in my heart.

"We all dream dreams in youth," I said, and then we returned to the house in silence.

He left us the next morning. After that I made preparations for my visit. No one opposed me, or suggested any change. Mr. St. John and his sister were very kind. It really seemed as if nothing had occurred, and that presently I would return and resume the old life. I could not bring myself to believe that this was to be the last; and my heart smote me for cowardly concealing my resolve.

Mrs. Lawrence parted with me most cordially. She had a faith, or affected it, that her brother could manage to restore part of my fortune, and began to plan gayeties for the winter. Mr. St. John drove me to the station. We exchanged a lingering good by. Was there any latent word that might still be spoken, any glance capable of changing the current of our lives? .

Alone in the car I dropped my travelling veil, although the day was warm. I felt weak and nervous now, and

16

the tears filled my eyes slowly. Was I as brave as I had made others believe?

The mental atmosphere pervading the house of Mr. Otis served to restore me. Anne's cheerful self-reliance roused me from the despondent mood into which I was falling. But my life was not to be quite as I had planned it. Mrs. Ingalls, offended it seemed at my delay, had accepted another person to fill the place. And from Philip I received a most kindly letter, enclosing an offer of a situation in a school to teach music, drawing, and painting. He urged me to accept it if I was still resolved upon the course I had marked out.

Mr. Otis had interested himself warmly in my lost fortune. Mr. St. John thanked him in a most cordial letter when he came to hear of the fact. A year might elapse before it was finally settled, and perhaps a few thousand dollars could be saved. As the time of my departure was drawing nigh, I informed Mr. St. John of the change in my arrangements, not omitting Philip's kindly interest. It was hardly worth while to return to Laurelwood, I added, if Mrs. Lawrence would allow Thirza to pack the remainder of my wardrobe, and send it to Baltimore. Anne insisted that henceforward I should consider her house as my home.

"You will remember that I am your sister now, and that it will not do for you to neglect me. I shall claim all your vacations," Anne said, with some tender tears in her eyes.

I thanked Heaven for this dear friend as I started out to try the world anew.

Elm Grove Seminary was situated in the western part of the State of New York. I could not help thinking of the tender care that had made so many journeys delightful to me; and by contrast this seemed tiresome and perplexing. Yet I had some curiosity to see my new home, and I thought a round of active duties would still this restless gnawing at my heart — crowd out the ghost of dreams dead forever.

The seminary was delightfully located, half a mile from the village, a lovely, sleepy place, that looked as if it might be taking a Rip Van Winkle nap. The white cottages were embowered with vines and trees, and the churches ivy grown. I was glad to find it different from anything I had ever seen.

The interior was no novelty. I had been used to boarding-schools, and the long halls, recitation-rooms, and rows of sleeping apartments greeted me with a most natural look. I was ushered into the reception-room, where Mrs. Ellingwood awaited me.

She was a tall, fine-looking woman, with great suavity of manner, but a cold gray eye, and a rigid mouth that bespoke strong determination. One would not be drawn to her in any friendly relation. She enlarged upon the order, strictness, and precision with which everything was carried on, her high principles and views of duty towards the young ladies intrusted to her care; in short, she made me understand that *she* was the head of the establishment, and that all were to respect her authority.

In return, I felt she was very well satisfied. I had come highly recommended, and, as she had a peculiar love for the best society, the fact of my having been a member of it, and met with a reverse of fortune, was a passport to her favor. I followed Laura Hastings's worldly-wise maxims, and made the most of myself and my accomplishments.

Friday was the first of September; but school did not open until the following Monday. I had time to look about me, and decided that it would be a very tolerable place. My room was pleasant, overlooking the south and the village; but what a contrast to the spacious one I had left! no soft carpet and curtains, no airy marble Graces, and the sweetness of countless flowers. It was not to be shared with any one, however, and I was thankful for that. So I hung up my dresses, arranged a few articles of *virtu*, turned my chairs, to take off the stiff, orderly look, and filled a shelf with some choice volumes.

There were quite a number of scholars, and during the next day they increased rapidly. I met most of my fellow-teachers, but there was not one that won me in the slightest degree. By Sunday evening I was as miserably lonesome as Mr. St. John could desire in his just wishes of retribution, if he thought of me at all. The years looming up before me grew frightful with grim phantoms. What an enchanting world I had left behind! Had fate alone shut me out of it?

I was glad to begin my duties. I threw the most earnest energy into them, and resolved to allow nothing to daunt me. Since I had chosen the path, I would take no weak, lagging step. I did find it tiresome, and not much to my taste; but I won Mrs. Ellingwood's commendation early in the battle. I resolved not to yield to any morbid desire to exaggerate my own trials and disappointments. I no longer expected life to be rose-hued; the carnival was over, and I was a sober, Lenten-robed pilgrim, on my way to another shrine.

After a month or two, when I was settled to my daily routine, an intolerable craving took possession of my soul. I tried a severe course of reading; but, though my eyes followed the lines for page after page, my thoughts went far astray. Music, which had once been my solace, was now connected with a sense of drudgery. Were the days Philip foretold coming upon me so soon? Had I no more courage or fortitude?

I certainly was not discontented with my situation : the salary was good, the treatment kind, and no stringent demands were made upon my time. I found that I soon gained the reputation of being haughty and reserved, and it suited me as well. I had no mind to listen to girlish complaints, or the vapid talk of sentimental women ; therefore I spent my evenings much alone, except when I was invited to the reception-room, which was not infrequently. Mrs. Ellingwood was rather proud of her acquisition, and showed a disposition to make the most of it. Except being rather tiresome, these small parties amused me. The other teachers generally managed to get into nervous spasms over what they should wear and whom they should see. The fifteen or twenty guests did not in the slightest alarm me. I was alike indifferent to their admiration or disfavor. Contrasting them with what I had known, made them seem poor and meagre indeed. A spirit of self-complacency pervaded many of these people. On the whole, I wondered if it was not a pleasant thing to hold one's self in high esteem.

Looking over the future, I could not but speculate upon it. Marriage, the great dream of most women, was not for me. If I had not loved in the past two years, I should not be likely to meet with any one in time to come whose charm would prove overmastering.

Then I tore down the flimsy subterfuge, and looked the truth boldly in the face. I *had* loved Mr. St. John — I did love him now. The peculiar influence he had exerted over me would always keep me from yielding to any other. Whether we were really antagonistic, or if it had been the result of some special fault in either, I was unable to determine; but I recognized the fact. That hope, therefore, had dropped out of my life.

My future was all my own : to spend it in slow years of

stagnation was simply impossible. What *must* I do? I could not go out into the world and make another fortune in the place of the one I had lost. I could not raise myself to any height: a simple, aimless existence, earning my daily bread and raiment.

Then I bethought myself of my book. I had commenced it in the happy solitude of Laurelwood, piqued into a mood of ambition by Mr. St. John's doubts and cynicisms. I recalled the fanciful dreams concerning those imaginary people, their loves, hopes, struggles, and the different ways by which they attained happiness and content. So I roused myself, and went at it again, thankful for the employment. Autumn came on, brown and chilly. I noted how the sun went lower, how the leaves lost their gold and crimson glory, and then winter, with its potent step, writing desolation everywhere.

It mattered little to me. My inner world was fast absorbing my very soul. Night after night I used to sit alone, taking a strange delight in these creations of my pen. How real they all became to me! I suffered in their sorrows, rejoiced in their joys, gave them faith when I doubted myself, made all things possible for them, while I felt bound hand and foot. In some lives there came just such seasons of rapture, after long and patient waiting; in others, despair and nothing. But since there is more shadow than sun in the existence of most people, we like the contrast, and enjoy the sun in pictures, rather than the shadow.

Then I began to watch the people around me with a new zest. Their peculiarities caught my eye at once. I speculated what they would do in certain situations, how they would endure trials; and found that for the many weak there were but few strong. Almost each one was continually shifting some burden on his or her neighbor.

Not much self-reliance and true courage. It was curious, too, that the people in the Laura Hastings mould generally won the day. How could men and women be so blind, so credulous?

One of my pupils awoke a strong interest in me presently; perhaps because she stood so entirely alone, was so repellent, and no favorite with the rest. Indeed, it seemed as if she was in disgrace half the time. The child — for she was barely sixteen — had a violent temper, and a quick, caustic tongue: an orphan; a friend was educating her; and, to render the terms more reasonable, she taught in one or two of the lower classes.

I believe she hated all but music. A strange, lithe little thing, with eyes and hair of the deepest hue, and a pale, clear olive complexion. Her features were small and regular; but her general expression was cold, faithless, and defiant, as if some way she were at war with half the world, and constantly watching for an opportunity to return the current coin of unkindness.

Yet at times, when she yielded herself to the charm of music, she used to startle me by her absolute loveliness. It was wild and weird, and made one almost shiver at the capabilities it revealed.

Every advance I made was repelled with a coolness that savored of disdain, and I presently ceased in my efforts, yet I was none the less interested. I had a curious presentiment that somewhere we would be strangely drawn together — one of those electric intuitions, for which one can give no reason. I fell into the habit of watching her, and involuntarily shielding her from the consequences of some of her faults.

"I wonder you can tolerate Miss Whitney," one of the teachers said to me; "she is the most disagreeable girl in school."

Magdalene. What did the name portend?

Spring was coming on apace. The time had not hung heavily on my hands, for I had been very busy. These warm days gave me a peculiar languor, yet I fought the spell of indolence with rigid bravery. Every week brought my book nearer completion. If it held some of my own yearning desires and unfulfilled hopes, who shall marvel? The world was full of these likenesses; phantoms sat in every corner of the heart, rarely clothed in glorious apparel. Life sprang up clear and sweet with its heavenly harmonies; but in the rude turmoil and jar of discordant voices, the pure strains were too often lost to human ears. What power was strong enough to reunite these broken links? Did God care when his children were weary and heavy laden?

The school that had gone on so methodically for nine months was now roused to a sudden tumult and fever. The graduating class was straining every nerve, and Mrs. Ellingwood was making preparations for some brilliant closing exercises. I was called out of my seclusion, and for a month was busy with the rest. The examinations passed very creditably, and then there was a general dispersion.

Mrs. Ellingwood was anxious to make an engagement for another year, and I assented; but my soul was buoyed up with a precious hope. If it were possible to win fame — and other women had succeeded — I would bend every energy to this pursuit. It was the choicest thing life held now.

I decided to remain at Elm Grove for a brief while. In those first days of quiet I finished my book, and wrote to several publishers in New York. I had promised my vacation to Mrs. Otis. Philip and Ellen had gone to Europe in May, so Anne was the only friend to whom my presence would be a positive pleasure. I remembered how, three years before, I had watched for vacation. How long ago! a past age it seemed. Then I was as careless and expectant as these girls were now. I felt old beside them, as if with eighteen had gone all the brightness and blossom of youth. Could·any hand restore the sweet hope? Not for me, I said, softly and sadly.

CHAPTER XVIII.

"O, how full of briers is this working-day world!"
ROSALIND — *As You Like It.*
"It is to live without the vanished light
That strength is needed."   MRS. HEMANS.

I PUT my room in order, locked drawers and desks, gave Mrs. Ellingwood a courteous good by, and commenced a new journey. No gay, satirical voice to laugh at me, no far-reaching eyes to hold me with subtle glances, no foolish quarrels and quick repentance. I was a sober, staid, business woman, with a most matter-of-fact air. Youth was nothing to me; girlishness I was glad to lay aside.

I went directly to New York. Of the five letters I had written, three had declined reading anything new on account of the press of matter on hand. The remaining two held out a slender hope. I weighed their respective merits, and finally decided by chance, though it was with some trepidation that I presented myself. One feels so different when one has nothing to ask of the world. It really appeared as if my earlier daring had all failed.

I met with a polite reception, that quite restored my courage. The book should be read, and my answer given in a week. Had I ever written any before?

"No; this was my first attempt."

"Not even stories or sketches?"

"Nothing at all."

"It was quite difficult to introduce a new writer of whom

the world had never heard. If the book had some particular merit—" and a very charming smile finished the sentence.

I could hardly claim that it was better than the majority of stories. Indeed, now I was seized with a fear that it was not so good; but we bowed hopefully to each other.

I realized the loneliness of a great city fully during that week of waiting. I had chosen the most retired hotel, and that was not overcrowded. Every one who could get away was at some pleasant summer resort, or country house. I was not at all sure that even Mrs. Westervelt was in the city. But I wanted no one to know my errand. If I failed entirely, the secret should be locked in the depths of my own soul. I desired no pity or sympathy. I watched the dawn of morning and the close of day in the most utter solitude, yet in a state of feverish expectation. At last the eventful time arrived, and assuming an air of indifference that I was far from feeling, I presented myself for this important verdict.

It is something, perhaps, for a man to be handsome and affable. My book was declined with the utmost suavity, I had almost said sweetness. While it betrayed unmistakable marks of genius, it was not at all in the popular style. If I had a reputation, it would do very well to make such a venture; indeed, in that case, it might be a perfect success. But he did not feel safe to undertake it. If I chose to try again I might be more fortunate. This story was very peculiar.

How brilliantly the sun shone as I stepped into the street! I shivered at the brightness, and longed to hide myself where it was never so dark and deep. Not even the loss of my fortune had affected me thus keenly. I began to understand how much of my future life had been staked upon this issue.

"Courage, heart," I said. "Some strong souls win heaven by force, how much more the things of earth."

So I ventured again. A grave, middle-aged man, with no smiles, but a kindly voice, received me. The same cautious story, — the difficulty of taking the first step. And although he took the manuscript, he prepared me for a fresh disappointment also.

"It was very dull with him just now, and he would read it immediately. Could I call in a few days?"

I assented. If I had thought the first week wearisome, this was doubly so. A wild impulse urged me to go to Anne's at once, but I persisted in my resolve. My heart sank within me, and every pulse quivered with the torture of suspense as I set out. I wondered how many times I should go on the same errand, or if I should accept this blow of fate as final.

I waited many moments in the little office. On the desk stood a few roses and geranium leaves in a slender bouquet-holder. These flowers appealed to me in a strange, tender manner, stirred my heart to sympathy.

I looked at the man's face as he entered, but it betrayed no secret. Yet it was so kindly, with all its gravity, that it inspired me with something like hope.

"I have been deeply interested in your story," he began. "It has much merit, but I am not at all prepared to say that it will be a success. It may prove a very fair introduction to the literary world, and it is quite necessary that a young author should try first for a name."

I bowed my head acquiescently; I could not trust my voice to speak.

"We are willing to undertake it, though we do not feel justified in making a very extravagant offer."

I drew a long breath of relief. Did I really hear aright?

Then followed the business part. I confessed that I did

feel satisfied with his proposal, though if I had thought more of fortune than fame, it would have appeared small. I felt, too, that I had made a friend, and that was a consolation. I agreed to his propositions unhesitatingly, my heart growing lighter with every breath.

But what was there so singular about the book? Was the yearning of a high, passionate spirit for that grand existence haunting most pure souls, a thing to astonish ordinary minds? What if the way was long and dark? what if failure did happen, was that improbable? or success, did that sound unreal? There comes a time to some few blest souls when they stand untrembling on the mountain tops. If it were not so, existence would be an utter failure.

The next day I reached Baltimore. There was great rejoicing in the happy household, for a little blue-eyed stranger had been added to their number — a sweet, darling girl, who had been received with the most rapturous emotion.

"You almost vexed me by your delay," Anne said, with her glad smile, that half contradicted her assertion. "I knew you would be surprised, and I could hardly wait. But, my dear, how thin and worn you are, quite unlike your usual self. You shall have nothing but rest and pleasure for the next month."

A most delightful prospect, truly. I thanked Heaven for this sweet friend, for these yet unbroken links in my chain. Anne's welcome was so cordial, and she bright and winsome with the old shy grace still clinging about her. The dearest and most perfect happiness had come to her, and no one could prove more worthy.

There was a small business matter awaiting me. Mr. St. John had secured three thousand dollars from the wreck of my fortune, and placed it in the hands of Mr. Otis. His connection as my guardian had of course ceased.

Besides these details, there was a letter very cordially worded, containing a message from Mrs. Lawrence, and inviting me to Laurelwood any time that I felt disposed to make them a visit.

In what mood Mr. St. John had penned these words I should never be able to tell. Of course I should not go.

"And Mr. Otis has an excellent investment for your money," Anne said. "I shouldn't wonder if you became a rich woman by and by, though it seems very little now."

"By the time I am old, and compelled to retire from active service;" and I smiled.

"I can hardly endure the thought of your being so far away. I've been wondering, dear, how it would answer to keep you here. You could have music pupils, you know, and probably do as well as at school."

"I have made a positive engagement for another year. Besides, I like the school very well."

"But you are certainly worked too hard."

"My darling, don't distress yourself about me," I replied, with a kiss, for her tender regard touched me to the heart's core. Had any one else ever loved me as well?

My month passed most delightfully. How many times I longed to give her my secret in return for her confidence, I can hardly say; but I doubted my own ability to achieve a thorough success. And if I did fail, better that it should be hidden from all pitying eyes. I was too proud to acknowledge a defeat.

Anne's baby was a source of unbounded satisfaction. Her sisters, fast growing into womanhood, held it in the highest esteem. Mr. Otis appeared to have taken upon himself a new dignity. He was slowly coming up to the heights of complete and ripened manhood. I remembered my first impressions of him with a feeling akin to

wonder that I could not have discerned his worth sooner.
To me he was the kindest of friends, unobtrusively solicitous for my welfare.

But youth is the season of quick judgments and over
hasty conclusions. And though my experience had been
brief, I was better able to distinguish between fine gold
and alloy. Already the rumor had reached Anne that
Aylmer Channing and his wife were not in a felicitous
state. The lady was high-spirited and rather inclined to
jealousy, while Aylmer still made himself as fascinating in
society. It was well fate had interposed and saved Anne
from the dreary state of a neglected wife. As for myself,
I still thought of my episode with a shiver. How weak I
must have been to yield to such folly. Perhaps Mr. St.
John was right in his estimate of me; but O, was there
no love in the world that could afford to be generous, to
forgive freely?

It seemed quite natural to go back to school, though
Anne was earnest in her entreaties that this should be the
last year. Unconsciously a new hope began to animate
me. If I could gain my old position, — and it seemed almost possible, — I should not hesitate to encounter old
friends. Yet I felt a little bitter to think how soon one
drops out of memory. Two years before I had been the
centre of an admiring circle; now I suppose this homage
was paid to a new star. I was no longer in the ranks.
Well, I had not made one appeal. I had taken fate at her
very worst, and meant to fight my own way up again, or
remain in obscurity.

And yet I confess a strange feeling of depression stole
over me. My tasks began to prove wearisome. I lived
in a constant fever of expectation that was not hope, and
began to realize how much I was counting on a slender
reed. If it should fail, what was left?

The number of new pupils was quite large, and most of them, it appeared to me, were exceedingly dull. Magdalene Whitney had come back; this was her last year. Some wonderful change had befallen her; not merely in disposition, but face and air were softer, sweeter. The girls had always teased her a good deal because she flashed into flame so easily, but now she shunned them. She seemed to desire solitude, and not infrequently I found her in the music-room when there was no practising.

One day I remember she turned suddenly upon me.

"Miss Adriance," she said, "why do you watch me so?"

It was the easiest to tell the truth.

"Because I am interested in you," I answered.

"Why?" The deep eyes seemed to pierce me through.

"I don't know that I can explain. You stand so much alone, you are so different from other girls."

"The difference will not repay your close study;" and her scarlet lips curled with the most superb scorn.

I made no reply. Why should I care about her, since she evidently desired no one's sympathy?

Going to the music-room quite late one afternoon, I disturbed her reverie. She appeared confused at first, then bowed coldly, and passed me. Something dropped from the folds of her dress. I picked up a note with a broken seal, but bearing no superscription. I took it to my own apartment, and as I laid it on the table the seal caught my eye fairly. "A. C.," with a quaint device that I knew well. I started in the utmost surprise.

The rules of correspondence were very strict, but I knew the system of smuggling letters was brought to a state of high perfection among school-girls. My duty was to hand this over to Mrs. Ellingwood, who would not scruple to read its contents. I had a more than passing interest in it, if it was as I suspected. I took the note out of its enclosure, therefore, and glanced at the heading, — "My dearest Magdalene," — in Aylmer Channing's light, graceful chirography. I could not mistake it.

I had not thought the man a deliberate villain before. With a girl of Magdalene's nature, the acquaintance could not be one of calm friendship, though that would be little to his taste. In his search for something new and piquant, I could see just how she had attracted him. Her spirit and daring, her fiery, passionate nature, her strange, suggestive face, had roused him from the tame duties of married life. I question if fidelity was possible to him. Some fatal desire for change swayed him with an irresistible impulse.

The next morning I summoned Magdalene to my room, as I had resolved upon my course. There was an apprehensive look in her eyes, and a nervousness quite unlike her usual demeanor.

"Does this note belong to you?" I asked. "I found it in the music-room soon after you had left."

"It does." I watched the eager working of the fingers, but I still retained it in my hand.

"I thought such things were forbidden here," I resumed, carelessly.

"Then you have read it; you had no right;" and her face was dark with intense passion.

"Perhaps you would prefer Mrs. Ellingwood's scrutiny?"

"O, you can give it to her," was the scornful reply. "I could defy you both, if I chose."

"Miss Whitney, I prefer to keep your secret. To be reprimanded can do you no possible good; besides, I have a deeper interest in the affair. Will you tell me where you met Mr. Channing?"

She turned pale at the mention of the name. After a long pause, she said, slowly, —

17

"I cannot tell you anything. I would rather suffer than break a promise, and a most solemn one binds me."

Then she folded her hands, and stood calmly waiting, her face settling into impassible lines.

"Is he your lover?"

The only answer was a faint flush.

"I have not read your letter," I went on. "I knew the seal, because I had some acquaintance with this Mr. Channing, and was once engaged to him."

"Then you hate *me*, as a matter of course!" with a bitter sneer.

"As little as I care for him. But he has no right to ask any woman's love, or to win it. He is already married."

A most indifferent and incredulous smile crossed her face.

"It is best that you should be convinced," I said. "His cousin was my guardian. I have a friend living in Balti-more who is distantly related to him, and through either party I could procure you positive proofs. But it would be better for you to write to him once again, and tell him from whom you had the story, and that Miss Adriance is one of the teachers in this place. There is the letter."

She bowed as she took it, and left the room without another word.

I wondered whether she would have sufficient courage for such a step. That she should take pains to shun me was in no wise remarkable, and I made no further effort to gain her confidence. Indeed, my own affairs occupied much of my thoughts. Every day was bringing me nearer the test of failure or triumph. It was so strange to bear it in this utter solitude — no one to uphold me with a smile.

Yet I believe I was a good deal surprised when the announcement was fairly made. It was the beginning of

December. A week later I received a parcel by express. I hurried it up to my room with a strange, faint sensation, as if the throbbing of my heart would strangle me. With what eager haste I tore off the wrappings! There, in its bright cover and clear type, was my treasure, the work of hours and moods that had run through the cycle of human joys, delights, fears, and almost despair. I was in a trance, a far-off world of my own; these faces around me were like some distant visions, these tasks a chain that dragged my body to earth, but did not touch my soul.

I must confess to an almost wild delight in its first perusal, for the fact of authorship had been hardly realized as yet. In my solitary life it was such a great event. It became love and hope, the solace that happier women find in their homes and children. It was a part of myself, henceforth indissoluble.

Lest I should fly to the heights of rapture, the publishers thought fit to moderate my expectations. Business was very dull, indeed; they had hesitated about issuing it at such an unfavorable time, but I might rely upon them to do their best, only I must not be too sanguine, or too deeply disappointed in case it was not a success.

When the first excitement had subsided, and I came back to common life, the whole atmosphere appeared dull and tame. My tense nerves relaxed, my busy brain yielded to a sort of stupor. I could not bring myself to care for anything; I seemed old and worn, past the pleasures of youth and hope. A dreariness took complete possession of me. I had made my great effort, like a gamester who plays his last card, and *not* won.

CHAPTER XIX.

" The homes we had hoped to rest in
    Were open to sin and strife;
  The dreams that our youth was blessed in
    Were not for the wear of life."
                    FRANCES BROWN.

" Miss WHITNEY is alarmingly ill," was said to me one
Saturday, as I came in from a walk.

I noticed that she had grown paler and thinner with the
hard work and holiday excitement, and perhaps another
cause. I had been so engrossed with my own thoughts
that I had not paid much attention to one who evidently
kept at a distance.

" Is it fever ? " I asked.

" No; hemorrhage of the lungs. The doctor has been
with her for nearly two hours. He has but just gone."

I sought Mrs. Ellingwood immediately. She was much
discomposed.

" A very unfortunate occurrence," she exclaimed, " for
which her violent temper is much to blame. The child
has no sense or reason, and I verily believe she would have
been glad to die on our hands. I never saw so strange a
being."

I went to the infirmary. On a cot lay Magdalene, still
deathly pale, and looking more ghastly by the abundance
of black hair tumbled about the pillow. She raised her
eyes faintly.

I bent over and kissed her. With a slow motion, she
slipped her hand in mine, and the unexpected token filled

me with surprise. There were four patients besides her, and as she was no favorite, I knew she would have the least care, so I offered to remain with her that night, to which the nurse gladly assented.

For several days there was little change in her, then she began to give evidence of rapid improvement. I proposed to Mrs. Ellingwood that she should be removed to my room, as the utmost quiet was indispensable. The lady stared in surprise.

"You are willing to take a great deal of trouble, Miss Adriance."

"She will recover so much faster," I returned, quietly.

As I had never allowed any intimacy with the pupils, she could suspect me of no treasonable design. I think she was rather glad to assent; so, after a little discussion, Magdalene was brought to my room and consigned to my supervision. She could sit up and help herself in many ways.

The deep eyes thanked me with wordless gratitude. I knew then that I had found the way to her heart.

"Why do you care about me, Miss Adriance?" she asked one evening, when I found her still in her easy chair, after supper.

"I can hardly tell," I answered, with a smile, "except from the fact of your being so nearly friendless."

"My own fault, I suppose. I am not an angel in temper; and the girls seem so shallow and insipid, most of them, or else deceitfully wicked. I ought never to have been placed in the world. No one suits me, and I please no one."

"Perhaps you have never tried."

"Miss Adriance," after a long silence, "how patient you are."

"It did not used to be reckoned one of my virtues."

And then I thought how Mr. St. John had called me unreasonable and impatient, and found no grace in me.

"Do you care to know how —"

She made so long a pause that I said presently, in the gentlest of tones, —

"Tell me what you like, Magdalene. I want you to feel quite at ease with me."

"About that letter. I wrote as you suggested, Miss Adriance. I was so confident that you were wrong. Ah, I can never tell you how I loved *him*. Remember that from babyhood no one has ever cared for me. I have been handed from one friend to another, until at last a cousin of my mother's proposed to educate me for a teacher. He is in California making a fortune, and this was merely a qualm of duty. Last summer I met *him*, Mr. Channing." She uttered the name with a great effort. "Did you ever *love* him?"

"No," I said, honestly, "but I was fascinated with his grace and beauty, and allowed myself to drift into an engagement. I saw a great deal of him, and learned my mistake in time."

"Well, I *loved* him. A year ago I would have ridiculed the idea of a broken heart, and what is it but a broken, hopeless life! It isn't hard to die, then. I met him by accident, and most of our acquaintance was unknown to any one. His passion roused and inspired me. I came to a new and glorious existence, just as if I had passed all my days in a dungeon, and some kindly hand had brought me out to light. Where it would have ended Heaven only knows. After this year I was to belong to him. The promise had but one meaning for me — marriage. I returned to school envying no queen upon her throne. I was wildly, madly happy, until that day. And even then I did not doubt him. I wrote in the pride of my perfect faith. Then I waited for an answer. Miss Adriance, did you ever *wait* for anything?"

I smiled faintly.

"I don't believe you know what it means. I was so sure at first. I couldn't count days nor hours. I did not attempt to make excuses for delay, but as I said, just waited. And that is all."

She leaned her pale brow against the pillow, fatigued by her long talk. I smoothed the heavy hair and chafed the cold, small hands. Was that *all* to this life? Alas, I feared so. What could I say to comfort her?

"Never mind about me," she went on presently. "I wish they had let me die; but since it was not to be, I shall get better. I do not want to be sent home. The place would be torture to me now, and there is no tender care for which I need long."

"My dear child, you must be quiet," I said, softly. "You are over exerting."

"One word more," and the wistful eyes sought to fathom mine. "Miss Adriance, will you love me a little? I'm humble now."

"My darling;" and I gave her fondest kisses for answer.

I think a resolute will helped Magdalene very much. She was soon able to go down stairs, and took her place in some of the classes. Yet I had a misgiving that it was not a sound restoration. She still shared my room, and we became strange, warm friends. Once she won from me the whole story of my acquaintance with Aylmer, then his name was dropped forever. Her love had been powerful in its strength and intensity. I felt as if I wanted Aylmer Channing to come and look upon his victim, and learn a lesson for all time — as if the man was capable of a deep and la ting impression!

When she was a little stronger I placed my book in her

way, and took a peculiar delight in the interest she mani-
fested. It had created no marked sensation; and I was
not enough in the world to understand the import of the
few notices that I saw. Perhaps it touched Magdalene
the more keenly from its sadness and truth. She literally
devoured it. This was sweetest incense, and soothed my
despairing heart. Should I confess to her how great a
failure I had made?

Mrs. Ellingwood insisted that Magdalene was well
enough to take her place in the school dormitory. I had
some fear, but a slight cold was the only immediate consequence. When she began to cough, I expostulated a
little. Alas! it was too late. One morning I found her
vainly trying to thrust out of sight a handkerchief stained
with her very life blood.

"Magdalene!" I uttered in an agony of apprehension.

"Hush. I did not mean you to know. I think I am
coming to the last. What does it matter? When I asked
for bread I received a stone. My heart has been starving.
Will God pity me a little, and give me rest?"

How rarely I had thought of Him!

"I don't want to go away. When I come to the worst
I want you to stay with me. It will not be long."

"Child," I exclaimed, in terror, "you must have immediate attention!"

"I saw the doctor yesterday. He assured Mrs. Ellingwood that I had only to guard against excitement and
over exertion, and should be quite well by summer. That
means I shall be asleep under the daisies. God knows
best. I shall be glad to go away from all the toil and
trouble. Don't wish anything else for me, Miss Adriance.
I am quite content."

Something about her awed me. She had changed so
much, grown absolutely dignified and commanding. For

several days I debated upon what course I should pursue; then a second attack decided the matter. By accident she was borne to my room, and there I watched her for nearly a month. In that time there came a deep and holy love between us. As if she had learned the secret of life at last, the faith that gains an abundant entrance into heaven.

During those watchful hours I told the dying girl my secret. Her eyes lighted up with a strange gleam of joy.

"You will be blest," she said, "in your power to carry joy to weary souls that faint on the highways. God must reward you for all you have been to me."

I smiled over these tender visions of her last days. It was too late for them to come true, but it was all that her love could give. And one midnight her weary soul fluttered up to the keeping of angels, leaving only a little death-cold clay in my arms. Seventeen brief years, and the sweetest draught of all turned bitter upon her lips. God help us to keep the faith, and not question too closely why these things are so.

The event made a great sensation. A death of this kind always fills one with awe, as if it could hardly be time for one to die in the very bloom of youth. Mrs. Ellingwood regretted that she had not sent her home immediately after the first attack.

But the break closed presently, and we all went on with our duties. Spring was filling up the hollows with the murmurous sound of unchained brooks. The brown hillsides changed to a faint glimmering green and drowsed sleepily in the sunshine. The pipe of birds sounded sweet in the early morn, and the air was fresh with dewy fragrance. What was it to me? I was sick and tired of the endless round. Of what avail was it for miserable souls to live at all!

My book had been a failure. The hope that I should

one day stand proudly in the place I had chosen for myself—reach the temple of fame with full hands, and lay my
gift upon the altar—was slowly perishing. And now I
told myself the truth—I could *not* endure the miserable,
aimless life I was leading; but what else was there for me?
To content myself with commonplace duties and events
was sure mental starvation. I seemed to be isolated, as if
there were a mark upon me, which, others seeing, might
avoid.

I was twenty-two. That was early in life to have the
worst of the battle. To sit on this monotonous bank,
watching the ebb and flow of life, and never going beyond
the dreary-looking shore on either side, was intolerable.

I was fast becoming irritable, but how could I resist this
constant feeling of rebellion? I could not shut my eyes to
the fact that I was out of place; that there was nothing to
call forth the energies within me that were absolutely
starving for want of proper nourishment and use.

I cannot make circumstances; I cannot even rule them.
I cannot understand life. Why are people created only
for misery? It does not sweeten their tempers or improve
their hearts, so far as my experience goes. Faith thrives
best in the genial warmth of happiness.

The old cry of the Psalmist rises to my lips, "O that I
had wings like a dove, for then I would flee away and be
at rest."

Still I kept on with my duties, and saw the change that
I dreaded approaching nearer and nearer. Anne was as
anxious as ever for my visit, and there was no reason why
I should not go, but I shrank from it with a curious intensity. Torpid as my brain seemed, it had some torturing,
sensitive nerves. The sight of her peace and happiness

would not soothe this wayward mood.   Sometimes I thought of a journey; but where could I go alone?   I had no ambition to guide me, no desires.

It is strange that in some seasons of life one seems to have several distinct individualities.   With one I performed each task mechanically.   Another seemed drifting about with every passing tide, while a third weakly rebelled, and yet had not sufficient force to marshal the others, or reduce them to obedience.

I wondered how many times Mrs. Ellingwood would go through the form of a new engagement.   Of course I should stay — all my life if she wanted me.   Then I packed my clothes, put everything in order, and said a few farewells.   The brightest vision of all was Magdalene at rest in her grave.

I had no desire to pause in New York, but went direct to Baltimore.   I found Anne alone, but bright and happy; her serene eyes marvellous wells of content.   Every event and sight that day is stamped so vividly upon my mind! Her cool, white dress, and a pale pink rose on her bosom, her baby smiling and winsome, the house with its usual neat adornment.   Everywhere repose and peace.

I had just time to change my dress for the late supper awaiting me, but I could not eat.   I sipped my tea languidly, and then took a long draught of cold water, that proved reviving.

" Your hands are hot and feverish," Anne said presently, " and your temples throb visibly.   Are you quite certain it is only fatigue ? "

" Foolish fatigue at that," I answered, almost sharply, as a keen, cruel sense of disappointment stole over me.   I had meant to come to her in such triumph this time.   It was she who was calm and strong, and I a rudderless bark, tossed about by every stray wave.

"My darling, have you come to any dark days?"

The sweet voice unnerved me. A choking spasm constricted my throat.

"Am I not your sister, your dearest friend? Can I not dispel the cloud?"

"One comes to the dregs of life occasionally, even if one is not utterly adrift."

"But there is One who can make the bitter sweet. No, don't look so faithless; you surely have not cast away this anchor?"

"Anne," I said, "it is not in the power of some hearts to believe at will. Was there never but one Hagar in the desert, who sat down to perish out of sight of all she loved?"

"And succor came to her."

"But in these later days one does not find it so easily."

"Sydnie, don't you believe that God is still merciful, and listens to all who cry unto him?"

"I have ceased to believe anything," I said, with sullen despair. "I have seen all my hopes perish miserably, and am ready to cry, Let me die with them."

"My darling, you are ill and dispirited."

"Anne," I exclaimed, vehemently, "you peaceful, happy women can never understand the struggles of others tormented before their time. Why is such continual suffering permitted? Why are people created with hearts that only the highest aspirations can fill, and then doomed to remain forever barren of fruit? Why do we wander in deserts, and clasp phantoms when we fold our hands together?"

"We would be less free if God did not permit us to stray and follow our own devices. But he is ready to bring us back when we earnestly desire it. And for the suffering and sorrow — why question if we do our part to relieve the oppressed?"

"I have exhausted life," I said. "I have come to the end, and all is darkness."

"I am not going to let you talk in this despairing fashion. Your nerves have been strained to the utmost, and it is folly to rasp the tender edges. You shall go to bed and rest."

She led me to my chamber, and the ministrations of her cool, soft hands tranquillized me. Then she kissed me and bade me sleep.

A broad sheet of moonlight lay on the floor like a silver lake. The peerless blue of the sky was broken by stars of faint gold, and the trees were edged with white as in a monochrome. I rose and went to the window, sitting a long while in the mild air, fragrant with night dews. But it could not cool the fever of my brain. Strange, distorted visions glimmered before my eyes. The old solitude of childhood oppressed me; then I was nearing my bridal with Aylmer Channing, and no hand was stretched forth to save me. Snowy robes mocked me with their softness. There was a dazzle of lace and satin, a smothering sweetness of perfume, and in my wildness I broke away from it all.

Then the vision changed. St. John and I rambled through the leafy groves at Laurelwood. Listening to his voice, I grew calm again, and though I knew it was a dream, the old spell reasserted itself. My heart, long cold and arid, softened to these tender tones. I seemed to realize now how this man had loved me, and what heavenly satisfaction life might have been with him. Yes, I had cast away my pearl because of some flaw in the setting.

Did I sleep then? I do not know. It was a long, blessed unconsciousness of pain or want, a sense of perfect rest. I was satisfied to be at peace at last.

CHAPTER XX.

"Cast off the weakness of regret, and gird thee to redeem thy loss;
Thou hast gained in the furnace of affliction
Self-knowledge, patience and humility."
PROVERBIAL PHILOSOPHY.

I REMEMBER rousing myself one day and glancing out of the window, surprised that it was not draped in moonbeams as I saw it last. Instead, a soft rain pattering on the leaves without.

I tried to rise, but my head fell back upon the pillow. Anne was beside me in a moment.

I experienced a weak, confused consciousness of having been ill, though then I felt well at heart.

"How long have I been here, Anne?" I asked.

"A month. But you are better now."

"Have I been very sick?"

She kissed me tenderly, her eyes swimming in tears.

I don't know why, but I felt glad and happy, just as if it were a pleasant thing to come back to life. She, seeing this, smiled.

I begin to understand some of these mysteries better. I have been groping about in the dark, intent upon my own way, trying to force a path through thorny hedges, while just outside lay the clear road. My imagination had been roused to some great achievement, rather than my soul awakened to the serious and earnest duties of life.

Lying there, day after day, too weak to talk much, but with a mind cleared from all its doubts and distraction, I was content merely to exist. Whatever the future held for me would come in its own good time. The calm that followed was delightful in its entire peace. Anne's slender figure, nearly always robed in white, angel-like in its harmonious movements, comforted me exceedingly. She had found the grand secret of a happy life, which must ever be more of a triumph than a happy death. Her whole study seemed to be how she could best minister to others. The highest and purest philosophy lies herein, for this broad, comprehensive charity alike blesses the bestower and the recipient.

I felt humbled as I glanced over my past. What had I ever done for another? Ellen's happiness had, after all, been more the result of circumstances. Poor Magdalene I had taken to my heart, but it had been purely material comfort — I had never been able to appeal to her soul, for my own was in the depths of doubt. I preferred to be wretched; I fanned each trivial circumstance into a withering flame that scorched, but did not consume. Though I had borne my misfortunes with outward equanimity, my heart had rebelled continually. I had exaggerated my ills, and transformed them into mountains.

I cannot say that I gave up my one great hope without a pang. Was the quality I had fancied genius a wretched impostor only? Did God mean that I should always keep to common ways, and glorify them by patience and love to my kind?

At last I said, "Not my will, but Thine." Not from apathy, but humility and resignation. And then I was ready to begin life again.

The first of September was coming on apace. I realized that I should not be strong enough to fill my old position, and wrote to Mrs. Ellingwood to that effect. Anne was overjoyed.

"I have a book for you to read," she said one morning. "Mr. Otis and I liked it so very much, and I have been waiting for you to improve sufficiently to undertake it. I can't tell why; but there is so much in it that reminds me of you. I should have written to you about it, only I wanted to watch the effect it would have upon you."

I smiled a little.

She came with it in her hand. "It is not merely for the sake of the story," she went on, and then my eyes caught the title. My own book! The crimson blood rushed to my face in torrents, and I trembled violently in every pulse.

"Why, what is the matter?" and her sweet eyes were filled with amazement.

"I have read it," I stammered.

"Do you know anything about it? It was published last winter; but I believe it did not begin to attract much attention until spring. The author seems to be enveloped in profound mystery."

I covered my face with my hands. That she should bring these precious tidings to me!

"I almost believe you wrote it yourself, and yet I never thought of that before. Confess!"

Her voice had a certain exultant ring that inspired me.

"It is mine," I said under my breath, scarcely daring to lay claim to it.

"My darling!" and with a glad cry there came a rain of kisses upon my forehead, baptizing me afresh. O, blessed sympathy of friendship, with the bliss, but not the torture nor wild desires of love! And then we clasped hands in that cordial tenderness that needs no words, but is a language unto itself.

"How blind I must have been! Nay, I think I had a dim perception that in it I saw your soul. When you taught these earnest, glowing truths, my dear friend, had they no voice for you?"

"Anne," I rejoined, "I have suffered much bitter self-upbraiding. I wrote the book in spells of something that appears to me now like inspiration. The rest of my life was wretched and dreary in the extreme. I had reached that utter weariness of heart and soul when all is black unbelief. I wanted fame — success. Pride was my dominant ruler and guide. I have been justly punished."

"But you *have* achieved success! Why, the book is everybody's admiration. You have only to confess, and you will find yourself famous."

Sweet words from the lips of love. Nothing ever thrills one so completely as that sense of first triumph, all the dearer and more satisfying for the many hours of despair that had preceded it. But my eyes filled with tears, rapturous, yet strangely sad, and for many moments we were both silent.

"I must hear all," Anne said at length. "How well you kept your secret! yet I shall have to exercise a good deal of Christian charity in order to forgive you for shutting me out of your confidence."

I told her the whole story. It appeared strange even to myself. Anne's sympathy was unbounded; more than once I saw the tears softly falling.

"O, my darling, how you have suffered!" she said at length, with a tremulous sob.

"You must not pity me, nor help me to make a martyr of myself. I am done with that forever. I turned wilfully away from the light, and God allowed me to wander in the darkness of my own making."

"I think there is a time in nearly all our lives when we go into the wilderness, and are tempted of the devil. It is only by keeping close to God that we escape."

18

I understood the peculiar light in her tender eyes. She, too, had known the anguish, the passion, and pain of standing a brief while without the portals of hope.

But the marvels for the day were not ended. I received a brief letter from Mrs. Ellingwood, expressing much regret that I would not be able to resume my place, and offering to wait a month. She enclosed a letter that had come while she was away, and had been mislaid. It was from my publishers. They were very much encouraged at the late success of my book, and proposed that I should come to New York, if it was convenient, as there were several points in the business they wished to discuss with me. It had been written a month before.

I was too tired and excited to sleep well that night, yet was not materially worse the next day. Some time elapsed before we recovered our usual serenity; indeed, the whole course of my life appeared changed. New plans and aims haunted me continually; but I tried to keep my expectations within bounds. It was only one little step in a long journey.

I made arrangements to go to New York as soon as possible, asking Mrs. Westervelt to take me in during my stay, to which she readily agreed. I longed to see the sweet, motherly face again. She was very lonesome, missing the society of Philip and Ellen very much. They did not expect to return until mid-winter.

Anne was loath to have me go, but she yielded her desires in her own sweet fashion. Her brother Walter had been in Italy nearly a year, and was making rapid improvement in health as well as art. "I shall have an interest in two famous people," she said, with her bright smile.

I found that Mrs. Westervelt had lost none of her charms. I was the better able to appreciate the exceeding loveliness of her character, and the refined and tender geniality of her temper. Crowds of olden memories thronged about me, filling the very rooms and halls with phantoms. I almost expected to see Mrs. Lawrence enter in all her airy grace and beauty, and meet Mr. St. John's deep, questioning eyes. There in the library a strange little episode had occurred; and I felt the blood mantling my brow at the very thought. Did he remember it? What spirit had possessed us in those days, in all days indeed? Had it been love, or simply desire to rule — to gratify a longing for power and influence? I wondered if we would ever meet again, and how? Mrs. Westervelt talked them both over in her delightful fashion, but what did she know of him? I smiled to myself.

Mrs. Varick, *née* Laura Hastings, was living in elegant style. Gertrude, also, had married, and Mrs. Hastings might well plume herself upon her success. I did not care to see either of them; indeed, I desired quiet and seclusion. I told Mrs. Westervelt the story of the past two years, or at least the main incidents, and surprised her greatly by the new triumph I had gained. After my first business interview, I felt quite assured that success *was* possible. I had gained a little fame and made a little money, but it was a very fair beginning. The prospect warranted my continuance; yet now I found myself wondering whether I should ever do as well again. I received the most gracious encouragement, and resolved that I would not fail for lack of trial, at least. There was much to do before I could repose in the shadow of my well-earned laurels.

I sometimes wonder whether there is any settled plan to life. I determined to return to Baltimore, and devote my winter to writing another book. I was making my last call at the little office that I had once entered with such trembling steps, when I met a sister of my publisher, a pale, sweet-looking woman, hardly middle age, but bearing marks of great fragility of constitution. She was on the eve of going abroad, but had met with some disappointment, I gathered from the few sentences I heard. As it did not concern me, I paid little attention to their conversation. I had just risen, and was about to leave them, when there was a flutter beside me, and a familiar face glanced into mine.

"O, Miss Adriance!"

Grace Endicott had been a pupil at Elm Grove Seminary. The similarity of names had escaped me.

"Have I kept you waiting, mamma?" she asked, eagerly. "I was detained unavoidably." Then to me, "Miss Adriance, I am delighted to see you. Mamma can bear witness that I have been won by your wonderful gift of music. It has actually inspired me."

She was one of the few girls it had been no trouble to teach; a great favorite with all in school; yet I had held myself aloof from the girls, and hardly felt familiar.

"This is *your* Miss Adriance, then?" her mother said.

The word, simple as it was, touched me profoundly. Had I unwittingly inspired this girl with regard?

"I wish she *was* mine," Miss Endicott exclaimed, impulsively; "then we would take her to Europe, mamma, and have no more worry. Miss Adriance, are you not going back to Elm Grove?"

"No," I replied.

"And are you quite at liberty?"

"My dear," her mother said, mildly.

"O, mamma, it would be just what we want. And maybe Miss Adriance would like to travel. I'm enchanted with the idea of going; and I never knew any one who did not sigh for Italy."

"I shall have to explain," Mrs. Endicott began, with a

winsome smile. "We expect to be abroad for two or three years; but Grace is so young that her father does not like to trust her altogether to foreign teachers. We want some one who is capable of exercising a supervision over her, and who would prove a companion for me. Just as we thought ourselves nicely suited, a break occurred in the negotiations, and we all regretted it extremely. It would be so much more pleasant to have a person who was not an entire stranger; but I suppose your arrangements would not permit of such an engagement, even if it should prove otherwise agreeable. Pardon us both for mentioning it."

There was something so refined and lady-like in her demeanor that it won me instantly. Then the proposal *did* look tempting. It would be many years before I could afford such a journey as a luxury; and in the life I proposed to myself the culture and knowledge thus acquired would prove invaluable. I had no tie to hold me here. Yet I could not decide thus suddenly.

"If it would not interfere too much with my plans in another direction, I should hardly hesitate," I returned, frankly.

"Mamma," Grace said, "suppose we take Miss Adriance home with us, and talk the matter over at our leisure."

Mrs. Endicott seconded the invitation so strongly that I acquiesced. Their carriage was at the door, and entering it, we drove to a quiet but aristocratic part of the city.

Grace was vehemently urgent. In vain her mother tried to restrain her. Still she was charming, and would prove a pleasant charge, I thought.

We discussed the matter at length. The duties would be light, leaving me much leisure time, if I could manage not to be distracted with the constant variety of travelling, though they expected to go to Florence immediately, and remain there for the first winter. The proffered salary was liberal, to say the least.

In return, I informed Mrs. Endicott of my desires. It certainly was one of those cases of mutual attraction, and seemed to promise a delightful acquaintance. I staid to lunch, and was then sent home in the carriage, the ladies promising to call upon me in a few days.

I related my odd encounter to Mrs. Westervelt that evening, as we sat alone.

"It looks very tempting to you, I dare say; but, my dear, I wish you had been more like ordinary women."

"Why?" and I laughed gayly. "In what respect am I different?"

"I should like to see you happily married and content."

"I shall have enough to content me, I am sure."

"Sydnie, you are still very young, and, may be, have not come to the great want of a woman's life — a cheerful household hearth. And though genius may be a fascinating possession, I am not sure but it brings in its train restlessness and dissatisfaction with common daily duties. We had other hopes for you, my dear child."

I understood the allusion, and colored faintly.

"It hurts me to hear a woman sneer against love, or treat it in the flippant manner so common among girls of the present day," she continued. "If any feeling is held in holy reverence, that should be."

"I shall always honor pure, true love," I said, with emotion.

She glanced earnestly in my face. I know we both thought of Mr. St. John; but there was nothing I could tell, and her delicacy forbore to question.

Grace came the next day, and spent an hour with me, quite delighting Mrs. Westervelt.

The longer I considered the scheme, the more feasible

it became. I went to Mr. Harold and asked his advice — for the grave, kindly face held a potent charm for me.

It was advisable that I should follow up my first success as soon as possible; but he thought the merits of the tour would outweigh its few disadvantages. He was extremely fond of his sister, and really desirous that I should go, though he would not urge. The interview decided me, however.

When Mrs. Endicott came, I gave her my answer, and she expressed her warmest satisfaction. They were anxious to start by the middle of October, which gave me but three weeks in which to complete my arrangements. It was best to return to Baltimore immediately.

Anne and Mr. Otis both congratulated me upon my improvement: I had begun to look quite like myself. I could not spoil my first day's pleasure by the announcement of my speedy departure, though I smiled a little over Anne's castle-building.

"I am so glad to have you back again," she said, the next morning. "I've planned such lovely times for the winter; and, as you write your new book, I shall read and criticise. Are you afraid, that you look so sober?"

"I shall not be here, my dear friend," I said, with a touch of sadness, for I had begun to realize how sweet it was to be so well loved.

"Not here?" she echoed, in dismay.

"I am going to Europe."

"Have you made your fortune, or is some one going to send you as a travelling correspondent?" she asked, in astonishment.

"Neither;" and then I explained what had befallen me.

"It is selfish to be sorry; but I had counted so much upon our enjoyment together! I am never to have you, it seems."

"There are a good many years yet to come," I rejoined.

"And hosts of friends, possibly a husband."

At this I shook my head.

"Have you taken a vow of celibacy?"

"Not exactly. Out of the three friends, one ought to remain single. You and Laura are married."

"And I used to think you would be the first to go."

"Undiscovered merit;" and I laughed.

"You really did not care for Aylmer?"

"Set your heart at rest. I am thoroughly ashamed of that episode. His cruelty towards Magdalene crushed out the last vestige of even friendly feeling."

"And you are quite fancy free?"

"Worshipping the hero of my dreams," I said, with a rising color.

Though Anne was grieved to the heart, she gave me all the assistance in her power. My wardrobe had not been replenished since the Laurelwood days, and many dresses needed only alteration and retrimming to make them presentable. Some I never should wear again. I seemed so much older and graver than when those marvellous robes of tulle and lace were fashioned. And the

> "Something sweet
> That follows youth with flying feet,"

was forever gone.

I was not hopeless nor dispirited, and yet there were moments when the years looked long and almost wearisome. After fame was gained, and the restless yearning for change satisfied, what then?

The partings were all ended at last, and I stood on the steamer's deck, catching last glimpses of New York. Once I had rocked to the plash of the tide up there in the river, viewing a sunrise. Everywhere something recalled Mr. St. John. He would hear of my departure, also of my debut in the world of literature, and be in nowise affected. Well, I had found a place in the world, and a work to do, and that ought to satisfy.

Does it?

No. Are women such weak, unreasonable beings that they must long continually for a crumb of love?

It humiliated me to confess it, even to myself; and yet, as Mr. St. John's wife, I should know more perfect, satisfying happiness in a month, than in all my solitary lifetime. I can see now my fatal, irremediable mistake.

CHAPTER XXI.

"Life will not flow as rivers flow, nor seas;
It is a flood but made of raindrops; days,
Hours, and moments; several, pitiless."

It is a long while since I have looked at this journal.

A life that is at once changeful, busy, and interesting leaves little time for retrospection. Mine has been crowded with delight and variety, and I have known more real enjoyment than I once thought possible.

In the Endicotts I found warm and delightful friends. Mrs. Endicott seems like an elder sister, for she has none of Mrs. Westervelt's motherly ways. Grace was piquant, charming, and full of girlish enthusiasms. In her I discovered many things that reminded me of myself, in my impulsive, undisciplined girlhood.

After seeing us domesticated at Florence, Mr. Endicott left for Paris and London, whither business called him. We were occupants of a picturesque old house that had doubtless been a palace in bygone years. At first I believe I was a little disappointed in the place. The narrow, irregular streets, and tall houses, with their sleepy, ruinous look, was so different from the busy life to which I had been accustomed. But in the distance the masses of hills sloped down to the lazily flowing Arno, while northward rose ranges of mountains. Here and there olive orchards waved their branches in the soft sunshine, gardens, vines, and flowers dawned upon us at every turn. We spent many a day in rambles about the sub-

urbs of this curiously historical city, and by degrees began
to feel at home.

The mornings were generally devoted to study. I
yielded to the spell of delicious languor, and for weeks
spent my leisure in reading aloud or idly dreaming. It
was delightful merely to breathe. I found my duties both
light and pleasant. We haunted the old churches, listening to masses as we had never heard them rendered
before. When I roused myself to work, the trance still
pervaded every fibre of my being, and under its enchanting influence I wrote of beauty, nature, and love.

Early in the summer we began to travel. Switzerland,
Germany, the Rhine, France, and a glimpse into Spain.
The second winter we spent at Rome. Mrs. Endicott's
health was much improved, and we had settled to a warm,
steady friendship. She was deeply interested in my pur-
suits, and delighted with my success. I hardly recognized
myself in this life of continual charm and variety.

One of my earliest friends in Rome was Walter Sutherland. He was still delicate with a high-bred spiritual
beauty that seemed almost unearthly in his moments of
enthusiasm. His whole soul was in his art, just as it had
been in boyhood. Mrs. Endicott became greatly interested
in him, but Grace found a stronger attraction in a companion of his, a young artist also. Arthur Wardleigh was
eminently calculated to please women, not with the superficial charm that had won Mr. Channing his successes, but
a true and earnest soul. She sat to him for a picture, and
he strolled in nearly every evening for music and a social
chat. How well I remember the long room with its antique furniture and polished floors, the piano at one end,
and those two youthful faces smiling, lighting up with a
word, or joining their voices in some sweet harmony. In
the centre, the table with its books, papers, and vase of

flowers, Mrs. Endicott in her great chair, and a group
gathered around, eagerly discussing art, science, poetry,
politics, or religion.   It was a kind of life nearly perfect in
its enjoyments, and influenced me in a peculiar manner.

Although we were not much in society, we had many
agreeable friends. One evening, I think it was during
Lent, Mr. Wardleigh brought a young American to call
upon us. We found him exceedingly entertaining. His
two sisters had been abroad several years, and he had but
recently rejoined them. It seemed like a little glimpse of
my native land, and was the more to me in that he had
met the Westervelts, indeed was quite well acquainted
with Philip.

"How really charming you were to Mr. Clifford," Grace
said, with a gay laugh. "I'm not sure that it is quite
right to make yourself so fascinating to susceptible young
men."

"Neither of us are in any danger, I think," was my grave
reply.

"Didn't he make you a trifle homesick with all that talk
about old friends? Once or twice there was such a soft,
strange light in your eyes. I do not want you to be seized
with a longing for home just yet."

I started at this, then said that I thought my reign as
governess would presently come to an end.

She colored at my retort.

We had counted strongly on the service of Passion
Week, and went to the Sistine Chapel every day. I do
not wonder that the gorgeous ritual wins many admirers.
It impressed me with a deep feeling of awe. Great pathetic swells of music, the dim lights, and air cloudy with
incense, the low-voiced priests and sombre penitential
robes, have a wonderful power over the imagination and
feeling in such a place, where sculpture, poetry, and paint-

ing lend their divine power.   And yet there must be times when nothing but true divinity will satisfy the hungering soul.

I remember glancing over the crowd, and coming to a face and figure that riveted my attention instantly.   What there was about it to affect me so curiously I could not tell, unless the long, searching gaze startled me and rendered me almost nervous.   This stranger was either English or American, tall, thin to emaciation, and deathly pale. His hair and beard were snowy white, and the contrast with his large, dark, inexpressibly mournful eyes, was indescribable.   Feeble and aged as he appeared, there was a lingering impress of power in every feature.   Again and again I encountered the look.

Grace remarked it also, and spoke of it afterwards.

" He appeared well-bred, and a gentleman, but he certainly did stare.   There's something suggestive about his face, as if I had seen it under different circumstances," she said.

" It affects me in precisely the same manner," I replied; and though I tried to dismiss it, I found that it still haunted me.

We were in our places the next day, and the unknown in his.   I began to have a strange presentiment of evil or misfortune.   Of late I had grown serenely happy; now I seemed to have come to the verge of change and danger.

The pomp of Good Friday was most solemn and imposing.   Just before nightfall we went to the chapel.   The setting sun made a dusky crimson twilight through the richly ornamented windows, and at the far chancel the tall candles sent their faint rays over the striking scene.   After the priest read the service, the mournful flow of music rolled like great sorrowful waves through the chapel.   One by one the candles were extinguished.   Then a plaintive voice took up the cry of desolation, touching every heart by its exquisite pathos, joined presently by a deep, tremulous alto, that rendered the sound more like a perfect agonizing wail.

Suddenly another sound broke the devotional fervor: a human exclamation of pain or grief. There was a stir in the vicinity of our unknown; indeed he seemed to have fallen heavily backward, but in the crowd we could not see any further movement. I was nervous, and discomposed; and though the remainder of the service was grand and touching, I hardly listened, and was glad to emerge from the darkened church into the open air and the lingering rays of daylight. We came, singularly enough, upon Mr. Clifford, assisting the very person in whom we had become so interested. His steps were tottering, and his face like death itself.

We merely exchanged glances. I was alarmed, and glad to find Mr. Endicott waiting for us.

Grace told the story, she being much calmer than I. And that evening, when Mr. Wardleigh came, it was repeated.

He smiled a little.

"I think it is Mr. Clifford's uncle, who is an invalid. He has quite large expectations from him, I believe. I have met the two sisters — Mrs. Dorrance and Miss Clifford."

"And the resemblance we could not account for, is to young Mr. Clifford," Grace said, relieved. "Yet there is a shadowy suggestion of something that I can't dismiss from my mind."

"We had better dismiss it altogether," I returned.

"How pale you are, Miss Adriance! And I'm stupidly nervous, for I see a resemblance in every one to those Cliffords, I believe. Just now your eyes had the exact expression."

"It is odd," Mr. Wardleigh said, "but the first evening Clifford was here I couldn't help thinking he looked like Miss Adriance. I suppose it was only a whim."

I went to my room presently, but somehow I could not sleep that night. Vague fancies haunted me, out of which I could make nothing tangible. I felt glad that we were soon to leave Rome, for I was tiring of its lonely magnificence. Indeed, a strange yearning for home came over me.

But my surprise had not reached its climax. The next morning, as I sat in my room writing letters, Grace entered with a face full of wonder.

"Mr. Clifford is here, and wishes to see you alone," she announced.

I started at this. "There certainly is some mystery about it," she went on. "If his uncle were not old and ill — "

"Hush!" I interrupted, silencing her playful badinage. Then I crossed the hall, but paused several seconds at the door, steadying my nerves.

Mr. Clifford stood by the centre-table, pale and agitated.

"You must excuse this unseasonable call," he said, with a faint smile; "but it is a work of necessity."

"Pray be seated," and I placed a chair for him.

"Miss Adriance," he began, slowly, after quite a pause, "I want you to exonerate me from all motives of impertinence or curiosity. I saw you yesterday as we came out of the chapel. I was assisting my uncle, who had been ill — "

"Yes," I said, as he waited.

"I mentioned your name then. It seems he had been attracted by a singular resemblance to a person long dead, a nephew dearly loved, who married a Miss Adriance. I do not know that it can have anything to do with you;

but he was most anxious to learn your antecedents. Of course, if Sidney Clifford had left a child its name would not be Adriance."

The room swam before my eyes. That old tragedy of love and death rushed through my brain. Sidney Clifford. I remembered that I had inherited my father's Christian name; by one of the odd incidents of fate, his family name I had never known, for my aunts had made Adriance legally mine. Mr. Anthon was probably aware, but he had not mentioned it.

"I must beg your pardon for startling you in this manner," he continued. "Uncle has some strange whims — but Miss Adriance!"

He came towards me suddenly. I was not faint, yet I gasped for breath.

"There was a little girl born to Sidney Clifford. This is her mother's picture." And he opened a locket.

I uttered a cry of joy and surprise. My own mother, as I had seen her just once.

"I think he is right. He always supposed the child dead, having been so informed. Miss Adriance, we are something nearer than friends — relatives."

I was in a maze of bewilderment, and hardly knew what to say. Was not the whole affair some idle vision, conjured up by an old man's diseased brain? But the picture!

"Yesterday, overcome by the warmth of the place, the power of the music, and perhaps his own feelings, he fainted. On leaving the church we met, as you know. He begged me to learn your name, and who you were. I explained immediately, and then he confessed he had watched you for the past week, drawn by some attraction it was impossible to resist. Last night he was very ill. He blames himself, I believe, for many of the misfortunes that befel your parents, and implored me to bring you to him, if I learned that you were really their child. He will tell you the story. I think there can be no doubt. It was one of those unfortunate secret marriages, but our main facts agree, and as he is all impatience I will not delay by further explanations. Will you accompany me thither?"

I assented, and went to make myself ready, promising to satisfy Grace on my return. I hardly knew whether I believed or not. And as we were rolling through the narrow street, in spite of the whirl of my brain I fancied that it would be ·pleasant to find some one on whom I had a stronger claim than mere friendship. But how many times in my short life I had been cast among utter strangers!

I repeated the few facts of my early history to Mr. Clifford. During the previous night, when his uncle had considered himself dying, he had spoken of some matters concerning which he had heretofore preserved the utmost silence.

"Of course," Mr. Clifford explained, " he could not imagine you were alive. The resemblance certainly is extraordinary. The first evening that I saw you, you reminded me of my sisters."

I had always supposed that I resembled my mother's family. I had a distinct remembrance of my two aunts, and I fancied that as I grew older I looked more like them. Was it the peculiar likeness between myself and the Cliffords that Grace had unconsciously remarked?

I was in a chaos of amazement and unbelief, or rather that strange sort of fear to which faith appears impossible. As if upon examination some conclusive link would be wanting, and the whole affair fall to the ground like a baseless fabric.

We arrived at the place presently — a lovely, olden-time villa, with a terraced garden, and great trees lining the carriage way as well as the walk. There was an air about it of going into slow decay, and yet it was exceedingly lovely. Mr. Clifford led me up the broad arched entrance, whose marble floor gave a faint echo to our tread. A lady, apparently thirty, tall and elegant in the black robe that clung about her with a kind of exquisite grace, came to meet us.

"I have brought her, Bertha," Mr. Clifford said, and then followed my introduction to Mrs. Dorrance. Although stately and commanding, she was very gracious.

"We owe you some apology for thus startling you with a family history," she went on, in a low, sweet tone. "But if it is true, as our uncle suspects, we shall endeavor to win your pardon by the welcome we shall give you as a relative."

"There can be no doubt about it, Bertha," Mr. Clifford said.

"Will you have Miss Adriance lay aside her bonnet and mantle, while I go and prepare uncle?"

I understood immediately that I would not be considered an intruder, and this gave me courage. Indeed, they both appeared so intent upon ministering to their relative that the mere influence brought me into the same mood. Mrs. Dorrance made a few explanations while her brother was absent, but he soon came to conduct me to the sick man's apartment.

CHAPTER XXII.

" Many things there are
That we may hope to win with violence;
While others only can become our own
Through moderation and wise self-restraint."

GOETHE.

A CURIOUS awe seized me as I entered the place. The lofty ceiling, frescoed walls, heavy crimson curtains that made a soft twilight through the room, the antique furniture and great canopied bed, seemed like a description in a story. The lighter appointments of the place I scarcely noticed then. As the sense of dimness cleared away, I caught a glimpse of the pale face amid the pillows, and started involuntarily.

"Sydnie Adriance!" he exclaimed, stretching out his hand with a majestic wave. "Let her stand there in the light, Gerald. My God! how like, and yet unlike. Child, come here, and forgive me before I die. I think I murdered your father!"

"Go to him," Gerald Clifford said, in a whisper.

I approached the bed-side. Something in the face appealed powerfully to me. I seemed to lose my own volition and be swayed by his desires alone. A motive I could not understand impelled me to say, —

"I do not think I have suffered much from the past mistakes of others."

"Ah, you are generous because you do not know. Gerald, give me some cordial, and leave me alone with her."

The young man obeyed, raising his uncle to a sitting

posture, and placing a chair for me. For the first few moments the silence was deathly. I glanced at the pallid face, so full of lines, the sunken yet strangely pathetic eyes, and the trembling hand grasping the counterpane for even that frail support.

"You don't know." The voice was weak and wandering. "If he could have given you a father's love and care — "

That touched me. I had never known neglect so far as my bodily wants were concerned, but the sweetness, the tenderness most children have by right of a blessed inheritance had fallen out of my life, leaving waste and desolate places.

"I want to hear your story," he said, presently. "I shall be better able to tell mine then."

I began with my earliest recollections, which were scarcely beyond that first conversation concerning my father. After that my guardian's visit and my first school experience; but at the death of my aunts I paused.

"Go on," he said, with some difficulty. "I want to hear all about this life that I might have made so much better."

I went briefly over the succeeding years — my school life, my introduction to the world, my subsequent loss of fortune, and the years since, with their varied incidents.

He had grown strangely interested. Through the latter part his eyes had scarcely wandered from my face. I marvelled that I should be able to talk with so little reserve, but I could see that it pleased him better. Every moment a strong, yearning sympathy drew me nearer to him.

"My poor child! If I could have known of your existence years ago, Heaven will bear me witness that I would have given you the tenderest care. It was I who visited your aunt, and she told me you were dead. I might have made inquiries elsewhere, but I could not suspect her of any motive for deception, though I could see that she cherished the most bitter hatred towards your father, even in his grave. Both of us sinned in our selfish love for the one nearest to us. Can it ever be forgiven?"

A strong impulse led me to clasp my hand over the thin white fingers. It was returned with trembling pressure.

"I must go back to my own early life to make you understand why I loved your father so well. There were two brothers of us, all that were left of a large family. Arnold and I were inseparable, and yet we were very dissimilar. He had a girl's delicacy and fastidiousness, while I was a great strong fellow, able to take life at its hardest or its worst. Why linger over that episode? We both loved the same woman, or rather child, a girl so fair, so pure and lovely in soul as well as in body, that all other women failed by comparison. I fancied she loved me in return; and I watched with keenest eyes, quickened, perhaps, by all I had at stake. With Arnold she was shy and reserved, I thought, shunned rather than sought him, while she came to me with so winsome a freedom that I laid my whole soul at her feet. Blind dolt that I was, not to see! but my passion absorbed sight and sense. One night Arnold came to me, his face fairly transfigured with delight, and his voice tremulous with joy. Muriel loved him, had confessed it, and promised to become his wife. In that moment I was plunged into the blackness and depth of despair. I could have cried out weakly in my agony, but for his sake I held my peace. But the torture of the next few weeks I cannot describe. Even now it comes back fresh and poignant. Muriel was so uncon-

'sciously sweet and sisterly. I knew then that my own blindness had misled me."

He made so long a pause that I looked at him in distress. Each respiration was labored and painful.

"You will injure yourself," I exclaimed, apprehensively.

"I have lived these scenes over continually during the last twenty-four hours. Life is nearly gone — what does it matter?"

What could I say? I cast about for some comfort, but none came.

"I could not stay to see them married. I happened to meet with a fine opening in a mercantile house connected with the China trade, and I resolved to go abroad. I spent nine years there, and amassed a fortune, added to the small one I had inherited. Then I set out upon a tour through all the wonderful countries of the old world — India, Persia, Arabia, and Egypt. I had reached the shores of Greece when I received word from Muriel. Arnold had died suddenly; and in one of the periodic financial convulsions nearly everything had been swept away. I had an abundance for them all, and I hurried back to my native land. I found Muriel lovelier than ever, but in a fatal decline. She grieved continually for her husband. I never saw deeper or truer devotion.

"There were two children, Sidney, the younger, named for me. There was a peculiar blending of father and mother in him; he had her soft dark eyes, and her almost heavenly smile, with all his father's delicacy of figure and constitution. From the first hour I took him to my heart. Richard, the elder, was proud, ambitious, and energetic, the kind of boy that appeals so strongly to the pride of most men; but Sidney I loved with a strange, tender passion.

"Well, Muriel died. She never knew my secret here upon earth, and in heaven the angels are pitiful. I took her children as my own. Richard prospered, and grew into a noble manhood. I settled him in business, and saw him married. Bertha, Gerald, and Alice, whom you have not seen, are his children. He, too, died young.

"Perhaps I was blind in my partiality for Sidney. I do not mean that I was ever ungenerous to Dick; but upon the younger I lavished all my love. He was so fond and clinging, so affectionate! O, why did I allow this sweet, fond heart to stray from me?

"One summer—he was barely twenty, and just through college—he took a fancy to ramble around with some young companions, as I thought. I had always supplied him liberally with money, and he really had no idea of its value. In most things he was a child. He met your mother, and the two fell headlong in love. After a while he wrote, confessing his attachment; and as she had been subject to what he considered a very cruel persecution on the part of her friends, he proposed to marry her immediately, and bring her home.

"And now comes my own bitter, humiliating confession. My jealous, absorbing love was goaded to madness. To lose him, to have another come between, and see him lavish upon her the boundless wealth of his affection! He was mine in a peculiar sense. I had given up his mother; but I would *not* relinquish him. I wrote, and commanded him to renounce his boyish folly, and return home at once. I blamed the girl as a designing schemer, and refused utterly to see her or receive her.

"My letter was delayed on its way; and when it reached him, Miss Adriance was already his wife, having clandestinely left her relatives. I was merciless in my anger, and his very tenderness for his bride exasperated me. I took a savage delight in announcing that he him-self had made the rupture between us; that he had proved weak, fickle, and ungrateful; and henceforth he need not look to me for assistance. Since he had chosen her, he must abide by his fate. Henceforward we would be utter strangers.

"Richard was provoked with his imprudent marriage also. Sidney begged him to intercede, that he might be restored to my favor; but I would not listen to a word in his behalf. For more than a year we heard nothing from him. I had been away several weeks on some busi-ness; and when I returned, my housekeeper met me with a strange story. Sidney had arrived one evening looking so ill and worn, and so disappointed at my absence, that she had asked him in. He would eat nothing, but begged to be allowed the privilege of going to his old room once more. At midnight, hearing a stir within, she had entered his room, and found him in a wild delirium. That was four days before, and he had alternated between fever and stupor ever since. The physicians despaired of his life.

"I was stunned by the tidings, and went immediately to him. My darling — but O, how changed! Worn to a skeleton, the thin cheeks a flame of scarlet fire, the soft eyes glazed with the fever that was consuming him. All my love rushed back in an instant. I would have given my life to save him. Alas! repentance — everything was too late! On the ninth day he died. I was holding him in my arms, and I know a faint gleam of consciousness overspread his soul. With one bright, glad smile his spirit went heavenward.

"For weeks I was plunged into a profound and pas-sionate grief. I scarcely slept, or ate, or thought. I had ordered a brief letter despatched to your mother; but my

heart was still bitter and unjust towards her. I blamed
her for all that had occurred. If she had displayed any
judgment she would not have rushed upon this evil marriage. I laid Sidney's death at her door.

"Some time afterwards, in looking over a long unused
drawer, I found the locket Gerald brought to you, and the
last note my poor Sidney had written — unfinished at that
— dated the evening on which he had returned. Some
presentiment of coming death had already foreshadowed
him. He implored me to be kind to his wife and little girl.
As your aunt told you, he had overtasked his strength in
his endeavor to keep them comfortable; and besides, he
had missed my love, and longed for it ardently. I cannot
tell you how this touched me. I studied the picture in
the locket — a sweet, girlish face, so lovely that I almost
forgave his fatal passion.

"As reason returned, I found that I had not been quite
free from blame. I had reared him in luxury and idle-
ness, given him expensive tastes and habits, and, at the
most critical moment of his life, thrown him upon his own
undeveloped resources. He had striven to do his best,
and the most severe judge could ask no more.

"In this softened mood I set out to find your mother.
In the city where they had been living all trace of her
was lost; but I remembered the name of the town where
he had visited her, and began to search for any one by
the name of Adriance. I soon found there were two
maiden ladies, living in strict retirement, and that this
unfortunate girl was their niece. I wended my way
thither, and had an interview with one of these women,
your great-aunt Hester, it seems. If possible, she was
more exasperated about her niece's marriage than I had
been, and inveighed most bitterly against her husband.
I spoke of the child, and of my intention to take it and

care for it; for, somehow, the thought of a little girl had
brought up the image of my lost Muriel. She stopped me
by announcing that the child had followed its mother,
and that I would forever be relieved of any care in that
direction; and there was a kind of haughty triumph in
her voice. I was too utterly overwhelmed to make any
further inquiries. My last hope of reparation had been
swept away. No atonement could be made for my cruel
injustice. But I cannot even now understand why they
chose to be so mysterious about you."

The weary eyes sought mine for explanation. The beseeching pathos nearly unnerved me.

"It was their pride to keep the last member of their
family. They had loved my mother with the same jealous
watchfulness;" and then I paused, fearful of wounding
him.

"But I would have forgiven all, and asked to be forgiven myself. Heaven knows I was humble enough then;
yet it is true I never could have left you entirely to their
care. What a life for a child! Still, I wonder that the
prospect of what I would be able to do for you did not
have some weight with them. They were not mercenary,
we must confess."

"They possessed sufficient for me;" and I gave a faint
smile to think how it had gone.

"And now you know all my sin. Child, do you despise
me?"

I buried my face on the pillow, overcome by a sudden
rush of emotion, and tears of the profoundest pity filled
my eyes.

"Sydnie! It takes me back to the old days. For his
sake you must forgive."

There was an indescribable entreaty in the tone.

"I forgive all," I said, in a tremulous voice.

"Strange that love should be at once the blessing and the curse of life; that our darkest and most unhallowed moments should be swayed by the passion in one form, and our hours of bliss in another. Come nearer, child, and lay your cheek against mine. What mighty voice spoke when I first saw you? It was no sickly fancy or superstition, but God's divine mandate. You will not leave me, Sydnie. It won't be long. I have passed the boundary of threescore and ten."

"If you wish me to stay — " and then I paused. How would my new cousins view this matter?

"I wish you to stay." His voice was so faint that I sprang up in alarm, and when I saw how ashen his lips were, I exclaimed, almost in terror, —

"What can I do for you? We have talked too long — "

"No," he interrupted. "Touch the bell yonder upon the table; it will summon Gerald."

Mr. Clifford came and administered some remedy.

"Gerald," he said, when he could speak, "this is your cousin, beyond doubt. I wish her to stay with us."

Gerald was not displeased with the announcement, I could plainly see.

"Bertha must make her feel at home. I shall have four children now."

He fell into a drowsy mood presently, and Gerald led me to the sitting-room, where his sisters were engaged with two young children. I felt a little awkward at first, but that soon wore away. I found them really charming, and disposed to be very friendly. Mrs. Dorrance was a widow, and the children were hers. Miss Clifford was not more than twenty, smaller than her sister in every respect, and exceedingly winsome — one of those appealing faces that win you simply because they seem to desire it so earnestly.

After a little the conversation turned upon our relationship, and the singular manner in which the explanation had come about.

"Uncle Sidney's early death always was a great grief to his more than father," said Mrs. Dorrance. "For many years afterwards he lived in seclusion, losing sight of the world altogether. When Mr. Dorrance died, he proposed that Alice and I should go abroad with him; and for a while his health improved very much."

An hour or two later I was summoned to the invalid's room again. He had been discussing my coming with Gerald, who had assented to his proposition. The larger part of his fortune was to go to the young man, and Mrs. Dorrance had been left in very easy circumstances. He proposed, therefore, to give me the same amount that Alice was to have, and which Gerald thought quite just.

"You are very generous," I said to him, in a low tone.

"We have so few relatives that it is not much tax, you see," and he smiled. "Besides, we take a certain pride in the relationship. You have already won quite a position, and, I think, to be placed above any necessity will leave you much more free to follow your inclinations. My uncle is most anxious that we should have a true and kindly regard for each other."

His manner had in it more of the brother than the lover. I was glad to see this.

I was compelled to return home that evening, for I knew Mrs. Endicott would feel alarmed at a longer absence; but I promised to make all necessary arrangements for a permanent stay with them. They expected to go to Nice shortly, and desired that I should accompany them.

At the Endicotts' we sat up half the night, talking. My story appeared more wonderful with every repetition of it.

"And you are actually related to the Cliffords," Grace

said. "How strange that it should have come about in this manner! Mamma, what will we do without Miss Adriance?"

Mrs. Endicott sighed a little.

I should be sorry to leave her. The tour had been delightful as well as profitable to me. I had enriched my mind with pictures of storied cities, works of art, sculpture, and music. I had seen society in the different nationalities, and to me this knowledge would be invaluable. I was reaching the height I had once planned for myself; yet it had not been altogether the work of my own hand. God does not mean that any human being shall stand entirely alone.

I felt strangely awed and humbled that night. I thought of my parents in their distant graves, their sad, broken lives, and my own eventful existence. I did not question God's providence now, or seek to wrest the inscrutable secrets of fate from him. I had learned to believe — to trust.

In the course of the next fortnight my change was complete. There was a very delightful home feeling with the Cliffords. Perhaps what won me the most was the genuine cordiality they evinced. No narrow or petty sentiment swayed them. Their natures were at once sweet and noble.

Arthur Wardleigh won a confession from Grace that I had more than half suspected. They were all to return to America by another autumn, Grace going as a bride. Consequently I would not be as much needed by the gay girl; but I was grieved at parting with Mrs. Endicott, she had proved such a delightful friend.

Uncle Clifford, as we all called him, improved slowly. He seemed to hold for me the most profound and tender regard. I shared the nursing with Gerald and Alice; in fact we three soon became the warmest of friends. I was so perfectly at ease with them. I liked this atmosphere of affection and refinement, and the once more being my own mistress.

CHAPTER XXIII.

" Open the chamber where affection's voice,
For rare occasions, is kept close and fine."

ARTHUR HALLAM.

WE are at Nice.

Uncle Clifford has quite recovered his usual health, for he was feeble before the shock he received at our accidental meeting. I sometimes wonder if the rest are not jealous, he clings to me so entirely. He walks up and down the shining beach, leaning on my arm, and we watch the ships that skim along in the glancing sunlight, or look over the blue rippling waters, that join a faint chorus with the fragrant murmurous air. Or we sit and rest on a rude rustic bench, talking over the past. He loves to speak of my father. I remember when my swelling child's heart first broke its bonds of thraldom, and was filled with love for him. Then he predicts a brilliant future for me.

What do I care for fame now? The great world is shut out. We have a sweet, sunny nook by ourselves.

Then I wonder at my former unrest. I think of the days of my pride and waywardness, when I left the Eden of my first love to become a wanderer. Is it blooming yet? What does it matter? I can never enter it again.

By and by we no longer walk to the beach, but watch the ships and listen to the fisher's song from our windows. What if there is another ocean nigh at hand, to be crossed by one alone?

Cannot human love make chains strong enough to hold

the dear one back? Ah, would it when the close of a long and wearisome pilgrimage is reached?

Every day takes him one wave nearer the haven of rest. The end is coming tranquilly, like a calm autumn season, whose spring shall open in the fields of light. Love is unbound from its chains of passion and selfishness, and grows into the likeness of the divine.

Then a time comes when he lies quiet and helpless. Fond hands minister to him. Now and then I sing some of the old hymns he loves so well, and the peaceful light in the tender eye thanks me with wordless gratitude.

At last we all stand beside him as the sunlight dies out over the far waters, and its last rays fall like an aureole around the marble-hued face. The hand I hold in mine is cold and pulseless. The lips move faintly. I bend over and kiss them softly, and there is a little quiver in the air, a flutter heard but unseen.

We who are left clasp hands with a sudden sense of desolation. He has crossed the swelling flood, to go no more out from the presence of the living God.

There was no reason why we should remain abroad after Uncle Clifford's death. Mrs. Dorrance was really anxious to return, and I was quite satisfied with my ramblings.

"Alice is to be married," she said to me one day, as we were making our arrangements. "She postponed it for the sake of accompanying Uncle Clifford, but her lover has grown impatient. I have a large house in New York, and shall be most glad to receive you there. We should be as sisters; and I have promised to do all in my power to make you happy."

I knew to whom her promise had been given.

"You are very kind," I said, from my full heart.

"Let us try it then. You shall be free to visit friends, but that will be your home."

When Alice heard the decision she was delighted.

"You see we mean to enforce our claim," she said, with a smile.

It was August when we reached New York. Everything appeared strange and unreal to me. And being called Miss Clifford, as that was one of the terms of my uncle's will, keeps me in continual doubt of my own identity.

As soon as the house could be put in order, Alice was quietly married. For the present her home was to be with her husband's mother. Then I made Anne a visit, and all the incidents since my departure had to be rehearsed, though I had written them in the order of their coming.

"And this cousin Gerald? I heard you had married him abroad."

"What an absurd story!" I exclaimed.

"I don't see any absurdity about it."

"Its very improbability renders it so."

"Is it so utterly impossible? You are not really own cousins, you know — if that is a scruple."

"We are very good friends, and can never be anything more. Gerald has an ideal as unlike me as you can well imagine."

"Young men change their ideals;" and she laughed.

"Well, I could never *love* him; and there you have all the truth."

"How odd you are!" was her simple reply.

Another baby had been added to the household, and two of Anne's sisters were married. They were still prosperous and happy. She made me describe Walter again and again, and was delighted with his prospects.

20

After all it was nearly Christmas before we became settled. I had two elegant rooms, and was left at liberty to
do quite as I liked. Mrs. Dorrance was generally busy
with her children during the morning, and I read or wrote
as the whim dictated; and after lunch we drove out, did
shopping, and made a few calls, or staid at home to receive them. Gerald was in nearly every evening.

I ought to have been entirely satisfied with this life. I
was an heiress again, with an assured position. I had,
moreover, established my claim to the world's favor, and
needed not to seek, but was sought. I could have reën-
tered society immediately; indeed, Mrs. Dorrance wished
to afford me every advantage in her power, though since
her husband's death she had lived in a very retired manner.

I had also resumed my friendship with the Westervelts.
Philip and Ellen were little changed, except the peculiar
change that occurs to most married people whose hearts
are strongly centred in their homes. Two children had
been born to them; and Ellen seemed to have small interest beyond her domestic cares and pleasures. I do not
mean that she had grown narrow or indifferent to the welfare of others; she was too thoroughly noble for that; and
yet some way we seemed to have drifted apart. Was I
growing cold and self-absorbed, I asked myself.

But one day an incident brought me quite back to the
old life. The servant announced that a lady wished to see
me in the drawing-room, and gave me a card. To my
surprise I read the name of Mrs. Varick.

I went down immediately, and had scarcely entered
the door when Laura's light laugh greeted me. She was
thinner than in her girlhood's days, and with a certain
fashionable affectation.

"My dear creature," she exclaimed, "I have been dying
to see you for the last three months, and martyred myself

by attending literary parties that were perfect bores, just in the hope of meeting you. At last I've had the courage to come."

"Then you have not forgotten me?" I said, amused.

"It always was my style to pay court to rising stars, you remember. I am as honest as ever; and you know that I liked you, odd as you were. Why, you've hardly changed a bit. I've faded frightfully; but it is rather a comfort to Mr. Varick to have me grow old. And so you're famous, and have another fortune, and are to marry very nicely, after all. I've heard quite a romance about you."

"The marrying is pure romance," I said.

"Nonsense; don't be modest. There are numbers of aspiring belles who would take Gerald Clifford, and say thank you in their secret hearts, though it might not be proper to express gratitude aloud. I fancied that was the reason you secluded yourself, in order to have time to attend to bride clothes."

"There is no truth in your surmise, and it offends me," I said, shortly.

"My dear, you haven't improved in temper, and the story came to me in that fashion; so I'm not to blame."

Her face was so altogether good-natured that I smiled, and then we both laughed outright. She reached over and clasped my hand.

"Dear old Sydnie," she said, "I'm not sure but you're the one true thing in this world of shams; but you are a mystery to me. Have you actually foresworn matrimony? Do you take your tea clear, and keep a discreet tabby? If you knew how I had longed to see you, you would certainly be real gracious. Don't you care a bit for me?"

There was something irresistible in this last sentence. I believe she really had a true regard for me.

"Come," she went on presently, "tell me all about yourself. I heard you had lost your fortune, and gone off to
teach. I never *could* understand why you didn't marry
Mr. St. John. And I never suspected your being a genius
at all; but I suppose that accounts for your dissimilarity
to common mortals. I was so glad when I heard you were
a rich woman once more. I want you to believe this."

I could not doubt the sincerity of her tone. We talked
for a long while, and I went briefly over some of the most
important events that had occurred since our separation.
To her the world had been all smiles.

"We have one little boy to heir the estate," she went
on, with a gay laugh, "and I confess I've had a most delightful time thus far. The longer I live, the more I see the
propriety of people being perfectly suited, and I have the
very things I enjoy so much. To have dropped into almost
any other groove would have made me miserable, bad tem-
pered, jealous, and all that. My graces thrive best in
prosperity. But, my dear, I have gossiped unconscionably.
And now I want to ask a favor. Don't deny me."

"That depends —"

"It's to come to a quiet little dinner-party. I know
half a dozen very admirable people who are dying to meet
you; and I don't see the slightest necessity for your making a hermit of yourself. Why, you're quite a young
woman yet; it is not worth while to fall into the ranks of
the grandmothers."

"I am still in mourning," I said, "which isn't party-like."

"I'll promise to have all things appropriate. I cannot
possibly give you up."

She actually persuaded me at last to appoint an evening
that would suit my pleasure.

"And I'll ask Mr. Clifford, so that you shall have an
attendant of your own. If you will come to call on me

to-morrow, I'll send the carriage for you. I want you to see my house; and we haven't but just looked at each other. Come to lunch. My dear, there isn't the slightest use of trying to resist me."

I confess some indefinable charm surrounded Laura — a power that enabled her to sway others in a singular manner. I yielded to the influence.

I went to lunch, and really had a delightful time. Laura's house was elegance itself. She has much shrewd, good taste, that stands her instead of the higher artistic quality. Her pictures were valuable and well chosen, her statuary rarely beautiful, and the rooms had the sumptuous air of a palace. She queens it royally. After all, she *is* in the right place, and has proved the best judge of her own capabilities. Mr. Varick looks ten years younger than when we first saw him at Newport. His little son is a perfect idol, a fine, healthy child.

Laura made her arrangements for the dinner with great delight. She mentioned several persons whom I knew it would be a pleasure to meet. Artists, writers, and men in high positions — every desirable man or woman appeared within her reach. I began to kindle with interest.

"What a handsome woman you are!" she exclaimed, with sudden vehemence. "If I were you, I would have half the world at my feet."

I smiled a little. The admiration was certainly honest.

Mrs. Dorrance and Gerald were gratified that I had accepted the invitation. But afterwards he lapsed into a reverie quite unusual for him.

"Are you tired?" I asked presently.

"No. Am I stupid, and is that a hint for me to go home?"

"Why, no," I said, in surprise.

He took several turns up and down the room, then he came and glanced into my face.

" Sydnie, do you believe in love at all ? "

" What a question ! " and I started, coloring violently. Were the surmises of others correct, and had I alone been blind ?

" Yes, it is odd, but don't we talk of everything? Sometimes I am afraid I bore you. I never had Bertha for a confidant; she was married when I was so young, and Alice went away just as she was growing companionable. But there's some peculiar quality in you that wins a person to talk of himself. You always seem to understand at a word."

" So you want me to commence a dissertation upon love —do you ? " I asked, gayly.

" No; only I was wondering if you had ever felt that which you describe so perfectly, so pathetically. It always seems such a strange, awesome thing to me, for there is a great deal of unhappy love in the world, and who can tell whether he is one of the few elect who are to be blessed ? "

" This is a new mood for you," I said, bringing him back to commonplace.

" Yes," with a nervous laugh. " But I'll say good night before I mystify you with my vagaries."

He kissed me as he went. It was a kind of family familiarity, but I did not observe that it meant any more on this night than it had for the past ten months. Still I was filled with a vague fear. Gerald had a tender, manly heart, capable of great happiness and much suffering, and I wanted the former, not the latter, to be his portion.

I did not see him again until the day before the dinner, when he was very urgent that nothing should keep me at home.

" You may be sure that I shall not disappoint Mrs. Varick, when she has asked her guests expressly on my account," I said.

I received a little note from her also, in which she begged me not to fail her, as she had a surprise in store for me.

So altogether I was rather curious. I arranged my hair and dress in a state of mind quite new to me. Not exactly expectancy, or fear, or distrust, but as if I were coming to some event that would change the current of my life again. My black silk dress did not admit of much ornamentation, but it was rich and heavy. How I recalled the old times, so long ago it seemed!

At last we started. Gerald was one of those tender, gentlemanly men about whose attentions cling an exquisite grace. Birth and breeding had both been his.

I was not dazzled or overcome by the company assembled. After the introductions, I felt myself quite at ease. We waited in the drawing-room for a few stragglers. Presently there was a stir. Gerald turned, and a sudden flush of color overspread his face. Two fairies, I should have said at the first glance, and then one wore a strangely familiar smile.

"My dear Miss Adriance!"

Mrs. Lawrence, as perfect in her grace and beauty as when I left Laurelwood, nearly five years before. The room swam before my eyes for a moment.

"I came expressly to meet you," she said, scarcely above a whisper, in her silvery voice. "You can never imagine how I have wanted to see you."

I could not doubt her sincerity, and felt convicted of something like ingratitude. Or was it that my new position won her favor as well?

"My niece, Miss Carme," she said, a moment after, making way for the tiny sprite beside her.

A lovely, shy girl, with great soft eyes like a gazelle's. A vision that one rarely beholds embodied in human form.

For it was not merely beauty of feature, but form and coloring and perfect grace. I almost held my breath.

"So Mr. St. John has not arrived?" Mrs. Varick said.

I had hardly thought of him in my bewilderment.

"No," in her sweet, gracious way, that I remembered so well. "It is barely possible that he may reach the city this evening. I left a note for him."

Was I pleased or not? I tried to decide as I sat listening to the talking, using the strongest exertion *not* to answer at random. . Everything about me appeared unreal; at times the blaze of light grew faint, and the voices sounded a long way off. Why, what a weak, silly woman I was! What if *he* did come!

I did not want to see him. Every nerve quivered at the thought of the interview. How could I endure it!

Yet Mrs. Varick's dinner-party was a success. Under other circumstances I should have enjoyed it wonderfully. I could not help being pleased as it was. To be appreciated in such a genial, delicate fashion, to know that I could still attract and interest, was indeed gratifying. And there was just the company to be mutually entertaining. Art and literature were discussed without pedantry. Most of those assembled had travelled, and visited the rich galleries of the old world. In spite of the dull pain at my heart, my spirits rose. I knew that my cheeks warmed and my eyes grew luminous.

Some time after we had returned to the drawing-room, Mrs. Lawrence and I floated together again. She was all ease and grace, as usual.

"How very little you have changed!" she said. "I have so often wondered if I should ever see you again, and I feel now as if I could scold you heartily for keeping away from Laurelwood. Do you not know that we should have been most glad to see you?"

She might, but Mr. St. John?

"Stuart will be so surprised! We came to New York without him, as he had some pressing business on hand. Elsie is so extravagantly fond of operas, and he didn't want her to miss one of the season."

"Your niece?" I said, inquiringly.

"Yes. Mr. Lawrence's sister married a Spaniard, you know. Elsie was her only child, and after her death, Mr. Carme married a second time. Stuart grew wonderfully interested in this child when he was in Cuba, and upon a second visit, some eighteen months ago, brought her home. She is the most charming little being you can imagine. I love her as if she were my own."

A sharp pang went to my heart. After all, why should it matter to me what course Mr. St. John's interest took? And yet all the old days rushed back, times when his approval and smile had been so much to me.

She chatted on. I had become a successful authoress, which did not at all surprise her; she had always fancied me peculiar. And I had really found some relatives — Mrs. Varick had been relating the singular circumstances. Some friends of Laura's were boarding at the same hotel with them, and the meeting of a few days before had been purely accidental. Mrs. Lawrence had asked if there were any tidings of me, and Laura had mentioned the fact of her call, and the intended dinner-party.

I felt easier when I heard this, though I found it would be impossible to avoid them now. I must summon all my courage. And I confess that after I had talked with Miss Carme, a strange desire took possession of me to know more of her. How extraordinarily lovely and fascinating she was! Gerald was as deeply interested in her as I; his face beamed with intense satisfaction.

The evening passed rapidly and pleasantly. Mr. St.

John's arrival had been given up by his sister, and my nervous apprehension was over. In a room at the end of the hall some of the younger members of the party had been waltzing. I watched Gerald and Miss Carine until my brain was in a maze. Indeed they attracted nearly every one's attention by the bewildering grace of their movements. Was Gerald absolutely fascinated? I had never seen such a light in his eyes.

Some impulse drew me away. It was too fateful to linger over. I turned and walked through the cool hall, and had just reached the staircase, when I paused, spell-bound. Mr. St. John stood before me!

"Does the feud last a lifetime?" he said, with his peculiar smile. "Have I offended you so deeply that you will not even speak or shake hands?"

I reached mine towards him; but it was cold and trembling.

"I confess this meeting is altogether unexpected," he continued, with a touch of embarrassment. "You have seen my sister?"

She came at that moment, and then the hall seemed suddenly to fill. Mrs. Varick pressed forward, and there was a sound of welcome. I mingled with the throng; but I heard no voice save his. He was explaining the detention of a train; then he and Mrs. Varick had a little badinage.

"Here is an old friend by a new name," she said, as soon as she reached my vicinity. "Miss Clifford."

He looked sharply at me. "I don't know that I ever remember a name changed in that manner," he said, pointedly.

"Changed for a fortune instead of love," Mrs. Varick answered, gayly.

Had he heard the absurd rumor, too? Well, he would

soon know, for I had told Mrs. Lawrence the particulars
of the strange story.

' "O, you have come?" Miss Carme exclaimed, her eyes
absolutely bewildering in their radiant light, and her face
flushed with warmth and excitement.

"Yes, at the eleventh hour. Have you enjoyed yourself?"

"O, so much! And I've been waltzing while the rest
talked."

Such a light, musical laugh! I thought I had never
heard anything so tenderly beguiling in all my life.

He gave her a fond glance, so quick that none besides
us saw it. But her eyes replied, and perhaps my heart.

I looked around for Gerald, and proposed returning
home. I fancied he would rather have staid, but he
assented. Then I was besieged for calls and promises of
various kinds; and the regrets expressed were extremely
flattering, to say the least.

I remember finding my way up the stairs to the dress-
ing-room in a strange, absent manner, as if my soul had
gone out of me. Then adieus were said, and Gerald
handed me into the carriage. We scarcely spoke during
our homeward drive; and if I had not been so absorbed
in my own reflections, I must have noticed his reticence.

At last I laid my throbbing head on my pillow. All
my hardest lessons to learn over again. O God, would I,
could I, ever forget?

CHAPTER XXIV.

"Therefore disturbing dreams
Trouble the secret streams
And founts of music that o'erflow my breast;
Something far more divine,
Than may on earth be mine,
Haunts my worn heart, and will not let me rest."

AFTER that night I was in a whirl of society. I had
preserved a tolerable seclusion before; but now I found
myself invaded at every point. It was gratifying to be
thus sought by people whose regard was worth cultivating; indeed, whose attention was the finest compliment
that could be paid me. And some way I took up my old
friendship with Mrs. Lawrence. Her charming niece was
a perfect marvel to me.

Between her and Mr. St. John there existed a very
peculiar attachment. She was frank and guileless as a
child, with a nature as sweet as an opening rose. She
always reminded me of flowers. He was to her the very
prince of men, and she offered him an unconscious adoration with every look. In time it might come to mean
love; but at present her heart was like an untroubled sea.
She took a strange fancy to me, that I did not at all understand at first. Gerald thought her quite beyond ordinary creations. Mrs. Lawrence was delighted with the
attention she attracted.

I began to fancy, after a little, that Mr. St. John
shunned me in some inexplicable manner. He called
occasionally with his sister, but never alone. When we

met elsewhere, although he paid me a courtly deference, we seemed leagues and leagues apart. He had forgotten those old passages then? It was my sorest punishment that I should still remember.

My fear concerning Gerald proved incorrect. It soon became understood that we were not to be married, to my great relief, though Mrs. Lawrence insinuated that I was about to miss another very good opportunity. She admired the young man exceedingly; and he was a most devoted cavalier to the two ladies. One evening I rallied him a trifle upon it.

A strange, sweet seriousness overspread his face.

"Shall I come to confession?" he asked, in a low voice. "My dear friend; have I kept my secret so well?"

"You love Miss Carme!" I exclaimed, startled by the sudden fact.

"I love her — my sweet, darling Elsie! Sydnie, I seem in a new world. From the first hour I saw her face my heart has been hers."

"The evening at Mrs. Varick's?"

"No, before that. Do you remember an evening, more than a month ago, that we just mentioned the subject of love, and I asked you how much you believed of its wondrous power? A few hours previous, while sauntering through the Academy, I came upon those two women — mother and daughter I thought them then. I heard the soft, beguiling tones of her voice, and her sweet laugh, so like a fairy echo. The loveliest picture there was that young girl. I sat entranced. It seemed as if my very soul went out of me; and when they were gone, I wandered about like one blind. Then I said, 'I will haunt every place until I see her again, and I shall never rest satisfied until she is mine.' By one of those odd freaks of fate I learned who they were, and, moreover, that they would be at Mrs. Varick's. Do you wonder that I was wild to go?"

He had uttered all this in a rapid breath; now he made a long pause. I understood the peculiar attraction she had possessed for him that evening.

"You have not spoken?" I inquired, hesitatingly.

"I have not spoken. It has been so sweet to linger upon the brink of fate; but I think she loves me."

"O, Gerald," I said, "you have my most earnest wishes for your success."

"They are going to Laurelwood soon. My precious darling—how can I endure existence without her?"

He paced the room softly. There was a sacredness in the simple story of this fervent passion that awed me. And then I thought how, sooner or later, love carried all souls captive—those, at least, who were not born blind and dumb. Yet I remembered one who stood alone. Had he ever known any pang, any divine thrill?

Now that Gerald had opened his soul there was no reserve. We had been such perfect friends that he was sure of not being misunderstood. I could not but choose to listen to the sweet confession; and I knew no reason why I should not hope with him.

For the next fortnight I saw a good deal of Elsie. Mr. St. John had gone to Laurelwood to make some spring arrangements, and Mrs. Lawrence depended upon Gerald for an escort. How could she have been so blind!

I called one morning to accompany her to an artist's studio, where she was having her portrait painted. Mrs. Lawrence came down to receive me.

"Elsie is ill," she exclaimed, with much concern. "She was very feverish and restless all night, and her head aches severely this morning. I wanted to have a physician, but she would not listen to it, and declares she will be better presently.   I'm so sorry Stuart is away.   If anything should happen to her —"

It was the first time I had ever seen tears in the lovely eyes of Mrs. Lawrence, and they moved me indescribably. "A sudden cold," I said, trying to encourage her. "Doubtless she will recover in a few days."

"I hope so.   She was out driving yesterday, and may have been a little careless; but I never knew her to act in this manner.   She is usually so sweet and gentle; now she will not have the slightest thing done for her."

I thought of Gerald's alarm when he should hear these tidings, and was quite disappointed that he did not call during the day or evening.

I sent to inquire after Elsie on the following morning. She had improved somewhat, but was not able to leave her room.

Gerald's continued absence filled me with a strange foreboding.   Even Mrs. Dorrance spoke of it.   I sent a note to learn the cause; and to my satisfaction he answered in person, by coming to lunch.

"Gerald, you have been ill!" Mrs. Dorrance exclaimed, as he entered the room.

He did look unlike the bright, handsome man we were used to seeing.   Yet I kept silence, for I knew it had another than a physical cause.

"Balls, and parties, and dissipations have proved too much for me, Bertha," he said, with an attempt at gayety. "I think of going to some quiet country place to recruit."

She looked grave, and presently said, —

"I hope your fortune will not prove a bane instead of a blessing."

"Nonsense, Bertha!" he replied, sharply.

It was an effort to keep up the conversation.   Perhaps I did less than my share, because I was so startled by the possible realization of my late fears. He was absent and dispirited, but after our return to the library, proposed a walk, to which I readily assented.

"Gerald," I said, after we had gone some distance, "this suspense is torture."

"My dear friend, forgive me. There is no longer any blessed suspense for me, and I have grown selfishly absorbed in my misery."

"It is all over then?" I returned, with a gasp, for I could see how he suffered.

"Hope is over, if that is what you mean;" and he gave a sickly smile. "But the rest can end only with life. Sydnie, I wonder if our uncle, in bequeathing his fortune to me, unwittingly transferred his own sad inheritance? I have thought of his life continually for the few past days. One blighted blossom in early youth, and no golden fruitage for the later years. Is love fatal to us Cliffords? My parents were happy, I believe, but yours soon came to the black shadow of a cruel fate."

In his pause I thought of myself. How strangely we were all linked together by suffering! Even Bertha's bright prospect had soon been overclouded by death.

"I think she loves me," he began, with sudden vehemence. "She could not deny it, though, for some reason, she would not confess. I believe no torture could draw it from her. Childish, impulsive, and eager as she is, there's something so grand and heroic about her that it fairly awed me. She never thought of my falling in love — and I know she was honest there. It's her fashion to be happy, and to make others so; and we have gone on for weeks in such a simple, familiar manner, that my proposal took her quite by surprise. I don't know as I should have found the courage if she had not spoken of her return to Laurelwood."

"But what reason does she assign?" I asked, much amazed at his words.

"She declared a marriage between us impossible, while she has nothing to urge against me, my position, or my fortune. I can't describe to you her manner, but her anguish rose from some deeper cause than the mere idea of giving me pain. I think she was hurt herself, though she would not own it. If she did not love me, I would endure it all in silence —"

"But I cannot see any reason sufficiently strong to sway her in opposition to her own feelings."

"It's some fancied duty, or an idea of right, that she clings to rigidly. All my persuasions could not move her, and she refused utterly to see me again. It was only misery to us both, she said. But I could not believe her decision final, and the next day wrote to her, entreating another interview. All in vain, however. What can I do?"

It was a case where I, certainly, was powerless to advise. What motive could urge Elsie to so mysterious a course? She was no foolish coquette, no finished actress. Indeed, her perfect simplicity had attracted me from the first. I seemed to be thrown out of my usual course of reasoning in every respect, and felt unable to counsel.

"I need not talk much of my love," he went on, presently. "You must know what it has been and what it will be to me; but to think of her as suffering — drinking some bitter draught that should have missed lips so sweet, is intolerable. Sydnie, must it be?"

"Gerald, Heaven knows that if I could be of any assistance to you, I would do anything in my power gladly. But I, too, seem helpless."

"You can see her. She has grown strangely fond of you. If her decision arises from a cause where change is

21

impossible, I must submit.   Women are better judges of
each other, perhaps."

"Suppose she shuns me also?"

"No, that cannot be.   At least, she will see you before
she leaves the city."

"I will do what I can," I said, moved by strong sympathy.   •

My promise was put to the test before the day ended.
An hour after my return home Miss Carme's card was sent
up to me, with these words, written in pencil: "May I
come to your room?   I wish to see you alone."

I waited in the hall for the lithe little figure to flutter
over the stairs with its dainty grace.   Not so bright and
vivacious as usual, and the glad ring had slipped from her
voice; but she kissed me with a kind of convulsive passion.

"I am glad to find you thus far recovered," I said, cheer-
fully.   "Are you quite well?"

"It was only a severe headache, and being tired out.
Auntie was so distressed — not but that it was very kind
of her.   I only wanted a little rest and quiet."

"Will you take off your cloak and hat?" I asked, as
she stood undecided; and then I assisted her.

There was an air of weariness and pain in every feature,
yet she strove to make herself appear natural.

"I wish you'd take me in your lap," she said, with childish pleading in her voice.   "I don't know why, but you
always make me think of those calm, sweet Sisters of
Charity, who, having overlived their own sorrows, can be
patient and tender with others."

I smiled a little at this as I took her in my arms.   The
fair head, with its silken tresses, was pillowed upon my
shoulder.

"What is the matter?" I asked, softly.

"That I should be such a baby? I feel just like being petted and soothed. I'm worn and weary, as if I were trenching upon the threescore."

"Are gayeties less pleasant without Mr. St. John?" I said, obeying an impulse that I could not account for the next instant.

A shiver seemed to run through the delicate form.

"I wish we had gone with him," she exclaimed, vehemently. Then in a slow, hesitating manner, "Miss Clifford, have you seen your cousin recently?"

"Gerald, do you mean? He was here to-day, and took lunch with us."

She started up at this, her face flushing and paling alternately. Then the hands clasped together with a pathetic gesture, and the eyes were turned away from me.

"I want to talk to you a little about him." She uttered the words with great difficulty, and made a long pause. "Did he tell you, or had you fancied that — he cared for me?"

She buried her face in her hands at this, and something like a hard, dry sob pulsated through her frame.

"I know all," I said, at a venture.

"O, Miss Clifford, don't hate me for making him unhappy. A fatal blindness must have led me on. Somehow I can't think of lovers, and whether any one is likely to care for me; and he seemed so like a brother!"

"*Why* couldn't you love him, Elsie?" I said, boldly, going to the root of the matter at once.

"Because I — Miss Clifford, I am engaged. I couldn't tell him the truth, but I want you to know it. And if I had suspected how it would be, I should not have received your cousin in the manner I did. But Mr. St. John liked him, and so was willing — "

Was she one of those specious women who crave admi-

ration, and delude themselves with the idea that they
are not really giving encouragement, while they accept
the most pointed attentions, simply because they do not
love?

"I think the fact might have been mentioned earlier.
It would have saved one tender and loyal heart from great
suffering."

"Don't be angry; and yet I suppose it is all right. I
ought to have known. You cannot help despising me.
It wasn't altogether my fault. Mr. St. John preferred not
to have the engagement mentioned — "

A sudden sharp suspicion caught me.

"To whom are you engaged, Elsie?" I asked.

"Why, to him."

"Mr. St. John!" I drew a long, quivering breath.

"Yes. He is so good and tender, so generous. Not
that Gerald lacks anything,"—and I thought she gave
the name a peculiar intonation,—"but I had promised
before. I did love him; I do love him now; and to make
him happy I would give my whole life. For though he
has always been prosperous, and the world might think
there was nothing for him to wish, he has never reached
the heights on which some men stand. He seemed to
have missed the one thing that brings highest joy, or had,
until — "

"Elsie, do you mind telling me how it occurred? — your
engagement, I mean."

For I was absolutely bewildered. Stuart St. John in
love with this child!

"He and auntie came for me, you know. There had
been some correspondence about it, and papa was quite
willing to give me up. Though my step-mother never
treated me ill, she loved her own children much better,
and when aunt Isabelle proposed that I should come

north, and finish my education, and remain with them if
I liked, mother urged me to accept. I had seen Mr. St.
John once when I was a little girl, and liked him so much!
Well, they came to Cuba, and brought me home with them
to Laurelwood. It's such a lovely place — isn't it? That
was nearly eighteen months ago. At first, for a while, I
had a governess; but Mr. St. John taught me my music.
I used to sit for hours and hear him play; I had never listened to anything so beautiful. Last spring and summer
he grew so sad that it pained me, and I wanted to comfort him. Just the tender melancholy that appeals strongly
to one; so I would bring my books and read to him, or
sing. We used to have such long, strange talks! and I
knew then that he wasn't happy or satisfied with what life
had brought him. At last — I don't remember how we
came to say it, but — he was glad to be loved, and I was glad
to love. I sometimes wonder that he should have chosen
me, he is so grand, so above me in everything. But he
doesn't love me to be grave, or make myself old. I've
been very happy."

Her eyes wandered dreamily to the farther side of the
room as she said this, and for a moment there was silence,
as the slow cadence of her voice died away.

"He thought I was too young to be married. Just before Christmas we all went to Washington, and spent two
delightful months there. Then we came to New York.
He told auntie it was best not to speak of the engagement
at all. I believe she thinks it rather foolish, and fancies
that I shall tire of it."

"And then you met my cousin?"

"Yes; that night at Mrs. Varick's. I'm so fond of dancing, you know, and Mr. St. John insists that I shall have
every pleasure. He is royally indulgent; but I mean to
give most of them up when I am married, and devote my-

self exclusively to him. I couldn't help liking Gerald. He's so fresh and winsome, and enjoys everything with such a peculiar zest. But I never thought — O, Miss Clifford, do believe that I did not purposely mislead him. And after a while tell him how it was, and try to make him find some happiness elsewhere."

"And you couldn't love him?"

Her lips quivered like a child's, and the tears just filled her soft eyes without overflowing.

"I had no right even to *try*. As soon as he spoke I knew how wrong it was. Perhaps I was cruel not to listen; but, O! every word smote my own heart so bitterly! All that first night I almost wished I had died before I had caused him such pain. You'll tell him how sorry I was."

"But Mr. St. John might release you."

"No; I shall never so wound him. It's a fancy of mine that somewhere along life he has received a keen, cruel wrench, and though he doesn't show the scar, it bleeds inwardly. Shall I tear it open afresh?"

She was sobbing in my arms. What a strange story! The incongruity of this marriage struck hard against a certain sense of mine, and I felt as if it should not be. But was it my place to interfere? *If* Mr. St. John loved her, would he not really hate me for my officiousness? And then the hot blood rushed to my brow. No; my lips must be silent, even if they all rushed to positive misery.

"My darling!" I said, trying to comfort her with kisses.

"O, Miss Clifford, I've been so wretched! but I know I am right. When we get to Laurelwood, I shall feel calm and strong again. I can't pain him, and blight his life. Gerald is so much younger, he may learn to forget me. Only if he will not think me deceitfully wicked. Don't let him do that."

"I will tell him the simple truth," I said, moved by the infinite pathos of her voice.

"And you think I am right?"

I would make one effort.

"Elsie," I said, tenderly, "it would be better to let Mr. St. John be the judge."

"No, no," and she shivered. "He is quite generous enough to yield his chance for happiness to another."

"Are you sure that you can make him happy?"

"Quite sure."

"But will you attain to the highest happiness yourself?"

"I shall do right," she said, bravely. "And now, dear Miss Clifford, forgive all the trouble I have caused you and yours. In a few days we shall leave the city."

"Let fate work out the problem," I said, fiercely, to myself. If God meant that this should be, I was powerless to turn the course of events. I could see where Elsie's sense of gratitude, justice, and pity were leading her astray. Yet to seek to convince her was useless. For Gerald to make an appeal to Mr. St. John might only complicate matters, even if he could resolve upon such a step. It must go on to the end.

We talked for some time, and Elsie grew gradually calmer. Still I could not help believing that her regard for Gerald was stronger than she would admit, and might blossom into the deepest passion of her life. She tried to soften the blow to him with many kind messages to be given after a while, but she remained steadfast in her resolve of not seeing him.

I called upon them twice before they left; and Mr. St.

John made a brief farewell visit with the ladies. Mrs. Lawrence tried to extort a promise that I would visit Laurelwood the next summer.

"I can no longer tyrannize over you in the capacity of guardian," he said, with a short laugh that had a bitter flavor.

CHAPTER XXV.

"Barely from off the desert of my life
I gather patience and severe content."
ALEX. SMITH.

GERALD did not submit to his fate easily. We both felt that Elsie was making an unwise, as well as dangerous experiment; and that when it was too late, she might learn her fatal mistake.

"I don't doubt that Mr. St. John will try to make her happy; but there is so much difference in their ages and temperaments. And she, in her rigid endeavor to cheat both him and herself, would die a martyr on the cross of love."

There was a settled melancholy in Gerald's deep eyes, and whenever he uttered such sentences, my heart was acutely pained.

And then I remembered my own many pangs. I strove to say that I would be satisfied to know that Mr. St. John was happy with another, but I could not so cheat myself. Years and absence had not extinguished that divine passion. Like Gerald, I had drank of its charmed waters for all time. There was no oblivion for me.

Some weeks later, Gerald joined a company of friends who were going to Central America. I knew the change would prove beneficial to him. Elsie's first letter was so tranquil, that I felt the faintest hope for him must be at an end forever.

It was quite impossible for me to return to my former

quiet mode of life. Society preferred its claims, and
would be heard. Why should I exile myself from all the
pleasures of the world? My friends rejoiced at my success,
and I experienced a thrill of gratification that was not
allied to vanity. Since this was to be the pleasure of my
future, I would accept it in peace.

Presently we glided over into May. The spring was
very forward, and the warm days made us think of finding
some airy summer resort. In the midst of these discus-
sions I received a sudden summons elsewhere — a note
from Mr. St. John, that contained these tidings: —

"My dear Miss Clifford: Since our return to Laurelwood, Elsie's health has gradually failed, and she is now
seriously ill with a fever. She begs for you continually;
and as it is for her happiness, I am emboldened to ask the
favor. Will you come to us immediately? With warmest
regards from my sister.   St. John."

To refuse was simply out of the question. I would
have done much for the dear child's sake. I felt that she
was nearing a fateful crisis. How would it end?

I telegraphed my answer, and made my preparations
immediately. How strange that I should be going back,
changed in many respects, yet in others the same! Nearly
seven years since I had first seen Laurelwood. What a
varied life mine had been!

Bertha insisted that I should return as soon as possible,
and I promised. A journey had no terror for me now,
and yet I seemed to tremble at every step. What would
be the result? For I felt as if I held the happiness of
others in my hand.

When I reached the station, I discerned a familiar figure
pacing the platform. My heart gave a great bound, that

was more of apprehension than hope. He was waiting for me, and took my hand as I stepped out.

"Miss Carme?" I exclaimed, in my awkward agitation.

"She is very ill indeed; nearing the crisis. I am glad you have come."

His face and manner were very grave, and there was a peculiar, stern resolve in every feature, that made a coward of me. Should I never be able to shake off this man's power?

"Did you find your journey tiresome?"

This time his voice was soft and sweet.

"Not particularly," I responded, and then glanced up with one of those sudden impulses. Did we both think of the first time I had come hither?

The carriage was waiting just beyond. He handed me in, and arranged the blanket with his usual carefulness, for the morning air seemed rather chilly.

"You said in your note that Elsie had not been well since you came to Laurelwood," I began, at length, for the silence grew oppressive.

"No. Her New York season was too fatiguing, I think. She was very glad to come away; and yet she has not been the same happy, care-free child that she was before. Miss Carme, of all others, needs a bright, satisfying life."

Did he begin to doubt his ability for making it satisfactory? A perplexed look lingered about his face like a fluttering cloud.

"There's something now that I don't understand; a kind of fear and reticence that I never saw in her before. Was she much with you during the last fortnight?"

"Very little," I replied, feeling that this was unsafe ground. "She was not well even then."

"I feel doubly anxious for her welfare, since it was our proposal that she should leave her own home. My sister is warmly attached to her."

It did not appear to me that there was much of the ardent lover in his look or tone. Would the man never be roused to that grand height of which I felt he was capable?

But we lapsed into silence again. Familiar sights and sounds stirred my heart and memory. The hope that had glorified the primal day of my life was not dead, only sleeping, and I already felt that it might be called forth with a word. Ah, I must thrust it back into its grave. The time had gone by when it would have been a welcome and cherished guest.

If Laurelwood had met with any change, it was only to grow more beautiful. I bowed my head with reverent awe, and let old remembrances join this new tide with a mighty rush. How little I had expected ever to return! and now I was here.

Mrs. Lawrence betrayed much emotion as she came forward to welcome me. She looked worn and anxious.

"I am so glad you have come!" she uttered, in a tone that I could not doubt. "But Elsie is much worse than when we first sent. She calls for you incessantly, but I doubt if she will recognize you."

"Miss Adriance has been travelling all night, and must have a rest before she enters the sick room," Mr. St. John said; and we both smiled over the old name. It did seem most natural here. I felt as if I had been away on a long masquerade, and had but just returned to my proper character.

I was compelled to yield to the kind care. After my breakfast, Mrs. Lawrence insisted that I should take a rest. Elsie was dozing and quiet, and Mr. St. John was going to watch her for a while. So it was nearly noon when I entered the apartment.

The poor child lay tossing restlessly upon her pillow, the wide open eyes unnaturally bright with fever, and the cheeks glowing in their dangerous scarlet.

"Miss Clifford has come," Mr. St. John announced, taking the wasted hand in his. She was very much emaciated, and her features, that had been so lovely in their roundness, now were sharp or sunken.

"I wanted to see her." The voice had a hollow, wandering sound, but she looked past me, rather than at me, while she seemed making an effort to remember something. "Did you tell him, Miss Clifford?" Do you think he forgave?—"

The rest was incoherent muttering. I felt a guilty knowledge of her secret rising to my face with a flush, and did not dare glance around.

"Where is she? Won't she take me in her arms, as she did once? I'm so tired, so tired!"

She stretched out both her hands imploringly. A beseeching look lighted up the restless eyes.

I came near and bent over her, soothed her with low words until she was tranquil, yet she did not appear to actually realize my presence.

"Suppose you leave me with her a little while?" I said, in a rather decisive tone.

Mr. St. John would fain have lingered. I knew that he had some dim suspicion of a secret. I could not think what I must do in this cruel strait, but resolved to guard her while it was possible.

When we were alone I let her talk without any restraint. She only gave vague hints, however, and restless mutterings, mentioning no name. If I could but keep Mr. St. John away!

At three the physician came in. An old friend that I had seen years before, and who appeared delighted with this encounter.

"You are just the one we need," he exclaimed, after his first surprise had subsided. "Mrs. Lawrence is nearly wild with excitement and fatigue, and it would be better if she were not allowed in here more than a few moments at a time. The nurse is excellent, but she hasn't that peculiar soothing power over her that you possess. If we can take her safely through until noon to-morrow, the danger will be past; and this sweet life is too precious to wither like a flower."

I promised to do my best, and succeeded very well — for from that time until nine in the evening, when he called again, she had said but little, though she had been exceedingly restless. One or two symptoms he thought improved.

"Watch her closely through the night," he said, and left directions for every change, with the kind of remedies that were to be used. He also had a long conversation with Mr. St. John in the adjoining room.

The nurse would have remained, but I did not care to have her. Mr. St. John proposed sharing my watch, but I was fain to dismiss him.

"At least I shall stay within call. It is too much for you to be alone; and we are under great obligations to you."

His tone was unnaturally cold, I thought, and he showed that he was laboring under some constraint. If Elsie could get through the night without betraying her secret!

Mr. St. John at length disposed of himself on the lounge in the adjoining room. I took my seat, having turned the light to a drowsy dimness, and bathed Elsie's burning hands, now and then cooling the throbbing brow, and turning aside the clustering hair. For a while she was quite calm, then she began to moan and murmur. I heard a step beside me. Mr. St. John looked much disturbed.

"Please do not feel distressed," I could not help saying.

"I am not utterly heartless," he returned, with a strange touch of spirit. "I cannot see you overtasking yourself—"

"Do not fear for me."

Elsie started that moment and sprang up, almost into his arms.

"Go away, Gerald," she said. "I cannot, cannot marry you; my promise has been given to another. No, don't kiss my hand even. Am I cruel? Heaven forgive me. I must suffer, too; but I shall be brave to bear it."

"Elsie!" I said, pressing my cheek against hers.

"Don't let him hate me. O, if I had known! But I never thought of his loving me. I must tear the sweet knowledge out of my heart. Gerald will never dream that I cared; and it is best—best. O, is any one happy in this world?"

He looked at us both. I was quivering in every nerve, hardly less than she. Now that the floodgates of her soul were loosened, there was no reserve. The secret that she would confess to neither Gerald nor me was told with all the wildness of delirium. How much she had suffered in her vain endeavor to keep to what she considered her duty, we both knew now.

It was a singular scene. The corners of the room were in shadows, the light sending its rays over the bed where she tossed and moaned, her face full of unearthly beauty, her hair glittering with every motion. The awe that always reigns at midnight affected me powerfully, and her strained, imploring voice, rising to highest pathos, then dying away to convulsive sobs. Mr. St. John stood with his arms folded, his face like chiselled marble. What pang of agony rent his soul?

Presently her strength was exhausted. I gave her the remedies the doctor had prescribed, and watched for many minutes. The next few hours might decide. I scarcely breathed in my intense anxiety.

Her eyes closed, her whole system grew more calm. The fever flush began to fade into deathly whiteness. I had been told every symptom so minutely that I drew a long breath of something like relief.

An hour, perhaps, we stood there, much of the time Mr. St. John's fingers being upon her wrist. Her respiration grew easier, and it was evident she was sinking into slumber. Once or twice Mrs. Lawrence, looking like a white wraith, had approached the door, but her brother would not allow her to enter.

"Sit down," he said to me; and I obeyed without a dissenting gesture. Then, after many moments, in the same cold, clear tone, "She is better — she will live," he announced.

I saw him move to extinguish the light and open the windows. He called me by a motion of his hand, and, following one of my old impulses, I went.

"Did your cousin propose to Miss Carme?" he asked.

To evade would be folly. How far it was necessary to soften the pang for him, I could not tell.

"He did," I answered.

"And she rejected him?"

"Yes."

"Did you know of this before we left New York? Did *she* tell you?"

"She did. I heard it from both."

"And you allowed her to make this monstrous sacrifice! You must have known that she loved him," he said.

"What could I do? She had already refused him, and was resolute in her endeavor to perform what she considered her duty. How could I go against her sense of right and honor?"

"Have you any tender, womanly soul at all? Do you care for your fellow-creatures? or are they like so many blocks of wood or stone? Both might have been saved much anguish."

"You are bitterly unjust," I said, roused, as in the old times. "I did point out the course that I considered best —that she should tell you, and allow you to become the arbiter. I could do nothing more."

"A word to me would have been sufficient."

"Did you expect *me* to say that?"

I turned suddenly, my face white with the effort I made to suppress my indignation.

"Heavens! no. You would sacrifice everything to your relentless pride. What have I done that you should hate me so persistently?"

"If I had hated you, I think I could have found a better opportunity to wound. I should have rejoiced in making you suffer through your love for her."

"My love for her has not been so selfish that I should have barred her out of any dearer happiness. I shall not attempt to justify myself in your eyes, knowing that can never be. She came to me a beautiful, guileless child, at a time when I had well nigh lost my faith in all other women. I did not design to win her heart; she was so young and fresh, so unconscious of all the dearer joys of life. But one day I found, or fancied, that I had roused a deeper than friendly interest in that hitherto untroubled heart. Perhaps the consciousness of being loved was as blissful to me as to another man."

22

I had no word to say, and so kept silent during the long pause he made.

"I said, perhaps God has sent this late joy to make amends for other dead hopes. I will take her to my heart, and shield her from all care, worship her as men do angels. I will watch the unfolding of this pure heart; and, if my name be inscribed on its innermost portals, I will cherish the gift with my whole strong soul; but if she finds that this was but a childish regard, and the deepest springs of her being are stirred, I will bless her and send her on her way. My own solitary fate I can endure."

"That was hardly love," I ventured.

"How many of us attain to our high ideal? In our early visions nothing but a royal banquet will satisfy us; later we sit down to humble fare with contented minds. I thought once that I had found the gold — instead, a glittering rock, than which no ice peak could be colder. Then I was willing to take the crumbs of daily life."

"You are not a humble man," I said, half bewildered by his tone and manner.

"Do you know what I am? would you know if a thousand years were given you?"

Elsie stirred, and we both were beside her in a moment. She was still asleep; her pulse, though weak, was growing more regular.

Mr. St. John summoned the nurse.

"You must go now," he said to me. And I hurried away, glad to be released.

But I could not sleep. A hundred conflicting emotions made perfect chaos of my brain. Was I never to be beyond the reach of this man's influence? Would he always be able to summon my soul with a word or a look?

After an hour or two I rose, bathed my face and arranged my hair, and went down to the breakfast-room. Mrs. Lawrence sat there alone.

"O," she exclaimed, "Stuart said you were to sleep till noon. The doctor has been here, and thinks the worst is over with our darling."

Her eyes were full of grateful tears.

"If I had a child of my own, I couldn't love it better," she said, vehemently. "I never cared so much for any human being."

I drank a cup of coffee, and then returned to Elsie's room. Mr. St. John was sitting by the window, his face bowed in his hand; but he neither spoke nor stirred.

How I lived through the day I can hardly tell. At times such a deathly sinking and strange fear rushed over me that I could hardly breathe at all — as if I had been tortured on the rack; and in the after moment of release my whole frame throbbed with intense anguish. If I could only be at peace once again!

Elsie, though very weak and low, was out of immediate danger. For several days she lay motionless, and with no desires, but in that shadowy, transition state. One morning she greeted me with a faint, sweet smile.

"How long have you been here?" she asked.

"About a week," was my answer.

"I am so glad you came! Did I talk much?"

"Not very intelligibly;" and I laughed.

After that she began to recover rapidly; but she could hardly endure to have me out of her sight. Her clinging love was inexpressibly sweet.

"Will you give me your cousin's address?" Mr. St. John asked me one evening. "He is abroad, I believe."

I wrote it on a card, and handed it to him. Since that night of our strange talk we had gone on in our usual manner; he being so self-contained that I really ceased to speculate upon him. I felt that he intended to summon Gerald back, but asked no questions.

The whole household, down to the smallest servant, rejoiced at Elsie's return to health. Mr. St. John was tenderly solicitous for her comfort and pleasure; yet I felt that it was not exactly a lover's care. *Was* he capable of a grand, absorbing passion, which would bring him out of his lofty self?

After a while Elsie's improvement ceased to be so rapid. She was well enough then to be taken out in an easy carriage; Mrs. Lawrence, or I, and Mr. St. John used to accompany her. But I noted the wistful sadness that would not infrequently steal over her face, and the longing eyes that looked into the far distance, seeing nothing. Mr. St. John watched her very closely also. I wondered within myself how it was to end.

At length I surprised her in tears.

"My darling," I exclaimed, "what has occurred to distress you?"

She leaned her head on my bosom, and wept bitterly for a while. At last she said, —

"Dear Miss Clifford, I have made my best friend miserable by my mad folly of the winter. I hate myself! I wish I had never come to Laurelwood to work such wretchedness. How did I happen to tell? All the first of my sickness I had such a horror of being delirious! That was one reason why I wanted you. I thought you would shield my fatal secret. But he heard it all."

"He could hardly help learning it, and must have suspected something by your manner, for it did make a change in you. It is better that it should be known, if you could only look upon it in this light."

"I look upon myself as a weak creature, with no stability of purpose, incapable of appreciating the most generous heart that was ever bestowed upon a woman. I have been deceitful, vacillating —"

"Hush," I said; "you shall not talk so. It was a mistake that any young girl might easily fall into. You thought you loved Mr. St. John —"

"And I did — I do," she interrupted.

"If there had been no Mr. St. John in the world, how could you have felt about Gerald?"

She flushed deeply, and said, with a weary sigh, —

"I don't seem to understand at all. I want Mr. St. John to be happy; instead of rendering him so, I have given him only pain, and made Gerald suffer also."

"What does Mr. St. John propose?"

"He talked to me so tenderly that it melted my heart. He will not admit that he shall be miserable in giving up the engagement, but I know no other hope will blossom to his life. Could I be happy in knowing he was sorrowful and desolate?"

"Could he be happy in knowing that the rich, spontaneous love — the best gift of a woman's heart — should in your case be another's?"

"Did you ever love any one?" she said, simply, raising her head.

The blood rushed in a torrent to my face.

"Forgive me." Her voice was very humble. "It seems so strange to care for two, though."

"Does it make no difference to you whether Gerald is happy?"

"O, Miss Clifford, it almost kills me sometimes when I think of his pain and anguish. And when I was first sick he was in my mind continually. Do you hear from him?"

"I have heard once."

"There is some fatality about me, I believe. I wonder that any one should care so much for me."

"My darling, no one can help it."

"Mr. St. John thinks it wiser to wait. He wants me
to be quite free in the mean while, and meet Mr. Clifford
again. But Gerald will never come back. I gave him
such a positive refusal."

Should I tell her what I suspected, that Gerald was
already on his homeward way? I did not know that Mr.
St. John had written, but I felt convinced that he designed
Elsie should come to her rightful inheritance.

I talked a long while, trying to make her look at the
case in its true light. She was so gentle, and longed so
earnestly to do right, that one could hardly call her strange
persistency obstinacy. She had proposed to herself a high
heroic task, and if it were swept away, her life at first would
appear aimless.

By degrees I believe Mr. St. John brought her to a
clearer mental state. She seemed merging into a sweet
and noble womanhood, and began to feel that her regard
for him was one of those exalted friendships, rather than a
profound love. He was delicacy and tenderness itself. If
he had ever treated me in this fashion —   .

One day he told her that he had sent for Gerald, and
received a telegram in return. Ere long he would be at
Laurelwood.

CHAPTER XXVI.

"The deepest ice that ever froze
Can only o'er the surface close;
The burning stream lies quick below,
And flows, and cannot cease to flow."

June had brought the roses to Laurelwood in richest profusion. I used to question if any other place in the world was so beautiful. Amid all my wanderings, that spot still seemed an Eden, and yet I was not happy. For I must begin my pilgrimage shortly again. Now that actual duty was over, the delay here was too dangerous and too dearly purchased.

We sat on the balcony in the late afternoon, where the westward sunshine was stealing through the swaying vines in grotesque shadows. Now and then one crowned Elsie, who had grown lovelier, if such a thing could be.

I was reading Lady Geraldine's Courtship to them, or rather had been, for now my voice paused at its ending, and there was a long silence.

"I think Sydnie is like Bertram," Elsie said, slowly, as if she had been revolving the subject in her mind.

"Do you?" and Mr. St. John smiled. "Because she is so proud?"

"Yes. He was more haughty than Lady Geraldine."

"But even he relented at last."

"Does that mean Sydnie wouldn't?" she asked, in a quiet tone. "And if she were in love —"

"Which she doesn't believe in."

"O, Sydnie, for once he is mistaken — is he not?" and

her eager face, with its glow of faith, was turned towards me.

"I never professed to doubt," I said, softly.

"It does not require open professions to test one in that respect. A little act is often sufficient."

"You don't mean that because she did not marry Mr. Channing —?"

"No, little one, I never considered that a love, or even a friendship."

There was a touch of sarcasm in his voice.

"Well, what then? I am curious," and she glanced into his face.

"I only know that once she was very proud. Perhaps she did not love at all. I suppose she did not, but she was loved."

I listened in a kind of breathless trance.

"O, tell me about *him*. I think I am always interested more in the unhappy ones, those who have a great trial or burden to bear."

He stooped to kiss her calm forehead

"There was once a man who loved her. He had lived much within himself, and rather distrusted the world in general. It may be that he was piqued to find a word or glance of hers could move him so easily. In all the wide world he feared nothing but her; because when he dared to dream, which was seldom, his visions were so entrancing, that sometimes he dreaded to have them swept away at a word. After her engagement was broken, she lost her fortune, you know. He took a little courage then, and offered her all that a man can give —"

"But she couldn't have refused him then, if she cared at all. It was so generous," she interrupted.

"I suppose she did not care at all; and so ends the story."

"O, Sydnie! I don't like it to end that way. Will he never come back to her? What became of him?"

"My little Elsie, men may be proud, as well as women."

"Didn't you care a little?"

"I was poor, and he rich," I said; but my voice sounded like a far-off dream. My very soul seemed to stand still. That I should listen to this story now, and know there was no step that I could retrace!

"He was noble and good, and I wish Sydnie had loved him."

Mrs. Lawrence sauntered out to us, and that ended the conversation. A few moments later Mr. St. John was summoned to the library by the arrival of a guest.

Mrs. Lawrence was very well satisfied with the turn affairs had taken. "It is the only real foolish thing that I ever knew Stuart to stumble into," she said, confidently, to me, concerning the engagement.

A servant was sent for Elsie. When I heard her low, glad cry, I solved the mystery at once. Mr. St. John came through the hall presently.

"It is your cousin," he said; and then he went to his own room. I talked to Mrs. Lawrence long after the stars came out. I wanted to keep away from myself and the sense of loss that overwhelmed me. Why must fate bring me back to be tortured afresh? Through this new tie we would be linked together again. How would I endure it? Every nerve shrank with an intense dread.

That Elsie was supremely happy I need hardly say. After that first interview her doubts were forever set at rest, and with her peculiar delicacy she confessed that Mr. St. John had been right, and decided wisely for all.

"That St. John of yours is the noblest man alive," Gerald said to me the next morning. "He is a veritable fairy prince; yet I wonder a little that Elsie should have loved me, for I cannot compare with him. I shall never be jealous, though;" and a bright, happy smile illumined his face.

One wave drifts us into bliss, and we are content; but we beat against the tide of sorrow continually, finding no haven of rest. We were all satisfied with the delight of these young hearts, and they settled into the rapture of lovers with hardly a thought for any one save themselves — the sweet selfishness of entire affection.

Gerald was browned by the tropical sun, but handsomer than ever. Mrs. Lawrence took him under her protection at once, and a marriage was discussed. He thought until autumn a sufficiently long probation, and Elsie really had no will of her own about it. I suspect Gerald tempted her by visions of foreign travel and Parisian operas.

All this was done in a week, and I proposed my departure. There was a general outcry, but I promised to be back at the wedding.

"If there isn't some fatality about it," Mrs. Lawrence said; and I knew my own unfortunate experiment came fresh to her mind.

"I don't see why you need go," Mr. St. John began, abruptly, as we were rambling through the shady walk.

"Business and necessity call me," I returned. "My duties here seem to be all performed."

"Duty and necessity! They are hateful words for a woman. She should have some sort of love or choice. Perhaps you have?"

There was a little sneer in the bland tones. For a moment I could not make any reply.

"Haven't your many ramblings hither and thither satisfied you? This unrest, this continual search for new pleasures, has been the bane of your life."

"Do you think every step I have been compelled to take has had direct reference to pleasure?" I asked, almost haughtily.

"Perhaps not pleasure, but a craving for new scenes and friends. Are they better than the old? And now that you have won fame, has it made you happy?"

"That was not my sole aim. Do me the justice to believe it."

"You always had a longing to mix in the world's fray. Some day you will learn that the crowning glory of a woman's life is not so much the position she sustains to the world, as to see her love and patience reflected in the faces she meets at the fireside. But I believe you cannot be content with the quiet joys that come to others."

"Mr. St. John, you are unjust — an old fault of yours."

"I am full of faults in your eyes!" He stooped to pull a branch of larch, and then began despoiling it of its clustering needles. "You distance us in your clear sight when you become philosophers. We protest a little at being stripped of the few graces romance has invested us with."

My pulses were throbbing under the rigid control in which I held them. I would not be made angry as in those foolish old days.

"I don't see why you go! For that matter, you might write a book here in these sylvan retreats, or turn poet. You are not fortuneless, that you need take up school teaching."

"I did that from urgent necessity," I answered, pointedly.

"No, you didn't. You had all offered you then that is ever laid at a woman's feet;" and his voice trembled with a strange excitement. "Home, fortune, and love! You refused them. I can never forget the word you used — *easily.* Is your heart a stone?"

An almost deathly spasm came over me. My very limbs tottered, and for an instant the shady path was like blackest night. Where should I go to escape this being, whose every word was torture? Then I rallied. I would fight my way out, hard as it might prove.

"I remember it," I said, with a calmness that sounded terrible, even to my own self. "No fortune could have bought me then, no gold ever will. And what was your love if it could be put in a few formal words? I will confess that I was proud and sensitive, sore too from the hard blow fate had given me; but even then that calm regard could not satisfy me."

"Nothing can. Nothing ever will."

There was a dreary cadence in his tone that smote me bitterly. We walked on in silence, side by side, but sundered as if the whole world lay between. Coming to the end of the path we both paused. What vain, wild incense I had offered at this man's shrine. Useless all!

"You will stay?"

Was the voice tender or beseeching? There was a rushing sound in my brain as if I had been leagues deep in the sea.

"I cannot."

He made room for me to pass. The last word had been said. I raised my eyes, as if mastered by some spell.

"Sydnie!"

I was weak and faint. If the strong arm had not caught me I should have fallen. And then one long, passionate kiss, one clasp.

"Go," he said, releasing me. "Since you prefer fame, and the honor the world can give, to love — my love," and his voice trembled with emotion, "I will no longer annoy you by my entreaties."

In that moment pride was swept away. Blinded by tears, and throbbing in every pulse, unable to speak, I stretched out my hands.

"Child," he said, with vehemence, "do you love me? do you need me? Have your false idols crumbled to dust? For if I have any, I want *all* your heart. No weak, irresolute passion will satisfy me. I *am* selfish and exacting in this."

"I need you," I replied, with the courage of a love I no longer feared, for the thought of reigning in his heart inspired me.

"Five years ago you went away, taking with you the dearest hope of my life. To-day you have brought it back. We will never part again."

O love, made perfect in faith! Why had I not known before? For now it spoke in the deep eyes suffused with tenderness, in the flush of the broad, kingly brow, the tremulous lips, the whole air.

"Is it no dream? My darling, let me hear from your own lips that you love me. How I have hungered for these blessed words!"

I said them not once, but many times. The eager, fervent eyes seemed to drain my soul to its very depths, and yet there was no void.

"Shall I tell you that, daring and resolute as I could be in all other matters, I have feared you almost beyond belief? From the very first, when you were a proud, wayward, undeveloped girl. I had never loved before, and all the fire of a strong nature was kindled. But I dreaded your triumph, and fancied in those old days that every other person pleased you more readily than I. Not even to my dearest friend could I have yielded you without a mortal pang. Perhaps love in natures like mine is cruel from its very intensity. I have been harsh and selfish, but Heaven knows the anguish I have suffered. Will you accept my expiation?"

"I could have loved you even then," I said, slowly, thinking of the many times he had swayed me against my will.

"Could you?" he returned, almost sharply. "How happened it, then, that my cousin's foolish trifling won you? From the first I had a fatal misgiving. A wild resolve urged me to fly to your rescue, and then the utter absurdity of the step deterred me. After you brought him home there were times when I was on the very verge of a betrayal. I never felt so certain of your regard that I dared risk a confession, for it seemed as if your ridicule was the one thing I could not endure."

"Your influence saved me in that dread time;" and I shivered at the recollection.

"Ah, I knew at last that you did not love him. But you counterfeited skilfully. Then, filled with doubt and mistrust, I asked myself how much truth there was in a woman. Faith received a cruel shock. Yet I fancy I understand how his sweetness and apparent generosity led you astray. But it maddened me that you should be so blind, and that my sister should stand ready to applaud and encourage. I refused my consent, in the hope that Aylmer would find some stronger attraction elsewhere. There were a few days of intense anguish, and then came that blessed respite. I read your secret—you were as much relieved as I."

"I hate myself for all that episode," I exclaimed, vehemently. "But you were bitter and cruel. How could I dream that you cared?"

"I spoke afterwards. Sydnie, if you had ever loved, how could you have been so cold and proud? When I went away, I thought I had won the great hope of my life. Our time for explanations was very brief, as you well know, and the sudden relief and joy dazzled me. I seemed to be borne down some swift tide of joy, and for the few hours stricken dumb, as it were. How often I attempted

to write I cannot tell you; but love like mine needed lips
as fond and warm to answer its questions. Haunted by
visions of rare, exquisite bliss, I counted every day's delay
with a jealous, longing heart. And when I returned —
ah, child! it was like a cruel stab from the hand of a friend.
The very servants came to welcome me, but no sound or
sign from you. I was amazed, chilled to the heart's core.
When necessity brought you into my presence, you were
distant and haughty as a princess. I tortured myself with
perplexing questions, and felt utterly at loss to account
for your coldness. That you should not misunderstand
the import of the words I had spoken before my departure,
I wrote you a note. What demon of icy pride possessed
you? Not a gesture of love, not a sign of tenderness, not
a word, until that bitter sentence — 'easily answered!' O,
Sydnie! were you human in those days, or only a beautiful, soulless statue?"

"I was poor. More than this — I had overheard a surmise that, having lost my fortune, I would be only too
glad to win your favor. The thought rankled until it
filled my whole soul."

"Not from my sister, surely?" he asked, in quick alarm.

"No. It was some foolish girlish gossip."

He smiled loftily, as if the fancy had been simply absurd.

"Did you hate to owe anything to me? Why, I would
have loved you, shielded you, made life as radiant as God
meant it should be to you. I thought then that having
gained one triumph over me, and brought me to your
feet, you were satisfied. I confess that you had always
held me in a strange state of doubt and fear."

"Forgive," I said, moved to tears. "I was afraid of
your pity and generosity. Since I had nothing save love to
give, I wanted that only in return. And you were proud."

"My darling, we have misunderstood one another fatally. I was sore and sensitive, and, with a man's spirit, one check was sufficient. I could not see my love trampled into the dust. Your going in the manner you did was another agonizing wound. It said that you wanted neither love, nor friendship, nor sympathy; that my very presence was distasteful to you. Still I kept watch of your movement. I knew how long you were at school; more than once I stole a glimpse of your pale, resolute face, still high and haughty. Why were you so unlike other women? And then your illness, your going abroad, and your literary venture. Did you gather anything from your own heart for that book? As I read, I seemed to understand your soul; yet having been once mistaken, I was wary. Then came the news of your marriage. I learned from a friend in Rome that you had gone to Nice with your husband's family. Until that time I had cherished a secret hope. Now all the romance of my life had burned to ashes, and lay a cold, gray ruin.

"I don't know that I can explain the peculiar charm Elsie exercised over me at this period. It was a child's sweet eagerness to comfort and cheer. Without a word she understood that my heart was heavy, and ministered to me in her own rare, delicate fashion. I knew I should never win love again; the fire and anticipation necessary for such an effort had died out of my nature. But this came to me in such an angelic guise that I opened my heart to the blessed visitor unaware. She thought she loved me, and I intended to be most generous with her. I would wait until she had seen the world — if she found a brighter and more youthful affection, I meant to yield my claim. I thought this would be so when I first heard her speak of your cousin.

"Meanwhile I had shut you entirely out of my life. I purposely avoided hearing the slightest mention of your name. Judge of my surprise, therefore, when I met you at Mrs. Varick's. And that night I knew no other had ever won your love. But I was bound!

"Was it wrong to expose Elsie to temptation? Heaven knows that I should have kept my word faithfully if it had been for her happiness. I suspected when I brought her home that something had gone wrong; yet I never dreamed of her making this sacrifice. My noble-hearted Elsie! She longed so for you that I sent; and I resolved then to fathom this mystery to the uttermost depths. But it was confessed in a way that I had not counted on; and that night I was as much in doubt as ever in regard to your love for me. Why did you never betray yourself? Your control is like adamant."

"Was," I said, softly. "It never can be again."

"My darling, will you let me reign? I believe most of my injustice has arisen from a fear of your love. Can I take it to my soul, and hold it as my very own, never to doubt again? Will you be patient until my wild passion is trained into tender, unselfish love? For it can be done."

I glanced into the deep, ardent eyes. Ah! was it not a dream? Could it be that I had gained the place better than all — a home in the heart of one who held my very soul in thrall? At rest and content. What blissful words!

We wandered up and down the shady walk, confessing the follies of those old days, and being absolved. · Was the joy less entrancing for coming late? We had both suffered, both waited, and learned some of the grand secrets of life.

"My dear Sydnie," Mrs. Lawrence exclaimed, an hour or two later, "is it true that you are going to marry Stuart? I am so bewildered by the announcement, that I hardly know what to believe."

23

"It is true;" and I blushed like a girl.

"I am so delighted! You and Stuart are both odd; so I think you will agree. Only—" she came near, and looked intently in my eyes—"are you in love? That used to be one of your stipulations;" and she smiled.

"I am in love," I confessed.

"Then you will be satisfied. I am sure that I wish you all happiness. I am glad matters have settled themselves so well, for Elsie's sake. I never did quite approve of the engagement, you know."

Elsie was wild with delight. She made Mr. St. John explain every mystery to her, and assured herself that he was on the verge of positive and complete happiness. As for me, I was passive, content to let another think for me.

What blessed days those were! Life rounded into perfect calm, after all its tempest and fierce tides.

I could hardly believe myself the object of this great tenderness. Not that Mr. St. John had suddenly lost all disposition to exert his power, but it was softened by his deep love, come to a late yet fragrant blossoming.

Mrs. Lawrence had reached the height of satisfaction. At last there was to be a wedding at Laurelwood. They overruled my faint objection, and determined that I should be married at the same time.

"You need not be afraid of old ghosts," Mr. St. John said, laughingly; "they are laid forever."

And so the preparations went on. Hosts of congratulations came to me; Philip Westervelt's, which brought tears to my eyes, as he rejoiced that his prayers for his friend had been answered; and Laura's, accompanied by a love-gift, one entirely characteristic of her. I managed to spend a week with Anne, and gave my cousins a few hours.

It is my bridal day.

Sitting here, adding a brief word to this record of my past, a step startles me. I am not so familiar with my happiness that I can take it calmly. Every pulse thrills to the sound of the low, fond voice.

The leaves are slowly turned in spite of my faint remonstrance. Tender kisses fall upon my forehead; then a stronger hand than mine takes the pen, and writes in a clear, bold manner —

"No longer *your* life, but *ours*."

I feel it; and my heart rejoices that its existence is to be merged into that of the beloved. With his hand clasped in mine, I shall not fear.

We have reached the fair land of human affection — we have only to go onward to the Eden of Divine love, and the way is fair, a path of roses with but few thorns, which God may give us the grace to miss.

www.ingramcontent.com/pod-product-compliance
Lightning Source LLC
Chambersburg PA
CBHW021110270326
41929CB00009B/814